The Social Context
of Premarital Sexual Permissiveness

IRA L. REISS

The
Social Context
of
Premarital Sexual
Permissiveness

HOLT, RINEHART AND WINSTON
New York • Chicago • San Francisco • Atlanta
Dallas • Montreal • Toronto • London

Acknowledgment is made to Harcourt, Brace & World for
permission to reprint the Kingsley Davis quotation from
Contemporary Social Problems, Robert Merton and Robert
Nisbet, eds., copyright © 1966 by Harcourt, Brace & World,
New York; and to Alfred A. Knopf for permission to reprint the
Robin M. Williams, Jr., quotation from *American Society,*
copyright © 1951 by Alfred A. Knopf, New York.

To My Parents, Philip and Dorothy Reiss

Preface

This is the first systematic sociological study of a national probability sample in the area of premarital sexual attitudes. Samples of students in American high schools and colleges are examined along with samples of adults. All the important empirical findings of previous researchers in this area are checked out by careful analysis of seven different samples. The findings cluster into seven areas, and a proposition summarizes the findings of each of these areas. Finally, the book integrates these propositions into one theory. The testing of various hypotheses, the formulation of the propositions, and the integration of them permeates the entire book. In this sense the book illustrates the process of theory-building in an area that is weak on theory. This may be useful even to those students of theory whose substantive interests are outside of the area of sex. The book should have utility for the student of methodology also, for in the course of this analysis of data, many methodological problems and the intricacies of the method of analyzing partial tables developed by Paul Lazarsfeld, Herbert Hyman, and others, as well as a new test for interaction developed by Leo Goodman, are amply illustrated.

The study utilizes aspects of both the structural-functional approach and the symbolic-interactional approach. The analysis related to a wide variety of specific theories, such as reference-group theory, anomie theory, cognitive-dissonance theory, social-class theory, social-change theory, and theories of deviant behavior.

Several new and potentially useful research tools are presented in this volume. Most important are the two twelve-item Guttman scales for measuring premarital sexual permissiveness. These scales more than adequately meet all Guttman-scaling criteria and should prove useful to researchers in many areas in the future. Equalitarianism can be indirectly measured by use of these two scales. Also presented is a ten-item romantic-love Guttman scale. These scales are the first of their kind to meet Guttman-scaling criteria.

To the reader interested in previous work in premarital sexual relationships the book offers a 250-item bibliography, and constant reference is made throughout the work to the major studies. The book is suitable for use by sociology majors or graduate students in courses in the sociology of the family or in deviant behavior, or in courses in other substantive areas where the methodological and theoretical aspects of the work would be important.

The wide range of possible causal variables examined in this study can be seen from the five major areas these variables were derived from:

1. General background factors such as class, religion, region, city size, age, race, and sex
2. Dating experiences and love conceptions
3. Sexual behavior and guilt reactions
4. Perceived permissiveness of parents, peers, and close friends
5. Family characteristics such as size, sex and age of children, and number of parents

This wide range of variables was tested on several probability-type samples of various age levels and residence. Such a broad coverage and the use of probability samples adds additional importance to these results for the interested sociologist, the student, and the intelligent layman who wants to learn more about the nature of human sexuality. The value of the work is best illustrated by the steps taken toward the achievement of an integrated theory that, hopefully, will aid in the understanding of the social context of premarital sexual permissiveness.

IRA L. REISS

Iowa City, Iowa
June 1967

Acknowledgments

My primary debt is to the four senior sociology students at the College of William and Mary who helped me begin the project as part of their senior research requirement: Ron Dusek, Martha Fisher, Richard Shirey, and John Stephenson. These students demonstrated the commitment college students are capable of by spending almost thirty hours a week on this research while carrying a full semester course load. At Bard College in New York, further valuable assistance was given by two senior sociology majors: Catherine Toye and Curt Swezy.

The bulk of the research analysis for this study was done at the University of Iowa, where, for six years, three graduate students were my major assistants. The most substantial debt of all is owed to Donald McTavish, who used his fine organizational abilities to set up a coding and indexing system and to develop computer programs extremely valuable to the project. In addition, he offered many valuable ideas. The smooth operation of the project was due largely to his skill in initially structuring the work. Highly skilled and important assistance was also given by Beverly Scott Davenport and Gary Hampe, who suffered through the many computer runs and tedious indexing and organizational tasks necessary to the research. They strengthened my faith in the ability of students to persevere in the face of many obstacles.

Even with the most dedicated assistance, the project would not have survived if it had lacked an economic base. The National Institute of Mental Health awarded three research grants to support this project over the years 1960 to 1964 (MH4045, 5566, and 05566). Their generosity was reinforced by their supplementary grant supporting participation in the amalgam national sample study commenced in 1963 by the National Opinion Research Center. This NORC program allowed several researchers to participate in one project and to share the cost, the questions, and the crucial data gained thereby. In this regard, thanks are due to Herbert Hyman, Paul Sheatsley, and Norman Miller for permission to use some of their questions.

The University of Iowa also aided the project by awarding me a Research Professorship and an Old Gold Fellowship to free me completely from teaching duties from February to September 1966. The University of Iowa also made available generous research assistance and valuable computer facilities, and the Computer Center cooperated in running the vast amount of data required by my work, even when this necessitated extra hours.

In addition to dedicated researchers and financial support, there was need for intellectual stimulation. This was ably provided by my colleagues at the University of Iowa. Special acknowledgment is paid to Theodore R. Anderson, who was quite helpful in discussions of the various statistical applications suitable for different types of problems, and to William Erbe, whom I submitted to a barrage of questions and opinions on the entire area of the analysis of partial tables.

Three fellow sociologists from other universities were kind enough to read the entire manuscript and give me the benefits of their detailed and insightful comments. My sincere thanks for this to Robert Bell, Lee Rainwater, and Clark Vincent.

The final necessary ingredient in the research project was emotional support. This was admirably supplied by my wife. She not only edited this book and helped type the manuscript, but also contributed many valuable suggestions regarding the ideas in the book.

The 2734 respondents in this study deserve thanks for their willingness to answer important questions about their private lives. No matter how much support one has in other realms, the cooperation of respondents is essential to this type of research. My gratitude also extends to the officials at the schools in the student sample whose cooperation helped make this project possible.

My debts, then, are many. I hope that this book will at least in part justify the vast amount of support that has come from so many quarters.

Contents

To the average normal person, in whatever type of society we find him, attraction by the other sex and the passionate and sentimental episodes which follow are the most significant events in his existence, those most deeply associated with his intimate happiness and with the zest and meaning of life. To the sociologist, therefore, who studies a particular type of society, those of its customs, ideas, and institutions which centre round the erotic life of the individual should be of primary importance.

BRONISLAW MALINOWSKI
The Sexual Life of Savages

. . . an orderly integration of the sexual drive with social life taxes to the utmost the normative machinery.

KINGSLEY DAVIS

. . . actions may deceive as well as words and there seems no reason for always giving one precedence over the other.

ROBIN M. WILLIAMS, JR.

1

The Scientific Study of Human Sexuality

The Neglect of Sex Research

Why should we study human sexual relationships? Judging by the long time it took sociologists to begin such a study, it might be concluded that there are few good reasons. Before World War II, research in this area was heavily confined to anthropologists, journalists, physicians, psychiatrists, and psychologists. Krafft-Ebing, Ellis, and Freud wrote the most influential books in this area in the half century from the 1880s to the 1930s.[1] Sociology was in its infancy during those years, and the contemporary literature shows very little sociological interest in studying the sexual relationship. The few books that did comment on sex usually made moral judgments regarding the increased acceptance of sex and added little of empirical worth.

Anthropologists showed interest in sex research before sociologists. Starting with the classic studies of the Trobriand Islanders by Malinowski, they began to document systematically the sex life of nonliterates.[2] But even in the

[1] Richard von Krafft-Ebing, *Psychopathia Sexualis.* New York: G. P. Putnam's Sons, 1965 (first published in 1882); Havelock Ellis, *Studies in the Psychology of Sex.* 6 vols. Philadelphia: F. A. Davis, 1905–15 (first published in 1897); and Sigmund Freud, *Three Contributions to the Theory of Sex.* New York: E. P. Dutton & Co., 1962 (first published in 1905). Aron Krich has edited readings from the above works entitled *Pioneer Writings on Sex,* Vol. 1 of *The Sexual Revolution.* New York: A Delta Book, 1964.

[2] Bronislaw Malinowski, *The Sexual Life of Savages in Northwestern Melanesia.* New York: Eugenics Publishing Company, 1929.

nineteenth century some social scientists, such as the social anthropologists Morgan and Westermarck, debated the possibility of an original state of sexual promiscuity and the role of sex in human society.[3] Thus, it seems apparent that most sociologists have only recently come to appreciate the value of studying the human sexual relationship. It should be added that even today there are but a handful of sociologists working in this area.[4] The most important postwar work has been done under the supervision of a zoologist (Kinsey), and it has only been in the past few years that the Institute for Sex Research has had sociologists on its staff. Kinsey's staff consisted predominantly of statisticians, anthropologists, and psychologists.

Why have there been so few sociologists doing work on sexual relationships? One reason is that professionals in psychology, anthropology, medicine, and journalism can more easily gain public justification for their research than can sociologists. The emphasis on pathology by psychologists, psychiatrists, and medical doctors helps to legitimize their investigations. They do therapeutic work that will lessen the number of people who perform sexually in other than conventional ways. The anthropologist is justified by the fact that he describes "savage," "pagan," "primitive," societies that cannot be expected to have fully learned the "advantages" of the civilized approach to sex. The journalist merely reports what he sees and almost always does so with moral undertones defending the conventional sexual morality. This is evident even in such sophisticated publications as *Time* and *Newsweek,* both of which have had series of articles on sex.[5] Despite these justifications for research, men like Freud and Ellis were often severely censured by the more conservative factions of society (for example, Ellis's book *Sexual Inversion* was indicted as "obscene libel," and this caused him to publish his famous *Studies in the Psychology of Sex* in America[6]).

The sociologist is in an even more difficult situation. His perspective is social, and thus his commentary is not about an emotionally disturbed person or a primitive society, nor is it a moralizing account of human shortcomings. It is a statement of what most people are like in their sexual relationships. Such an approach tends to be blunter and potentially more explosive. In short, the sociologist is a person who would intrude on our privacy and who might discover embarrassing facts that could weaken our faith in the conventional sexual morality. Without medical, therapeutic, or

[3] For some of the basic ideas see Lewis H. Morgan, *Ancient Society*. Chicago: Charles H. Kerr and Company, 1877; and Edward Westermarck, *The History of Human Marriage*. 3 vols. New York: Allerton Book Co., 1922 (first published in 1891).

[4] Sixteen sociologists have been located who, it would seem, have a major commitment to, and have done sociological research on, the human sexual relationship. Most of these were men under the age of forty-five. This is evidence that there is a recent trend toward more investigation of this area.

[5] See *Time,* January 24, 1964, and *Newsweek,* April 6, 1964.

[6] Krich, pp. 21–29.

moral motivations and justifications, the sociologist stands suspect as a disturber of the moral order or at least as someone about to upset the low level of awareness that exists in the current system of sexual relationships. Such a position may have made sociologists feel that sex is not a "safe" or "prestigeful" area to study.

In point of fact, much of the early work on sex by sociologists was performed in the "safe" fashion; that is, it consisted of predominantly moral essays supporting the existing system and condemning all deviants as immoral and as taking very harsh risks.[7] The intrusion of morality into sex research should have been expected. Only in very recent years, the last ten or twenty at the most, has there been any lessening in the moralistic, nonempirical approach by sociologists in this area.

Of course, part of the reason for this unscientific approach and the late development of the sociological interest in sex can be attributed to the fact that sociology is one of the youngest of the social sciences. It would seem natural that older disciplines, like medicine and psychology, were the first to approach this area. Also, explanations of sexual behavior were generally accepted as being of relevance to these older fields. Such behavior was not looked at in terms of sociological factors but rather in terms of psychological or physiological factors, and it is possible that sociologists themselves may have not approached this area because they shared this conception and felt sexual relations were not in their province. Despite the fact that in the 1890s Durkheim had shown the relevance of sociology to such a "psychological" phenomenon as suicide, it appears that the profession was not ready to lay claim to legitimate rights in the sexual sphere.

The intense public censure of Kinsey's first two reports is explained by the argument above.[8] Kinsey undertook the kind of research that sociologists might have tackled. However, sociologists are less likely to share his reductionist view of human behavior.[9] He exposed much that many people wanted to remain concealed or that could not easily be accepted. Even professional sociologists do not always understand what Kinsey found and how he did his research—so strong and widespread was the cultural reaction. Not many sociologists knew that the American Statistical Association undertook a study of the first Kinsey volume and published a report basically

[7] For a criticism of this moral approach and a discussion of an objective approach see Ira L. Reiss, "The Treatment of Premarital Coitus in Marriage and Family Texts," *Social Problems*, 4 (April, 1957), pp. 334–338; also Ira L. Reiss, "Personal Values and the Scientific Study of Sex," *Advances in Sex Research*, Hugo Beigel, ed. New York: Harper & Row, Publishers, 1963, pp. 1–10.

[8] Actually, most Americans approved of Kinsey, but only the minority was vocal. See Jerome Himelhoch and Sylvia Fava, eds., *Sexual Behavior in American Society*. New York: W. W. Norton & Co., 1955, sec. 11.

[9] For comment on this see Manford H. Kuhn, "Kinsey's View of Human Behavior," *Sexual Behavior in American Society*, Jerome Himelhoch and Sylvia Fava, eds., pp. 29–38.

praising the relative merits of Kinsey compared to previous researchers.[10] Also, many sociologists misunderstood Kinsey's use of accumulative incidence and his trend statements.[11] But because of Kinsey or because times were changing toward greater liberalism, research into sexual behavior became more common and public opposition seemingly subsided. In the past few years, sociologists doing population research have reported that questions regarding sexual behavior are answered more easily than questions regarding family income.[12]

What has been said above about the study of sexual relationships is to some extent applicable to the entire field of the sociology of the family. The sociological approach to the family has often been moralistic, and theoretical and methodological sophistication has suffered.[13] This too has changed in recent decades, and in some areas at a very rapid pace. However, there is still a general invidious comparison made, and the family area is often viewed as an area of low prestige because of its non-empirical history.

The fact that most sociologists are male may have tended to make them shy away from study of the family, for it has a "feminine" connotation in our society and thus may be less acceptable as an area for men. Many sociologists who do choose to work in the family area are sensitive to this low-prestige heritage and do their utmost to choose a specialization in this field that is as acceptable as possible. Relation of social class to family forms, the types of family systems best integrated with the occupational system, and the interrelation of the family and the political institution are all "respectable" areas of study. These approaches have relatively high prestige and thus help make study of the family a legitimate area and help the researcher raise his self-concept. However, the area of sexual relationships still bears the stigmas of the older moralistic writings, of the hint of some personal deviant motivation on the part of the investigator, of possible social opposition, of having the low-prestige factor of practical application, of being commonplace, and thus it is relatively ignored. There has been some

[10] William G. Cochran, Frederick Mosteller, and John W. Tukey, *Statistical Problems of the Kinsey Report on Sexual Behavior in the Human Male.* Washington, D.C.: The American Statistical Association, 1954.

[11] For a brief explanation of accumulative incidence see Paul H. Gebhard, *et al., Pregnancy, Birth, and Abortion.* New York: Harper & Row, Publishers, 1958, pp. 7–8.

[12] For reports of this see Ronald Freedman, Pascal K. Whelpton, and Arthur A. Campbell, *Family Planning, Sterility and Population Growth.* New York: McGraw-Hill, 1959, p. 14. Mirra Komarovsky reports a similar finding mentioned on p. 415, fn. 20 of *The Journal of Marriage and the Family* (August 1965). See also Mervin B. Freedman, "The Sexual Behavior of American College Women," *Merrill Palmer Quarterly,* 11 (January 1965), p. 34.

[13] See Harold T. Christensen, ed., *Handbook of Marriage and the Family.* Chicago: Rand McNally & Co., 1964, chapter 1; also, William J. Goode, "The Sociology of the Family," in Robert K. Merton *et al., Sociology Today.* New York: Basic Books, 1959, pp. 178–191.

improvement in this situation due to the general increase in the status of the entire family field. This is occurring more rapidly today due to the strong public interest and demand for knowledge regarding sex and family life in general.

The Importance of Sex Research

An equally important question is, Regardless of what people think about sex research, is there reason to think it is important for sociologists to investigate this area? More specifically, What theoretical, methodological, or empirical justification is there for the sociological study of the premarital sexual relationship?

The sexual relationship involves a situation wherein individuals constantly make choices regarding their sexual attitudes and behavior. From very early years onward, the individual is confronted with the choice of what he or she is willing to accept and what he or she is willing to do. Unlike most other species, the human species, both male and female, has a relatively constant sex drive and the ability to engage in sexual behavior at all periods of the year. Given our courtship system, an individual and his dating partner have ample opportunities to do what they please regardless of the view of their parents or those in power in the society. Sexual relationships are everywhere socially regulated, and thus this situation of "constant choice" provides an excellent test of internalization of norms, changes of norms, relation of norms and behavior, as well as a chance to measure the relation of sociocultural factors such as social class, religion, region, and race to sexual attitudes and behavior. The entire area of deviant behavior is relevant here, for few areas offer as good an illustration of the problems of socialization and conformity.

The sexual standard an individual holds is important in the sense that it relates to the social groups to which he belongs and can affect marital decisions. If the sexual beliefs and behaviors of the other person are not agreeable, the likelihood of a rift is increased. Thus, to understand mate selection one must understand human sexual attitudes. In a broader sense sexual relationships are important to understand because they affect the basic fabric of our lives. Sex is one key motive in human behavior. Sexual customs relate to our conceptions of love, religion, and family life, and have indirect ties to the political and economic systems.[14] An individual's conception of the male and the female role may well affect his choice of an appropriate occupation, his attitudes toward schoolwork, and his basic self-concept.

[14] For an excellent discussion see Kingsley Davis, "Sexual Behavior," in *Contemporary Socail Problems,* 2d ed., Robert K. Merton and Robert A. Nesbit, eds. New York: Harcourt, Brace & World, 1966, pp. 322–372.

The vast network of interrelations can be visualized by imagining what would happen if we were to change our society by altering the sex ratio, or by altering the female's interest in sexual relationships, or by changing the sexual standards of various segments of our society. Such changes in the sexual sphere would drastically affect other areas, such as marriage and family institutions, and the relation of the family to the political, economic, and religious institutions, to name but a few.

Sexual relationships offer the sociologist an opportunity to study a universal aspect of social systems and to try to discern the ways in which it fits into a particular society. It gives him an excellent opportunity to study that most basic sociological question, How is social order possible? Such a study gives insight into actors in the social system and into the ways in which society shapes powerful organic tendencies and fits them with other features of the social system. This also has a direct bearing on understanding the mental health of various groups, for through the study of sexual relationships a sociologist can learn a great deal about human society on the microscopic level of dyadic interaction as well as on the macroscopic level of sociocultural factors. The fabric of our social existence in almost every institutional area is affected by our standards and behavior in the area of sex, and thus it is all the more amazing that so little has been done to investigate the human sexual relationship.[15]

What We Know at Present

The key focus of this book is on premarital sexual relationships, although marital sexuality will be touched upon. It is hoped that future researchers will deal with other types of sexuality. Since parental attitudes toward premarital sexuality are dealt with, data with implications for marital sexuality are presented, and the propositions and theory that are developed reflect this connection. Within the area of premarital sex the focus is on the explanation of the various degrees of heterosexual permissiveness embodied in our premarital standards. Questions of homosexuality, masturbation, self-concept of masculinity and feminity will be dealt with only when relevant to this primary interest.

We know a good deal about the premarital sexual *behavior* of respondents in nonprobability samples and very little about their attitudes or about those of others. A unique feature of this book is that it contains the first probability sample of the nation that has been used for a sociological analysis of the sexual relationship, and it is the first book to fully focus on sexual attitudes and not just behavior. Terman, Burgess and Wallin, Kinsey, Ehr-

---

[15] David A. Ward and Gene G. Kassebaum report the key role of sexual behavior in the social structure of prison. See *Women's Prison*. Chicago: Aldine Publishing Co., 1965.

mann, Kirkendall, Vincent, and Christensen—the authors of the most comprehensive existing works on the sexual relationship in America—did *not* use probability samples.[16] Michael Schofield, in his study of English teenagers, did employ a large-scale probability sample.[17]

However, despite the sampling limitations of many studies, there are some basic facts that seem to persist and that have been assumed to be accurate for America. For example, there is widespread agreement that premarital coitus is more common for males than for females and for Negroes than for whites.[18] There is also widespread agreement that affection is a more important factor in motivating the female to perform sexually than it is in motivating the male.[19] Further, it is generally assumed that different social and cultural factors produce different sexual behavior and attitudes, although the literature is not unanimous as to just what these factors are and how they work. Several researchers have found that those relations wherein the male has higher social class than the female are much more likely to involve premarital coitus than those relations wherein the female has higher status than the male.[20] Religiousness in several studies was found to be an inhibiting influence on sexual permissiveness, that is, religious persons are less likely to engage in sexual intimacies.[21] There is also evidence

[16] Lewis H. Terman, *Psychological Factors in Marital Happiness.* New York: McGraw-Hill, 1938; Ernest W. Burgess and Paul Wallin, *Engagement and Marriage.* New York: J. B. Lippincott Co., 1953; Alfred C. Kinsey, Wardell B. Pomeroy, and Clyde E. Martin, *Sexual Behavior in the Human Male.* Philadelphia: W. B. Saunders Co., 1948; Alfred C. Kinsey, Wardell B. Pomeroy, Clyde E. Martin, and Paul H. Gebhard, *Sexual Behavior in the Human Female.* Philadelphia: W. B. Saunders Co., 1953; Paul H. Gebhard, Wardell B. Pomeroy, Clyde E. Martin, and Cornelia V. Christenson, *Pregnancy, Birth, and Abortion.* New York: Harper & Row, Publishers, 1958; Paul H. Gebhard, John H. Gagnon, Wardell B. Pomeroy, and Cornelia V. Christenson, *Sex Offenders.* New York: Harper & Row, Publishers, 1965. Winston W. Ehrmann, *Premarital Dating Behavior.* New York: Holt, Rinehart and Winston, 1959; Lester A. Kirkendall, *Premarital Intercourse and Interpersonal Relationships.* New York: The Julian Press, 1961; Clark E. Vincent, *Unmarried Mothers.* New York: The Free Press, 1961; Harold T. Christensen and George R. Carpenter, "Value-Behavior Discrepancies Regarding Premarital Coitus," *American Sociological Review,* 27 (February 1962), pp. 66–74.

[17] Michael Schofield, *The Sexual Behavior of Young People.* Boston: Little Brown & Co., 1965.

[18] For a recent statement see Ira L. Reiss, "Premarital Sexual Permissiveness among Negroes and Whites," *American Sociological Review,* 29 (October 1964), pp. 688–698. Almost all the studies cite male-female differences, and Gebhard cites racial differences in *Pregnancy, Birth, and Abortion.*

[19] Ehrmann is the best source here. For similar findings on English youth see Schofield.

[20] Ehrmann, pp. 144–169; Burgess and Wallin, pp. 340–341 (evidence here only supported less intercourse when the woman has a higher education; there was no difference between women having the same or less education than their fiancés); Eugene A. Kanin and David H. Howard, "Postmarital Consequences of Premarital Sex Adjustments," *American Sociological Review,* 23 (October 1958), pp. 556–562.

[21] Kinsey *et al., Sexual Behavior in the Human Female,* pp. 304–307, 331; Burgess and Wallin, p. 339; Ehrmann, p. 94.

that the consequences of coitus vary according to the standards an individual holds.[22] Many studies support the contention that an increase in sexual behavior of several types occurred during the 1920s.[23] Ehrmann reports ways in which love and dating experiences affect sexual behavior.[24] General findings have also been frequently reported regarding similarities of sexual standards and behaviors in certain social groups, such as class, educational, and so on.[25] The bulk of types of findings that are most solidly supported by more than one study are covered by this short list, although it is by no means exhaustive.

In *Premarital Sexual Standards in America,* the major research in this area was reviewed with the goal in mind of trying to organize the findings in terms of filling the gap that existed in our knowledge of standards.[26] The general conclusions were that we know very little about sexual behavior compared to other areas of study and that we are particularly lacking in information concerning sexual standards as opposed to sexual behavior. The fact that engaging in sexual intercourse in one group may cost a high price psychologically and that in another no price whatever has been largely ignored in previous work. However, there is some knowledge of this matter, since Ehrmann did deal with standards on a small scale in his 1959 book, as did Christensen in his cross-cultural comparison of college students in Indiana, Utah, and Denmark.[27]

The time was ripe for someone to investigate this area using probability samples to discern some basic correlates of premarital sexual permissiveness in American society, and to develop ways of measuring this phenomenon. The National Institute of Mental Health solved the financial problems attached to such a research venture and supported the project from 1960 to 1964.[28]

Brief Overview of This Study

Given the state of knowledge in this area, it seemed appropriate to formulate a general approach and to test a wide variety of hypotheses covering most of the fruitful aspects. Work started at the most abstract level, with the theory that groups differing in their premarital sexual permissiveness

[22] Christensen and Carpenter, "Value-Behavior Discrepancies Regarding Premarital Coitus"; Ira L. Reiss, *Premarital Sexual Standards in America.* New York: The Free Press, 1960, chaps. 7 and 8; Kirkendall, chaps. 8 and 9. For general evidence of the role of learning in sexual relations see chap. 1 in Reiss.

[23] The Kinsey studies are the best source for this statement. See also Termann.

[24] Ehrmann, chap. 4.

[25] Ehrmann; Kinsey, *Sexual Behavior in the Human Male* and *Sexual Behavior in the Human Female.*

[26] Reiss, *Premarital Sexual Standards in America.*

[27] Christensen and Carpenter, "Value-Behavior Discrepancies regarding Premarital Coitus"; Ehrmann, chap. 5.

[28] Public Health Service Research Grants 4045, 5566, and 05566.

would also differ in other social and cultural characteristics. These other sociocultural characteristics that were felt to be potential "causes," or independent variables, were (1) general background factors, such as social class, religion, region, city size, age, race, and sex; (2) dating experiences and love conceptions; (3) sexual behavior and guilt reactions; (4) perceived sexual permissiveness of parents, peers, and close friends; and (5) family characteristics, such as number, sex, and age of children, and number of parents.

The empirical justification for choosing these factors as potential independent variables was of uneven quality. Evidence related to several of the most tested relations in these five areas has already been discussed. Other items were selected primarily on the ground that they had "promise" and were relevant to a basic understanding of this area. For example, concerning the background factor of region, folklore has it that the South is the region with a strong double-standard emphasis, and thus the permissiveness of southerners should differ.

The second major area was chosen because the relation of dating experiences, love conceptions, and premarital sexual relationships had been pointed out by Ehrmann and others.[29] The third area was added because the relation during adolescence of attitudes, behavior, and guilt is of crucial importance to any theory of sexuality.

The fourth major area—the perception of the attitudes of parents, peers, and close friends as important independent variables—is indirectly related to the research Ehrmann and Bell have done in this area.[30] Also, Kinsey[31] has shown that there is consistency in sexual behavior of different education groups, and the general literature regarding socialization stresses that parents, peers, and close friends are of great importance in the development of any attitude.[32]

The final area, family characteristics, was selected because the work of Bossard, Boll, Elder, Bowerman, and others has shown the causal effects of such factors for promoting various types of attitudes and relationships.[33] Also, the effects of divorce, death, and desertion on children has often been cited. Orville Brim has shown that having an older sibling of the opposite

[29] Ehrmann, chap. 4.

[30] Ehrmann, chap. 5; Robert Bell and Jack V. Buerkle, "Mother and Daughter Attitudes to Premarital Sexual Behavior," *Marriage and Family Living,* 23 (November 1961), pp. 390–392; and by the same authors, "The Daughter's Role During the 'Launching State,'" *Marriage and Family Living,* 24 (November 1962), pp. 384–388.

[31] Kinsey, *et al., Sexual Behavior in the Human Male.*

[32] Frederick Elkin, *The Child and Society: The Process of Socialization.* New York: Random House, 1960; George Herbert Mead, *Mind, Self, and Society.* Chicago: University of Chicago Press, 1934. These are very general references for this idea. More specific ones will be cited later.

[33] James H. S. Bossard and Eleanor Stoker Boll, *The Large Family System.* Philadelphia: University of Pennsylvania Press, 1956; Glen H. Elder, Jr., and Charles F. Bowerman, "Family Size, Sex Composition and Child Rearing," *American Sociological Review,* 28 (December 1963), pp. 891–905.

sex affects the degree of an individual's masculinity or feminity, so birth order may well affect sexual permissiveness.[34]

It should be apparent that it is necessary to begin research in the area of sexual relationships with the few *ad hoc* findings that are available and with hunches regarding what other factors are worth investigating.

Many of the investigations made were necessarily exploratory. Therefore, several measures of each variable often were used in order to explore fully the utility of a variable; for example, over a dozen ways of measuring social class were employed. To supplement data on the number of times an individual has been in love, a ten-item Guttman scale of romantic love feelings was devised. Also, each version of every independent variable was checked with several different types of cutting points to examine further its relation to the dependent variable of premarital sexual permissiveness. In addition, these checks were made separately for each of the five schools in the student sample, and a very wide number of control variables in both the student and the adult sample were used. In short, the task was the exploration of a wide variety of possible independent variables to be carried out in an exploratory fashion. The general technique of analysis used was the analysis of partial tables as developed by Lazarsfeld, Hyman, Zeisel, and others.[35] Specifically, this means that each relationship of sexual permissiveness to some other factor was looked at to see if it would hold up for older as well as younger people, for males as well as females, for the lower class as well as the upper class, and under other conditions.

Specific hypotheses were formulated regarding the ways in which these independent variables would affect the dependent variable of premarital sexual permissiveness. These will be discussed throughout the book. The ultimate aim was to integrate the findings into several propositions and, hopefully, to integrate these propositions into a theory of premarital sexuality. In this way, it was hoped, the field would be left somewhat more organized than it had been found.

Although behavior is dealt with in this study, it was decided to focus more on the measurement of attitudes than on behavior.[36] First, it was as-

[34] Orville G. Brim, Jr., "Family Structure and Sex-Role Learning by Children: A Further Analysis of Helen Koch's Data," *Sociometry,* 21 (March 1958), pp. 1–16.

[35] Patricia L. Kendall and Paul F. Lazarsfeld, "Problems of Survey Analysis," *Continuities in Social Research,* Robert K. Merton and Paul F. Lazarsfeld, eds. New York: The Free Press, 1950, pp. 133–196; Paul F. Lazarsfeld, "Interpretation of Statistical Relations as a Research Operation," *The Language of Social Research,* Paul F. Lazarsfeld and Morris Rosenberg, eds. New York: The Free Press, 1955, pp. 115–125; Herbert Hyman, *Survey Design and Analysis.* New York: The Free Press, 1955; Hans Zeisel, *Say It With Figures.* New York: Harper & Row, Publishers, 1957; Hubert M. Blalock, Jr., *Causal Inferences in Nonexperimental Research.* Chapel Hill: University of North Carolina, 1964.

[36] The question of definitions is an important one. An elaborate set of definitions has not been attempted for the terms "attitudes," "norms," and "values," but instead they are used in the following, rather common, fashion. "Norms" are defined as

sumed (and this proved to be the case) that resistance to asking behavioral questions of young people would occur among high school principals in some of the samples. Secondly, it was assumed that less deception would be attempted concerning questions of attitude.[37] Third, the attitudes of young people have been much more neglected than the sexual behavior of young people. Fourth, it would have taken a considerable addition to an already long questionnaire to check fully both attitudes and behavior, so one of these had to be minimized. Nevertheless, some questions regarding sexual behavior were used later in the study, and these focused on the relation of behavior and attitudes (Chapter 7). Finally, it should be noted that Kinsey showed that little change had occurred in coital behavior since the 1920s, whereas attitudes have apparently changed more since then.[38]

Hopefully, by this time in the development of social science we have discarded the primitive notion that behavior rather than attitude is more of a "true" measure of a relationship. Behavior may be just as deceiving as attitude. Behavior in the sexual sphere may result from many cross-pressures and may involve what the individual fully accepts or what he almost fully rejects. An individual may do only what he accepts or he may do more or he may choose to do less by not indulging at all, even when he thinks it is right to do so. Thus, behavior is no more a "real" measure of sexual relationships than is attitude; both are complicated and both are, together or separately, legitimate realms for investigation.

In this study a Guttman scale is used to measure premarital sexual attitudes.[39] The unidimensional and ordinal qualities of this scale, and a priori judgment that premarital sexual attitudes would fit into the cumulative scale model that Guttman-scaling requires, were the main determinants of this decision. It seemed important to develop a measuring instrument that would

---

standards for behavior that are held by a group; "values" are that which a group believes ought to be desired, and "attitudes" are tendencies to act that are presumedly based on one's norms and values. For elementary definitions see Kingsley Davis, *Human Society.* New York: Crowell-Collier and Macmillan, 1950. See also Clyde Kluckhohn, "Values and Value Orientations in the Theory of Action." *Toward a General Theory of Action,* Talcott Parsons and Edward Shils, eds. Cambridge, Massachusetts: Harvard University Press, 1954, pp. 388–433.

[37] On the advice of the professors running consumer finance studies, Lenski used attitudinal rather than behavioral questions in the area of spending and saving. See fn. 27, p. 96 in Gerhard Lenski, *The Religious Factor.* New York: Doubleday & Co., 1961.

[38] Ira L. Reiss, *Premarital Sexual Standards in America,* p. 230; see also Ira L. Reiss, "The Sexual Renaissance in America: A Summary and Analysis," *The Journal of Social Issues,* 22 (April 1966), pp. 123–137.

[39] The best sources for Guttman scaling are Samuel A. Stouffer *et al., Studies in Social Psychology in World War II,* vol. 4. Princeton, New Jersey: Princeton University Press, 1950 (chaps. 1–9 are written by Stouffer, Suchman, and Guttman); Louis Guttman, "The Cornell Technique for Scale and Intensity Analysis," *Educational and Psychological Measurement* (Summer 1947), pp. 247–280; Edward A. Suchman, "The Logic of Scale Construction," *Educational and Psychological Measurement* (Spring 1950), pp. 79–93.

be usable on a variety of samples, and that would fit the Guttman-scale model, and that could thus have predictable properties. Further, the scale was to be tested on a variety of samples so as to discern its utility for widespread use.

As the initial sample, a probability sample of four high schools and colleges was selected, and after a small pretest they were given a self-administered questionnaire.[40] One high school and college was all Negro, and one high school and college was all white. The schools were all located in Virginia, within twenty miles of each other. An equal-probability sample of the colleges was taken, and the entire junior and senior classes of the high schools were used.[41] These four schools differed considerably in age and race and afforded a diverse check on the workability of the scales. Only single, never married, undergraduate students were used. The rate of return was 88 percent. The majority of the nonreturns may have been people who were not contacted, for in the Negro college the interviewers hired did not bother to give out the questionnaire to those who lived on the top floors of the dormitories, even if they were supposed to be in the sample. The total number of returned questionnaires from the four schools was 692. Beside the scale questions, the questionnaire included questions on the major areas noted above as being crucial sources for independent variables. (See Appendix A for this questionnaire.) The four schools were contacted in March 1959. In October 1959, a fifth school, a small white college in New York, was added. This school gave an even greater range of responses to the samples, for it had a long-standing reputation for being an extremely liberal school in terms of sexual beliefs. Thus, in a way, it was a validity test of the scales. Two hundred eleven more cases were added from that school, which was an 88 percent return of those contacted. All single, white students were contacted. The few Negro students were not used. Thus, overall, the five-school sample had 903 cases.

In December 1962, the National Institute of Mental Health granted additional funds to pay the National Opinion Research Center of the University of Chicago to administer the sexual-attitude scales and other questions to a probability-type sample of adults, twenty-one years of age and over, representing the country.[42] About eighty percent of this sample were mar-

[40] Every *n*th student was chosen from an alphabetical list of names of the students in the two Virginia colleges. Thus, "equal-probability sample" is the best description of the sampling technique. Each chosen student was handed a questionnaire in his dorm, and it was picked up within twenty-four hours.

[41] The white high-school principal refused to allow contact with freshmen and sophomores, for he was afraid of parental reaction. The Negro high-school principal cooperated after the researcher indicated his negative position on segregated schools. Both principals called all juniors and seniors into the auditorium, separated them in seats, and then gave them the self-administered questionnaire to complete. There were no refusals and no parental objections.

[42] The national sample was a probability-type sample based on block level and represents a quota sample from within each block. (For example, blocks of a city

ried. This afforded an additional test of the scales and an adult sample for comparison. The total sample contacted in June 1963 by NORC was 1515. (See Appendix C for this questionnaire.)

At about this time a crucial probe of the relation between attitudes and behavior began with a non-random sample of 316 students from a white college in Iowa. An additional purpose of this investigation was to probe the possible effect on scalability of the item order of asking the sex questions. (See Appendix B for this questionnaire.) The Iowa sample is the only nonprobability sample and is used mainly in Chapter 7 as a check on the relation of behavior and beliefs. The probability student and adult Samples are used much more generally throughout the book.[43] The question of the validity and the reliability of the scales and the samples are taken up in the next chapter and in Appendix D.

Table 1.1

NUMBER OF CASES IN VARIOUS SAMPLES[a]

White Virginia college	274
Negro Virginia college	202
White Virginia high school	151
Negro Virginia high school	65
White New York college	211
White Iowa college	316
National Adult Sample	1515
Total	2734

[a] All are probability-type samples except the white Iowa college.

Thus, there are three major samples in this study: the Five-School Student Sample, or what shall be called the student sample, the National Adult Sample, and the Iowa College Sample. When a relationship was tested on the student sample as a whole, it was always checked on each of the five schools in this sample. The relatively large number of samples is an important aid in testing hypotheses. If a relation holds up in several samples, one has more faith in it.

Overall, the research had two basic purposes: (1) to develop and test Guttman scales to measure premarital sexual permissiveness and (2) to examine the sociocultural correlates of premarital sexual permissiveness.

---

were chosen at random, and the interviewer was told how many men or women of what age or race to interview in the chosen blocks.) This type of sample of fifteen hundred is equivalent to a simple random sample of a thousand. There is no way of estimating refusal rate in such a sample.

[43] The National Adult Sample was checked with the 1960 census on a large number of characteristics. It proved to be quite close on almost all variables compared. The Iowa College Sample was taken in sociology classes and had no refusals.

However, it was even more fundamental to develop the theoretical structure of this area. Toward this goal chapters 3 through 9 offer a proposition to "explain" the key findings of each chapter. Chapter 10 provides a broad theory that subsumes these propositions. It is hoped this will aid future researchers in this area. Although individual characteristics and motivations have been dealt with in part—and in this sense a psychological approach is included—the main approach is sociological, for explaining social facts by reference to other social facts has been the basic approach of this research.[44]

It is undoubtedly true that correlation and causation are two different, although related, things and that the latter is much more difficult to demonstrate with confidence. It is also true that the direction of causation is a formidable puzzle to solve. Causation is particularly difficult to deal with in a cross-sectional study such as this. Longitudinal studies afford much clearer insight into crucial relationships through time. Nevertheless, causal notions have been introduced here, for a pure listing of correlations is rather sterile. Hopefully, introducing causal notions will encourage the growth of theoretical explanations in any future tests done on these findings.[45] Since premarital sexual permissiveness is the subject of this study, it has been treated predominantly as a dependent variable, and thus feedback and consequences of this variable have not been systematically treated. Thus, if the author at times sounds as if he possessed full causal knowledge, this warning should be kept in mind, and it should be noted that causal descriptions are a heuristic device and a natural part of science that helps to extend theory at least partially into the dark realm that looms in front of the limits of empirical data.

[44] For the classic statement of the sociological approach see Emile Durkheim, *The Rules of Sociological Method*. New York: The Free Press, 1938 (Originally published in 1895).

[45] The .05 level of significance is used as a general limit to chance throughout this study. However, results at the .10 level will be listed as such because of frequent prediction of an expected direction.

2

The Premarital Sexual
Permissiveness Scales

Premarital Sexual Standards

The key focus of this study is upon sexual *permissiveness* as measured by Guttman scales. However, it is suitable to start this discussion by a brief glance at studies of sexual *standards*. After this discussion the Guttman scales will be presented and analyzed as an important way of measuring premarital sexual permissiveness.

A few studies in recent decades have probed the area of sexual attitudes rather than taking the more usual approach of focusing on sexual behavior. Bromley and Britten, two female journalists, studied attitudes among college students during the 1930s.[1] Although their samples were not probability samples, it is interesting to note that they found 25 percent of the females and 52 percent of the males to be nonvirginal—rates that have frequently been reported in more recent studies up to the 1960s.[2] Bromley and Britten divided their virgins and nonvirgins into subcategories depending on their attitudes, but the classification was not mutually exclusive and included married and homosexual categories. They called many of their male nonvirgins "hotbloods" and many others "pragmatists" (the exact meaning of such terms is hard to determine). Interestingly, they reported that half of the virginal female pop-

[1] Dorothy D. Bromley and Florence Britten, *Youth and Sex.* New York: Harper & Row, Publishers, 1938.

[2] For a recent statement see Mervin B. Freedman, "The Sexual Behavior of American Colege Women: An Empirical Study and a Historical Survey," *Merrill-Palmer Quarterly of Behavior and Development,* 11 (January 1965), pp. 33–39.

ulation approved of intercourse outside marriage even though they had not yet experienced it. The Bromley and Britten study, however, was not an attempt to develop a scientific classification of sexual standards but rather an attempt to afford a popular understanding of college sex life in the 1930s. Thus, it is only of peripheral interest in the search for a classification of sexual attitudes.

A more scholarly attempt at classifying sexual attitudes was published by Rockwood and Ford in 1945.[3] They used two classification forms; the first had four categories of attitudes, one of which the respondent was to check as being in agreement with: (1) equal freedom for both, (2) complete chastity for both, (3) complete freedom for men, and (4) complete chastity for women. Clearly, these categories are not mutually exclusive. An individual could believe in the double standard and check either "complete chastity for women" or "greater freedom for men." He could believe in abstinence for both and agree with either "equal freedom for both" or "complete chastity for both." Rockwood and Ford recognized some of these shortcomings and revised this form. Table 2.1 presents the revised set of categories and the results obtained on the basis of 173 Cornell students.

Table 2.1
SEXUAL STANDARDS OF 173 CORNELL STUDENTS

	Percentage		
SEXUAL STANDARD	MEN (N^a = 73)	WOMEN (N = 100)	BOTH (N = 173)
Sex relations for both	15	6	9
No sex relations for either	49	76	65
Sex relations for men only	23	11	16
Sex relations for engaged	11	6	8
Question left blank	1	2	2

Source: L. Rockwood and M. Ford, *Youth, Marriage, and Parenthood,* New York: John Wiley & Sons, copyright © 1945, p. 40.
[a] In this and all subsequent tables *N* stands for the number of respondents.

However, this set of categories is still not completely adequate. The first three standards cover the three logically possible attitudes that any culture may take toward premarital coitus. A culture may accept coitus for both sexes, for neither sex or predominantly for one sex.[4] Thus, it follows that all additional standards are subtypes of these three standards. Such subtypes must be spelled out, for they give the particular flavor to a society's values

    [3] Lemo D. Rockwood and Mary E. Ford, *Youth, Marriage, and Parenthood.* New York: John Wiley & Sons, 1945.
    [4] Ira L. Reiss, *Premarital Sexual Standards in America.* New York: The Free Press, 1960. Chap. 3 contains a full discussion of this area.

in this area. The only subtype in this table is "sex relations for engaged." This is logically a subtype of "sex relations for both." The lack of subtypes means sexual beliefs that are quite different are being lumped together. "No sex relations for either" includes people who will pet to orgasm and those who will not even accept kissing. "Sex relations for both" includes people who will have coitus only when in love and those who accept coitus more casually. Also, there are important sexual standards that are left out entirely; for instance, in what category could an individual be placed who believed that men had more sexual rights than women but that women were allowed to have coitus when in love or engaged? If such a person checked "sex relations for both," then the equalitarian aspect is overestimated; and if he checked "sex relations for men only," the equalitarian aspect is understated. This is a popular standard in our culture, and yet there does not seem to be a clear-cut category for it in the Rockwood and Ford classification schema.

Shortly after the Rockwood and Ford study, Judson Landis questioned five thousand college students from twelve different colleges, using the same fourfold breakdown of standards.[5] The results of his research are presented in Table 2.2, together with a summary of the original results obtained at

Table 2.2

PERCENTAGE OF STUDENTS CHECKING EACH OF FOUR STATEMENTS
REPRESENTING ATTITUDES ON PREMARITAL SEX STANDARDS

APPROVED STANDARD	11 COLLEGES 1952–1955 ($N = 3000$)	MICHIGAN STATE U 1947 ($N = 2000$)	CORNELL 1940 ($N = 173$)
	Males		
SEXUAL RELATIONS			
For both	20	16	15
None for either	52	59	49
For men only	12	10	23
Between engaged only	16	15	11
	Females		
For both	5	2	6
None for either	65	76	76
For men only	23	15	11
Between engaged only	7	7	6

Source: Judson T. Landis and Mary G. Landis, *Building a Successful Marriage,* Third Edition, © 1958, p. 215. Reprinted by permission of Prentice-Hall, Inc., Englewood Cliffs, New Jersey. Table has been rearranged.

[5] Judson T. Landis and Mary G. Landis, *Building a Successful Marriage,* 3d ed. Englewood Cliffs, New Jersey: Prentice-Hall, 1958, chap. 11.

Cornell by Rockwood and Ford. The results were relatively similar, but due to the aforementioned shortcomings, it is difficult to establish the validity of these measures.

More recently, Winston Ehrmann analyzed the sex codes of almost a hundred of his University of Florida students.[6] As can be seen in Table 2.3, the

Table 2.3

PERCENTAGE OF SINGLE AND DOUBLE STANDARDS IN THE PERSONAL
CODE OF THOSE SUBJECTS WHO HAD BEEN IN LOVE

STANDARDS[a]	MALES (N = 45)	FEMALES (N = 42)
Double	33	0
Conservative single	20	86
General liberal single	42	7
Lover liberal single	5	7

Source: Winston W. Ehrmann, *Premarital Dating Behavior,* New York: Holt, Rinehart and Winston, copyright © 1959, p. 189.
[a] "Conservative single" standard is the same as rejecting coitus for both male and female. "General liberal single" is the acceptance of coitus for male and female when in love or when not in love. "Lover liberal single" refers to the acceptance of coitus for both male and female but only when love is present.

results seem to stress the male's emphasis on the double standard and to deemphasize the female's support of that standard. However, this difference is partially due to the method of classification used by Ehrmann. He counted all women who wanted to remain chaste as belonging in the "conservative single" standard, even though some of them would allow men to have coitus with other women and thus would not really hold a "single" standard,[7] in the sense of a standard that applies equally to both sexes. The categories used by Ehrmann are only slightly different from those used in the other studies, and thus they are also subject to the same criticisms. Also, there is no clear place in this schema for the person who accepts coitus for the male at any time but for the female only when in love. This particular variation is quite popular, as evidence will presently show. In addition, there is a need for subdivisions within all standards.

It is not the purpose of this critical analysis to take away from the value of the above studies, but to point out that there are several important premarital sexual standards that are not classifiable by these approaches. It has not been attempted here to cover all previous work, but instead to

[6] Winston Ehrmann, *Premarital Dating Behavior.* New York: Holt, Rinehart and Winston, 1959, chap. 5.
[7] Ehrmann, p. 304, fn. 13.

select the studies most widely known and most typical of the work in this area.[8]

An attempt was made to overcome some of the limitations of previous studies by composing a set of standards that better fit the existing major premarital sexual standards in American society. As can be seen in Exhibit 2.1, four standards were decided upon: abstinence, double standard, permissiveness without affection, and permissiveness with affection.[9] The abstinence standard is divided into four subtypes, depending on whether an

Exhibit 2.1

PREMARITAL SEXUAL STANDARDS IN AMERICA

1. Abstinence (premarital intercourse is considered wrong for both sexes)
   (a) Petting without affection (petting is acceptable even when affection is negligible)
   (b) Petting with affection (petting is acceptable only in a stable, affectionate relationship)
   (c) Kissing without affection (only kissing is acceptable, but no affection is required)
   (d) Kissing with affection (only kissing is acceptable, and only in a stable, affectionate relationship)
2. Double standard (males are considered to have greater rights to premarital intercourse)
   (a) Orthodox (males may have intercourse, but females who do so are condemned)
   (b) Transitional (males have greater access to coitus, but females who are in love or engaged are allowed to have intercourse)
3. Permissiveness without affection (premarital intercourse is right for both sexes regardless of the amount of affection present)
   (a) Orgiastic (pleasure is of such importance that precautions are not stressed)
   (b) Sophisticated (pleasure is stressed, but precautions to avoid VD and pregnancy are of first importance)
4. Permissiveness with affection (premarital intercourse is acceptable for both sexes if part of a stable, affectionate relationship)
   (a) Love (love or engagement is a prerequisite for coitus)
   (b) Strong affection (strong affection is a sufficient prerequisite for coitus)

Source: Adapted from Ira L. Reiss, *Premarital Sexual Standards in America.* New York: The Free Press, copyright © 1960, p. 251.

[8] For another recent report see chap. 4 of Rose K. Goldsen *et al,* eds., *What College Students Think.* Princeton, New Jersey: D. Van Nostrand Co., 1960.

[9] It should be clear that the concern here is not with homosexual relationships or masturbation nor with marital or postmarital sexual relationships. Rather it is exclusively with heterosexual premarital sexual standards, attitudes, and behaviors toward kissing, petting, and coitus. These other important topics require separate careful treatment. Only what our culture defines as our basic sexual standards before marriage have been selected here. Names for the four basic standards were chosen that would convey the meaning of the standard and would not be purely a description of behavior. This was done because attitudes and not behavior were being dealt with, and thus "permissiveness with affection" seemed a better name than "coitus with affection."

individual accepts petting or kissing and whether or not he requires affection to be present. The double standard is divided into the "orthodox" subtype, which does not, under any conditions, accept coitus for women, and the newer, "transitional" subtype, which allows women to have coitus, but only when they are involved in a love relationship. The permissiveness-with-affection standard is divided into those who accept coitus for both men and women but require love and/or engagement to be present and those who require only strong affection to be present. The permissiveness-without-affection standard is composed of those who contend that physical attraction and pleasure are sufficient justification for coitus. The "orgiastic" subtype is less likely to take precautions against consequences such as venereal disease and pregnancy than is the "sophisticated" subtype.

This more refined breakdown has an advantage over the traditional four-fold basic breakdown of standards; it allows for more precise definitions of the four basic standards and their subtypes, so as to avoid overlapping classifications of individuals, and thereby aids in more accurate classification. Of course, even finer subtypes could be composed and finer distinctions made—for example, between mammary and genital petting and between those abstinent individuals who are equalitarian and those who are not. Part of this breakdown was actually used in the analysis presented in Chapter 6.

Such an extensive typological approach to premarital sexual standards also has its limits. At times it is difficult for an individual to have analyzed his sexual beliefs well enough to be able to see himself clearly as holding one or another of the sexual standards presented. In short, a typology calls for a global judgment that is often difficult for a person to make. In addition, a typological approach involves a mixture of dimensions, and it is difficult to compare all standards along any one continuum. It was for these reasons and others that it was decided to try and develop Guttman scales for this study that would measure premarital sexual permissiveness and also afford a basis for judging what sexual standard an individual held. Such scales would be unidimensional and thus allow all respondents to be compared in terms of being more or less permissive. Furthermore, such scales would involve many specific questions, which might well be easier for a respondent to answer and which could ultimately be used to categorize a person into one of the sexual standards. Thus, Guttman scales would yield a unidimensional measure of premarital sexual permissiveness, would present questions easy for the respondent to answer, and ultimately would allow the researcher to judge the sexual standard of the respondent.[10]

The dimension to be measured was premarital sexual permissiveness,[11]

---

[10] For an approach showing ranking regularities regarding sexual customs among various cultures see Julia S. Brown, "A Comparative Study of Deviation from Sexual Mores," *American Sociological Review* 7 (April 1952), pp. 135–146.

[11] For an early presentation of findings see Ira L. Reiss, "The Scaling of Premarital Sexual Permissiveness," *Journal of Marriage and the Family,* 26 (May 1964), pp. 188–198.

for the degree of permissiveness seemed to be of primary importance in any comparison of sexual belief. Another key dimension was equalitarianism. An indirect measure of equalitarianism was worked into the study of permissiveness by having two separate scales, one with questions only about males and one with questions only about females. The similarity or difference in response to these two scales could be used as a measure of equalitarianism without ever asking any direct questions on equalitarianism.

It was felt that in American culture, permissiveness in sex was not only a matter of physical activity but also of the conditions under which the individual would accept such physical activity. Permissiveness depended, therefore, on both the intimacy of the physical act and the conditions under which it occurred. The key condition was judged to be the amount of affection present in the relationship. The bare question, Do you accept premarital coitus? would not be unidimensional in American society, since it would not have a singular meaning to all respondents. A clearer way of probing this area seemed to be to ask questions like, Do you accept premarital coitus when in love? when not in love? and so forth. Consequently, the Guttman scales are based on questions concerning the individual's acceptance of various physical acts under various conditions of affection.

For the purpose of this study physical acts were divided into three categories: kissing, petting, and coitus. Conditions of affection were divided into four categories: engagement, love, strong affection, and no affection. Each of the three physical conditions was qualified by each of the four affection-related states, making a total of twelve statements which the respondent was asked to agree or disagree with either strongly, moderately, or slightly.[12]

Exhibit 2.2

MALE AND FEMALE PREMARITAL SEXUAL PERMISSIVENESS SCALES[a]

The following questions concern some attitudes of yours regarding courtship behavior. We realize that you may be tolerant of what others do and think, but we are not interested now in that. We are interested in your own personal views about the questions we will ask. These questions do *not* concern what you do—they concern what you *believe* about courtship. On this sheet we would like you to circle the degree of agreement or disagreement you have with each statement. Just answer these statements on the basis of how you feel toward the view expressed. Your name will never be connected with these answers, so please be as honest as you can. We use the words to mean just what they do to most people, but some may need definition:

Love means the emotional state which is more intense than strong affection and which you would define as love.

[a] There are some very slight differences in the wording of this scale in the student and adult samples. The wording above is the preferred form and was used in the adult sample.

[12] Engagement is considered to be an affection-related state involving a higher degree of affection than is present in other love relationships that do not also involve engagement, and thus it ranks at the "top" of the affection-related conditions.

Strong affection means affection which is stronger than physical attraction, average fondness, or "liking," but less strong than love.

Petting means sexually stimulating behavior more intimate than kissing and simple hugging, but not including full sexual relations.

Male Standards (Both Men and Women Check This Section)

1. I believe that kissing is acceptable for the male before marriage when he is engaged to be married.
   Agree: (1) Strong, (2) Medium, (3) Slight
   Disagree: (1) Strong, (2) Medium, (3) Slight

2. I believe that kissing is acceptable for the male before marriage when he is in love.

   (The same six-way choice found in statement 1, follows every statement.)

3. I believe that kissing is acceptable for the male before marriage when he feels strong affection for his partner.

4. I believe that kissing is acceptable for the male before marriage even if he does not feel particularly affectionate toward his partner.

5. I believe that petting is acceptable for the male before marriage when he is engaged to be married.

6. I believe that petting is acceptable for the male before marriage when he is in love.

7. I believe that petting is acceptable for the male before marriage when he feels strong affection for his partner.

8. I believe that petting is acceptable for the male before marriage even if he does not feel particularly affectionate toward his partner.

9. I believe that full sexual relations are acceptable for the male before marriage when he is engaged to be married.

10. I believe that full sexual relations are acceptable for the male before marriage when he is in love.

11. I believe that full sexual relations are acceptable for the male before marriage when he feels strong affection for his partner.

12. I believe that full sexual realtions are acceptable for the male before marriage even if he does not feel particularly affectionate toward his partner.

Female Standards (Both Men and Women Check This Section)

(The same twelve items occur here except that the female is the sex referent.)

These twelve statements are the basis of both the male and female premarital sexual premissiveness scales; the only difference in each is the sex referent. In order to avoid ambiguity, some key terms used in the scales, such as *love,* and *petting,* and *strong affection,* were defined. The graphic portrayal in Table 2.4 shows the logic of the scales. A simple comparison of the responses to the male and female scales affords a measure of equalitarianism. A respondent can be classified in several ways: (1) how he responds to the scale statement of his own sex, (2) how he responds to the scale statements of the opposite sex, and (3) how equalitarian his responses are to both scales. On the basis of these types of responses to the scale statements, each respondent may be placed into one of the sexual standards

Table 2.4

GRAPHIC PORTRAYAL OF QUESTIONS
IN THE MALE AND FEMALE SCALES[a]

Affectionate Condition	Type of Physical Activity		
	KISSING	PETTING	COITUS
Engaged	1	5	9
Love	2	6	10
Strong Affection	3	7	11
No affection	4	8	12

[a] The same twelve items occur in both male and female scales except that the sex referent in the former is the male and the sex referent in the latter is the female.

listed in Exhibit 2.1 without ever having been asked directly to make a "pigeonhole" global judgment of himself.[13] For example, a respondent who only agreed with the first three "kissing" statements on both the male and female scales would be a kissing-with-affection subtype under the abstinence standard. If the respondent also agreed with the fourth "kissing" statement for both the male and female scale, he would be a kissing-without-affection subtype. If he agreed with the same number of affectionate petting statements (5, 6, 7) for both scales, he would be a petting-with-affection subtype and if he also checked statement 8 he would be a petting-without-affection subtype. The orthodox double-standard male would allow some degree of coitus for himself but not for the female, and thus he might check all twelve items on the male scale with agreement but agree only to the first five or six items on the female scale. The transitional double-standard (see Exhibit 2.1) subtype might agree with one or more of the "affectionate coitus" items on the female scale but with more of these and with item 12 on the male scale. Permissiveness-with-affection subtypes would be detected as those who agree with the affectionate-coitus items on both scales, and permissiveness-with-

[13] A respondent's sexual standard is arrived at by first examining his responses to the four "coital" statements in both the male and female scales. If he has agreed with one or more of these statements then a check is made to see if the response is the same on both the male and female scales. If it is, then the respondent accepts coitus equally for both men and women and would be either an adherent of permissiveness with affection or permissiveness without affection. If the respondent gave a different response to the "coital" statements on the male and female scales, then he would be classified in one of the double-standard categories. Those who disagreed with all coital statements on both the male and female scales would then be examined on the four "petting" statements in a fashion similar to that on the four coital statements. Finally, those who also disagreed with all petting statements on both the male and female scales would be similarly examined on the four "kissing" statements. In such a basic fashion respondents can be logically classified into the sexual standards and their subtypes.

out-affection subtypes as those who agree with all twelve items on both scales.

The only subtypes that cannot be detected in terms of the standards in Exhibit 2.1 are the subtypes of the permissiveness-without-affection standard. These subtypes are unique in that they do not relate to affectionate states but rather to the amount of precautions taken. They involve a different dimension than that measured by these scales. Thus, all permissiveness-without-affection adherents are counted as one group.

The empirical data revealed some other standards that had not been incorporated into the original schema. One was the nonequalitarian subtype of the abstinence standard that typically involved the acceptance of petting on the male scale but only of kissing on the female scale. More than one out of every six abstinence adherents, particularly females, accepted this subtype. In addition, it was found that some respondents displayed a slight "reverse" double standard, that is, they gave greater coital sexual freedom to the female. This latter response is almost certainly an error. Assuming that people do not have their answers to all twenty-four questions perfectly worked out in their minds, it is not surprising that some should unwittingly agree with one more question on the female scale than on the male scale. However, the matter was checked further. Using several hundred students from an Iowa college (the Iowa College Sample; see Appendix B and Chapters 6 and 7), a checklist was composed of the standards in Exhibit 2.1 and of the reverse double standard. No respondent checked the reverse double standard as his choice, despite the fact that these same respondents produced response patterns that were reverse double standard in their replies to the male and female scales. This is further evidence of the inadvertent nature of this response pattern. These reverse double-standard respondents seem to fit very well within the general category of double-standard respondents in many characteristic ways. The "reverse" image was largely accidental and due to lack of precisely worked-out views in the area. Similarly, a reverse nonequalitarian subtype under the abstinence standard was found, and was shown by the Iowa sample to be a subtype that no one would directly choose and thus consisted mainly of error responses due to lack of clarity on the issues raised in the questions.

Tables 2.5 and 2.6 show the breakdown of the various standards within each of the five high schools and colleges comprising the Five-School Student Sample and show how this varies by sex. The vast differences among these five schools shows up clearly here.[14] More will be said about this

[14] Two other all-white college student samples have been used to test these scales. One was an Iowa sample, and the other was from the state of Washington. In both cases the scales met all Guttman-scaling criteria. The responses fitted generally with those of the other student populations, with the Iowa school showing more liberality than the white Virginia college but less than the New York college, and with the Washington school showing about the same type of response achieved from the white Virginia college. The Washington school was known for being a conservative college,

Table 2.5

PERCENTAGE ACCEPTING EACH PREMARITAL SEXUAL STANDARD
IN FIVE SELECTED SCHOOLS IN STUDENT SAMPLE[a]

STANDARD	WHITE VIRGINIA COLLEGE	WHITE VIRGINIA HIGH SCHOOL	WHITE NEW YORK COLLEGE	NEGRO VIRGINIA COLLEGE	NEGRO VIRGINIA HIGH SCHOOL	TOTAL STUDENT SAMPLE[b]
1. *Abstinence*						
Kissing with affection	6	12	1	4	4	5
Kissing without affection	5	8	1	0	2	4
Petting with affection	36	22	12	15	5	21
Petting without affection	2	2	2	0	0	2
Nonequalitarian	10	15	1	4	7	7
Reverse nonequalitarian	3	6	2	2	2	3
Total	62	65	19	25	20	42
2. *Double standard*						
Transitional	10	5	21	19	11	14
Orthodox	14	10	6	14	4	11
Total	24	15	27	33	15	25
3. *Permissiveness with affection*						
Engaged and/or love	6	6	11	12	16	9
Strong affection	2	4	20	13	21	10
Total	8	10	31	25	37	19
4. *Permissiveness without affection*						
Total	3	2	14	8	16	7
5. *Reverse double standard*						
Total	3	8	10	9	14	7
Number of respondents	(264)	(147)	(188)	(165)	(57)	(821)

[a] To obtain a column total of 100 percent use only the five "total" percents. The rounding-off procedure may cause this total to be off one or two points.

[b] The percents in this column are calculated on the entire student sample. They are not simply averages of the percent in each of the five schools because the schools represent subsamples of various sizes that must be properly weighted.

later.[15] For the present, some general observations will suffice. Thus the general popularity of some of these standards, such as the petting-with-affection subtype of the abstinence standard, and the wide range of acceptance of abstinence, from 65 percent in the white high school to 19 percent in the New York college, was noteworthy. (Thus it would seem that the hoped-for diverse type of sample on which to test the scales was achieved.) Negroes seemed generally more permissive than whites, although

and this result adds to the validity of the scales. The scales have been translated into Swedish under the direction of Professor Floyd Martinson of Gustavus Adolphus College, and they were administered in Sweden in the summer of 1966. Results have not yet been fully analyzed.

[15] Only those respondents who answered all scale questions were used in the study. Fortunately, over ninety percent of those in all the samples did answer fully.

Table 2.6
PERCENTAGE ACCEPTING EACH PREMARITAL SEXUAL STANDARD BY SEX IN THE STUDENT SAMPLE

STANDARD	WHITE VIRGINIA COLLEGE		WHITE VIRGINIA HIGH SCHOOL		WHITE NEW YORK COLLEGE		NEGRO VIRGINIA COLLEGE		NEGRO VIRGINIA HIGH SCHOOL		TOTAL STUDENT SAMPLE	
	M	F	M	F	M	F	M	F	M	F	M	F
1. *Abstinence*												
Kissing with affection	3	7	2	21	1	1	1	7	3	4	2	8
Kissing without affection	2	8	5	11	1	1	0	0	0	4	2	5
Petting with affection	26	43	22	22	7	16	4	24	3	8	14	28
Petting without affection	4	1	3	1	3	0	0	0	0	0	3	1
Nonequalitarian	4	14	9	20	0	1	4	4	3	12	4	10
Reverse nonequalitarian	3	3	5	7	1	2	4	1	0	4	3	3
Total	42	76	46	82	13	21	13	36	9	32	28	55
2. *Double standard*												
Transitional	20	3	11	1	17	26	24	15	19	0	18	10
Orthodox	12	16	9	10	6	6	9	19	0	8	9	13
Total	32	19	20	11	23	32	33	34	19	8	27	23
3. *Permissiveness with affection*												
Engaged and/or love	10	2	12	1	11	12	10	14	6	28	10	8
Strong affection	4	1	6	2	21	19	19	7	28	12	14	7
Total	14	3	18	3	32	31	29	21	34	40	24	15
4. *Permissiveness without affection*												
Total	5	1	5	0	22	5	14	2	25	4	13	2
5. *Reverse double standard*												
Total	5	1	12	4	9	11	11	7	13	16	9	6
Number of respondents	(116)	(148)	(65)	(82)	(94)	(94)	(79)	(86)	(32)	(25)	(386)	(435)

the white New York college equaled the Negro schools. Table 2.6 shows some striking male-female differences, such as twice as many females as males accepting abstinence, male preference for the transitional double standard versus female preference for the orthodox double standard, and permissiveness without affection as very heavily a male position.

The National Adult Sample shows similar features, as can be seen in Table 2.7. To make the results comparable to the student sample race and sex were controlled. The same type of differences between Negroes and whites, and males and females, appeared here. However, the greater conservatism of the adult sample is plainly visible in this table.

Probably the most important point that these findings bring out is that there is a way of measuring premarital sexual standards by use of Guttman

Table 2.7
PERCENTAGE ACCEPTING VARIOUS PREMARITAL SEXUAL STANDARDS
BY RACE AND SEX IN THE ADULT SAMPLE

STANDARD	WHITE MALE	WHITE FEMALE	NEGRO MALE	NEGRO FEMALE	TOTAL MALE	TOTAL FEMALE	TOTAL ADULT SAMPLE
1. *Abstinence*							
Kissing with affection	11	25	12	21	12	25	18
Kissing without affection	8	13	2	6	7	12	10
Petting with affection	22	20	9	14	21	19	20
Petting without affection	10	5	2	3	9	4	7
Nonequalitarian	12	20	0	6	11	18	15
Reverse nonequalitarian	5	9	5	15	5	10	7
Total	68	92	30	65	65	88	77
2. *Double standard*							
Transitional	6	1	11	4	7	1	4
Orthodox	7	3	9	4	7	4	5
Total	13	4	20	8	14	5	9
3. *Permissiveness with affection*							
Engaged and/or love	3	1	7	7	3	1	2
Strong affection	4	1	14	6	5	1	3
Total	7	2	21	13	8	2	5
4. *Permissiveness without affection*							
Total	8	3	23	10	9	3	6
5. *Reverse double standard*							
Total	5	1	7	6	5	1	3
Number of respondents	(594)	(622)	(57)	(72)	(651)	(694)	(1345)

scales. It is now pertinent to deal with the Guttman scales themselves, which are the basic measure of the dependent variable (premarital sexual permissiveness) used in this study. Although standards will be discussed, the main emphasis throughout this study is on the dimension of permissiveness measured by the scales. The key question of the entire study is: What sociocultural factors help explain the difference between high- and low-permissive groups?

Premarital Sexual Permissiveness

The question of whether arriving at standards via the twenty-four scale questions is more effective than via a simple checklist of the standards was tested on about three hundred Iowa college students. Roughly eighty percent of the students felt the scale questions were easier to answer; twenty percent felt they were equally difficult; virtually no one thought the checklist was easier to answer. The Guttman scales directly measure one dimension—namely, the individual's amount of premarital sexual *permissiveness;* this is most frequently used as a measure of the dependent variable. Premarital sexual *standards* can be indirectly measured by these scales, as has been already shown, and they serve as another measure of the dependent variable. Measuring premarital sexual permissiveness directly by the scales allows all respondents to be placed on a continuum of more or less acceptance of permissiveness and allows the continuum to be cut wherever wished. These qualities make permissiveness more useful and simpler than sexual standards. Of course, as shall become apparent, there are problems for which we must look at sexual standards, and both of these dependent variables were checked in all the analyses performed.

The twelve statements that make up each scale were selected because it was felt that they covered the dimension of premarital sexual permissiveness from its low to its high points. However, this can only be certified by testing the scales and by observing the order in which the items scale. The checks made on these scales in the student and adult samples show that the items do cover almost the full range of this dimension, the first item in the scale (see Exhibit 2.2 for description of items) receiving about ninety-five to ninety-nine percent agreement and the last item only receiving about seven to twenty-one percent agreement (see Table 2.8).

Table 2.9 shows the rank order of acceptance of these items in the two major samples. Basically, items 4 and 8 scaled in other than the order in which they were asked. Items 1, 2, and 3 also showed some variation, but the difference was so slight, involving only one or two percentage points, that it was not significant. Clearly these first three "kissing" items are so close to one another that it is best to treat them as one item. In comparing the two samples it can be seen that the student and adult samples scale dif-

Table 2.8

PERCENTAGE AGREEING WITH EACH ITEM
IN MALE AND FEMALE SCALES IN THE ADULT
AND STUDENT SAMPLES

QUESTION NUMBER	ADULT SAMPLE TOTAL PERCENT	STUDENT SAMPLE TOTAL PERCENT
	Male Scale	
1	95.3	97.5
2	93.6	98.9
3	90.2	97.2
4	58.6	64.2
5	60.8	85.0
6	59.4	80.4
7	54.3	67.0
8	28.6	34.3
9	19.5	52.2
10	17.6	47.6
11	16.3	36.9
12	11.7	20.8
N	(1390)	(811)
	Female Scale	
1	95.0	98.5
2	93.3	99.1
3	88.1	97.8
4	50.1	55.2
5	56.1	81.8
6	52.6	75.2
7	45.6	56.7
8	20.3	18.0
9	16.9	44.0
10	14.2	38.7
11	12.5	27.2
12	7.4	10.8
N	(1411)	(806)

ferently with regard to items 4 and 8. These two items ranked higher (obtained higher relative support) in the adult sample than in the student
sample. This is particularly true for item 8.

Item 8 refers to the acceptance of petting with someone for whom there
is no particular affection. The lower support of this item, relative to other
items, by the student sample, indicates a greater willingness on the part of
students as compared to adults to accept coitus when affection is present
(items 9, 10, and 11) than to accept petting when affection is absent (as
in item 8). The adult sample reversed this priority and accepted petting
without affection (item 8) before they would accept coitus with affection
(items 9, 10, and 11). This is an important difference in ranking, for it

Table 2.9

SCALE ORDER OF QUESTIONS ON MALE AND FEMALE
SCALES IN THE ADULT AND STUDENT SAMPLES[a]

RANK	ADULT SAMPLE TOTAL QUESTION ORDER	STUDENT SAMPLE TOTAL QUESTION ORDER
1st (highest support)	1	2
2d	2	1
3d	3	3
4th	5	5
5th	6	6
6th	④	7
7th	7	④
8th	⑧	9
9th	9	10
10th	10	11
11th	11	⑧
12th (lowest support)	12	12

[a] Same results were obtained for both male and female scales.

would seem to be a characteristic difference distinguishing high- and low-permissive individuals.

This high-permissive–low-permissive difference can be seen by comparing the white and Negro groups in the adult sample in Tables 2.10 and 2.11. Negroes show higher percentages accepting the more permissive items and also rank items 4 and 8 lower (less relative support) than do whites. This is a comparable situation to the relative ranking between the total student sample and the more conservative adult sample as seen in Table 2.9. The Negro segment of the adult sample has almost the exact same high-permissive scale order of items as the total student sample. (Compare Tables 2.9 and 2.11.)

Dividing the student sample into the five different schools also bears out this low- and high-permissive difference. Tables 2.12 and 2.13 show the percent accepting each item and the rank order of each item by school. The schools that seem to have a high level of permissiveness among their students give less relative support (low rank) to items 4 and 8. The Negro schools and the white New York college are the three high-permissive schools. In the male scale, item 4 ranks ninth and tenth in these schools but ranks sixth in the two low-permissive schools. Item 8 ranks eleventh in the high-permissive schools but ninth in the low-permissive schools. This means that the high-permissive schools give more support to having intercourse with someone you are in love with than to kissing someone you don't care for (item 4) and give more support to intercourse with someone you have strong affection for (item 11) than to petting with someone for whom

Table 2.10

PERCENTAGE AGREEING WITH EACH ITEM IN THE MALE AND FEMALE
SCALES BY RACE IN THE ADULT SAMPLE

QUESTION NUMBER	TOTAL ADULT SAMPLE	TOTAL WHITES	TOTAL NEGROES
		Male Scale	
1	95.3	95.6	92.1
2	93.6	94.4	86.3
3	90.2	91.5	79.1
4	58.6	59.9	47.5
5	60.8	60.0	67.6
6	59.4	58.5	66.9
7	54.3	54.0	56.8
8	28.6	28.7	28.1
9	19.5	16.9	43.2
10	17.6	14.9	41.7
11	16.3	13.9	38.1
12	11.7	10.6	22.3
N	(1390)	(1251)	(139)
		Female Scale	
1	95.0	95.6	89.6
2	93.3	94.4	84.0
3	88.1	89.4	76.4
4	50.1	51.0	42.4
5	56.1	55.2	63.9
6	52.6	51.3	63.9
7	45.6	44.3	56.9
8	20.3	19.7	22.9
9	16.9	14.3	40.3
10	14.2	11.7	36.1
11	12.5	10.3	31.9
12	7.4	6.2	18.1
N	(1411)	(1267)	(144)

you do not have affection (item 8). The low-permissive schools reverse these rankings and give the priority to affectionless kissing and petting. It is important to note that these high- and low-permissive differences hold regardless of whether whites and Negroes or students and adults are compared.

There seems to be some sort of compensatory behavior operating here. Those who are high on permissiveness differ from those who are low on permissiveness primarily by their greater willingness to choose a higher level of physical intimacy with affection as more desirable than a lower level of physical intimacy without affection.[16] In place of greater physical

[16] This does not mean that high permissives will have a lower percent supporting, say, item 8. Rather, it means that in a high-permissive group item 8 will have a lower percent than item 9, and that this will be much less the case in a low-permissive group.

Table 2.11
SCALE ORDER OF QUESTIONS ON THE MALE AND FEMALE SCALES BY RACE IN THE ADULT SAMPLE

RANK	TOTAL QUESTION ORDER	TOTAL WHITE QUESTION ORDER	TOTAL NEGRO QUESTION ORDER
	Male Scale		
1st (highest support)	1	1	1
2d	2	2	2
3d	3	3	3
4th	5	5	5
5th	6	④	6
6th	4	6	7
7th	7	7	④
8th	8	⑧	9
9th	9	9	10
10th	10	10	11
11th	11	11	⑧
12th (lowest support)	12	12	12
	Female Scale		
1st (highest support)	1	1	1
2d	2	2	2
3d	3	3	3
4th	5	5	5 ⎫ tie
5th	6	6	6 ⎭
6th	4	④	7
7th	7	7	④
8th	8	⑧	9
9th	9	9	10
10th	10	10	11
11th	11	11	⑧
12th (lowest support)	12	12	12

intimacy with affection the low permissives allow themselves greater access to affectionless behavior that is less intimate, while the high permissives prefer the more intimate affectionate behavior. For example, it seems that the low permissives feel the stronger taboo against coital behavior and thus will even resort to affectionless petting in order to stay away from coitus.[17] The high permissives do not exhibit such a taboo on coitus and thus prefer coitus with affection to affectionless petting. This is not by any means an inevitable result, for the high permissives could have been much more acceptant of affectionless kissing and petting.

Some other features stand out in these scale results. The great importance of affection as a means of increasing acceptance of sexual behavior is

[17] Harold Christensen found that the low-permissive group (Mormon) was most likely to have "terminal petting." See his "Scandinavian and American Sex Norms," *Journal of Social Issues,* 22 (April 1966), pp. 60–75.

Table 2.12
Percentage Agreeing with Each Item in the Male and Female Scales in the Student Sample

QUESTION NUMBER	TOTAL STUDENT SAMPLE	WHITE VIRGINIA COLLEGE	WHITE VIRGINIA HIGH SCHOOL	WHITE NEW YORK COLLEGE	NEGRO VIRGINIA COLLEGE	NEGRO VIRGINIA HIGH SCHOOL
			Male Scale			
1	97.5	99.2	97.2	99.5	93.8	94.6
2	98.9	99.6	98.6	99.5	97.5	98.2
3	97.2	98.9	94.4	96.8	98.8	92.8
4	64.2	74.1	60.1	65.6	56.9	44.6
5	85.0	84.8	66.4	95.2	91.3	80.3
6	80.4	76.8	60.8	93.7	86.9	83.9
7	67.0	55.5	49.0	86.8	76.3	73.2
8	34.3	31.6	23.8	43.9	37.5	32.1
9	52.2	31.9	25.2	78.3	71.9	71.4
10	47.6	30.8	21.0	76.7	63.1	51.8
11	36.9	20.5	16.8	60.3	50.0	48.2
12	20.8	15.6	8.4	31.7	25.6	26.8
N	(811)	(263)	(143)	(189)	(160)	(56)
			Female Scale			
1	98.5	99.6	97.9	98.9	98.1	94.6
2	99.1	100.0	98.6	99.5	97.5	100.0
3	97.8	99.2	97.2	97.3	96.9	96.4
4	55.2	63.8	53.8	56.7	46.0	41.1
5	81.8	82.9	57.9	94.1	85.1	87.5
6	75.2	72.4	52.4	91.4	82.6	71.4
7	56.7	42.0	40.7	81.3	60.2	73.2
8	18.0	13.2	17.2	28.9	13.7	17.9
9	44.0	22.2	22.1	74.3	54.0	71.4
10	38.7	16.3	18.6	72.2	47.8	55.4
11	27.2	9.3	11.7	49.7	34.2	53.6
12	10.8	5.8	6.9	19.2	9.9	17.9
N	(806)	(257)	(145)	(187)	(161)	(56)

quite visible. This can be seen most clearly by looking at the "affectionless" statements (items 4, 8, and 12). All groups rated the behavior indicated in item 4 as at least more permissive than some petting behavior, and all groups except the adult whites rated the behavior indicated in item 8 as at least more permissive than some form of coitus. In addition, the "strong affection" statements almost always rank as less-approved, or higher on permissiveness, than do the "engaged" or "love" statements. (See Tables 2.11 and 2.13.) *To summarize—when affection decreases, the same sexual behavior is viewed as considerably more permissive. This is particularly true for high-permissive sexual groups.*

The tendency of the behavior indicated in items 4 and 8 to move into a "higher" type of sexual behavior (petting or coitus) is of research value.

Table 2.13

SCALE ORDER OF QUESTIONS ON THE MALE AND FEMALE
SCALES IN THE STUDENT SAMPLE

RANK	TOTAL STUDENT SAMPLE QUESTION ORDER	WHITE VIRGINIA COLLEGE QUESTION ORDER	WHITE VIRGINIA HIGH SCHOOL QUESTION ORDER	WHITE NEW YORK COLLEGE QUESTION ORDER	NEGRO VIRGINIA COLLEGE QUESTION ORDER	NEGRO VIRGINIA HIGH SCHOOL QUESTION ORDER
Male Scale						
1st (highest support)	2	2	2	2 } tie	3	2
2d	1	1	1	1 } tie	2	1
3d	3	3	3	3	1	3
4th	5	5	5	5	5	6
5th	6	6	6	6	6	5
6th	7	(4)	(4)	7	7	7
7th	4	7	7	9	9	9
8th	9	9	9	10	10	10
9th	10	(8)	(8)	(4)	(4)	11
10th	11	10	10	11	11	(4)
11th	8	11	11	(8)	(8)	(8)
12th (lowest support)	12	12	12	12	12	12
Female Scale						
1st (highest support)	2	2	2	2	1	2
2d	1	1	1	1	2	3
3d	3	3	3	3	3	1
4th	5	5	5	5	5	5
5th	6	6	(4)	6	6	7
6th	7	(4)	6	7	7	6 } tie
7th	4	7	7	9	9	9 } tie
8th	9	9	9	10	10	10
9th	10	10	10	(4)	(4)	11
10th	11	(8)	(8)	11	11	(4)
11th	8	11	11	(8)	(8)	(8) } tie
12th (lowest support)	12	12	12	12	12	12 } tie

For example, if for some reason the researcher cannot ask questions about premarital coitus to a group of respondents, then item 8 can be used to obtain some information concerning coitus without ever directly asking about it. It can be predicted (for all groups except white adults) that over ninety percent of those who agree with item 8 will also accept coitus when affection is present. This is so because item 8 ranks higher in permissiveness than do some of the coitus-with-affection items (9, 10, or 11), and the cumulative quality of a Guttman scale guarantees that in about ninety percent of the cases agreement to a higher-ranking item involves agreement with all lower-ranking items. It should be added, however, that this rule does not work both ways—that there are people who will accept coitus when affection is present but who will not accept petting without affection; and thus item 8 does not give information on all who accept coitus. Nevertheless, it is a way of gaining some information on attitudes toward coitus without ever asking the question directly. In an analogous fashion, item 4 would allow one to gain information on petting without ever directly asking questions on petting. In this way a less controversial item may be used to predict a more controversial attitude.

The scale order (rank order) of items in both the male and female scales is virtually identical in all adult and student groups when the highly "mobile" items, 4 and 8, are left out. The only exceptions are those cases where the difference is due to a few respondents, such as in item 1 in the student sample. The universal order is 1, 2, 3, 5, 6, 7, 9, 10, 11, 12. Furthermore, the movement of items 4 and 8 have empirical value in that they allow us a basis for judging the level of permissiveness of the group being measured.

Universal Permissive Scales

The universal order of items, which holds up in all samples, may be used for comparative purposes. However, it is simpler to combine some items. For example, since over ninety-five percent accept items 1, 2, and 3, these separate items might well be dropped, and those who only accept one or more of these three items might be called scale-type zero. Then, since items 5 and 6 are so close in percentage agreement, they can be combined into one scale type, and all those who also agree with one or more of them could be called scale-type one. Scale-type two would, in addition, accept item 7, and scale-type three would, in addition, accept either item 9 or 10 or both. Scale-type four would also accept item 11, and finally, scale-type five would accept also item 12. This short universal scale would then consist of five items, or combined items: (5, 6), 7, (9, 10), 11, 12. A scale-type-zero person would disagree with all of these, and a scale-type-five person would agree with all of these. (For a fuller discussion of these scale types see Appendices D and E.)

Table 2.14 presents the race and sex breakdown on this short universal form for the adult and student samples. For the sake of simplicity, this scale has been dichotomized to designate scale-types zero, one, and two as "low" and scale-types three, four, and five as "high." In effect, this means that those who accept coitus will be called high and all others low. In actuality, all tables were run with the scale open and with other cuts, and it was found that this made little difference. Most of the relations with permissiveness show a linear quality, and thus the aforementioned dichotomy is suitable. Where a curvilinear relation occurs, it is presented accordingly.

Table 2.14

PERCENTAGE DISTRIBUTION OF GUTTMAN-SCALE TYPES ON UNIVERSAL
FIVE-ITEM SCALE BY RACE AND SEX
FOR THE STUDENT AND ADULT SAMPLES[a]

	LOW 0	1	*Permissiveness Scale Types* 2	3	4	HIGH 5	N
			Student Sample				
White Male	7	11	20	18	19	25	(287)
White Female	26	27	20	14	10	2	(324)
Negro Male	4	4	7	17	31	37	(115)
Negro Female	14	16	25	30	11	4	(118)
Total	15	17	19	18	16	15	(844)
			Adult Sample				
White Male	22	7	40	7	8	15	(607)
White Female	54	15	25	2	2	3	(649)
Negro Male	18	5	13	15	21	29	(62)
Negro Female	32	17	21	7	10	12	(81)
Total	37	11	31	5	6	10	(1399)

[a] The male-standards scale was used to compute scale types for men, and the female-standards scale was used for women. Thus, this scale scores the individual on self-permissiveness.

In order to obtain a "self-permissiveness" score, the scale was used with men being scored by their answers to the male scale and women being scored by their answers to the female scale. This presents the self-permissiveness of the person rather than the permissiveness for the opposite sex or than an average general permissiveness. Throughout this study the universal scale is used to measure self-permissiveness, and thus the respondent is scored on the scale of his or her own sex.

Appendix D gives full details on this universal scale as well as on the basic twelve-item scale. It is unnecessary to say more here than that without dropping or adding any items, the original twelve items formed a Guttman scale that met all Guttman-scaling criteria to quite a high degree. This includes a check on item intercorrelation, coefficient of reproducibility, coefficient of scalability, minimal marginal reproducibility, percent pure scale types, and other checks. The same was true of the six-scale-type universal scale described previously. Appendix E explains a simple way to use this six-scale-type universal scale in empirical work.

Summary and Conclusions

The Guttman scales have worked successfully in every sample in which they have been used. This method of measuring permissiveness is believed to have advantages over more "global" approaches, for the items used in the scale are easier to respond to, and the scale has a unidimensional quality that makes comparison simple. Also, the scale may be used to classify people according to standards as well as according to degree of permissiveness. This can be done by comparing the respondent's score on both the male and female scales, thereby adding the dimension of equalitarianism to the dimension of permissiveness.

It was noted earlier that there was a compensatory behavior that distinguished high- and low-permissive groups; that is, the high-permissive groups gave a lower relative rank to kissing and petting without affection than did the low-permissive groups, who to various degrees ranked such behavior as more acceptable than intercourse with affection.

The specific standards are discussed later at greater length, particularly in Chapters 6 and 7. It is enough to say here that the exact percent of adherents in each standard should not be taken as more than a general indication of the standard's relative popularity. The attempt was to get at informal, operational standards instead of at formal ones. The extent to which this was accomplished is also discussed later. Finally, it should be noted that the self-permissiveness score that is dichotomized into high and low is generally used as the key measure throughout the study. The basic attempt is to explain some of the sociocultural factors related to being high or low on permissiveness. To aid in this process, the empirical findings of the next seven chapters have been integrated into seven propositions, and in the final chapter an attempt has been made to integrate these propositions into one theory. The basic task of this study, then, is to utilize the scales developed to present empirical findings and to integrate those findings into propositions and a theory.

3

Racial and Sexual Differences

Introduction to the Analysis of Tables

The response to the statements in the male and female scales noted in Chapter 2 makes it quite clear that Negroes and males are respectively more permissive than whites and females. This relationship holds up in both the student and adult samples. This chapter will explore some correlates of these differences.[1]

One of the significant findings of this study is that racial and sexual differences are not simply differences in degree but reflect a rather basic difference in the sociocultural situation of these groups. Other studies have pointed out the greater permissiveness of Negroes.[2] However, most of

[1] Some early comments on this area can be found in Ira L. Reiss, "Premarital Sexual Permissiveness Among Negroes and Whites," *American Sociological Review,* 29 (October 1964), pp. 688–698.

[2] Among the many books on the American Negro, the following are most relevant to understanding Negro sexual behavior and beliefs: Harry S. Ashmore, *An Epitaph for Dixie.* New York: W. W. Norton & Co., 1957, and *The Negro and the Schools.* Chapel Hill: University of North Carolina Press, 1954; Jessie Bernard, *Marriage and Family Among Negroes.* New Jersey: Prentice-Hall. 1966; Brewton Berry, *Race and Ethnic Relations.* Boston: Houghton Mifflin Co., 1958; William Brink and Louis Harris, *The Negro Revolution in America.* N.Y.: Simon and Schuster, 1964; Allison Davis and John Dollard, *Children of Bondage.* New York: Harper Torchbooks, 1964; Allison Davis, Burleigh B. Gardner, and Mary R. Gardner, *Deep South.* Chicago: University of Chicago Press, 1941; John Dollard, *Caste and Class in a Southern Town.* New York: Doubleday Anchor, 1957; St. Clair Drake and Horace R. Cayton, *Black Metropolis.* 2 vols.; New York: Harper Torchbooks, 1962; E. Franklin Frazier, *The Negro in the United States.* New York: Crowell-Collier and Macmillan, 1957 and *The Negro Family*

these are intensive psychological studies or participant-observation studies of a community. The few that are more like surveys report little more than that this greater permissiveness exist. Race and sex differences were elaborated, and some data on this from the present study were presented, in several of the tables in Chapter 2. In particular, the relation of these race and sex groups to certain religious and courtship institutional structures is examined in this chapter. This should begin to explain the crux of the differences between these race and sex groups.

The tests reported on in this chapter (and in most of the other chapters) use the six-scale-type universally ordered scale, and as noted in Chapter 2 (see Table 2.14), the respondents are characterized by their responses to the scale that corresponds to their own sex. The tables show this scale dichotomized between scale-types two and three, or divided into respondents who accept coitus under some condition and those who do not accept coitus under any condition. This is approximately the place that is suggested by intensity analysis as a suitable cutting point. (See Appendix D.) It should be clear that the test for almost all the tables computed in this and all other chapters were run with different and more-varied cuts in order to be sure of the linear quality of the relationship and in order to be sure that the results were not due simply to an arbitrary cut of the scale.[3]

As mentioned earlier, the method of analysis employed was that of partial tables. Simply put, this means that "controls" such as race were used and that the resulting partial tables were compared to see if the partial table for whites differed from that for Negroes. In this way the relation of various factors to premarital sexual permissiveness could be examined, and a check could be made to see if the relation held up using such a control as race.

The usual way to decide if two partial tables differ from each other is to see if the relationship being examined is significant for one category of the

---

in the United States. New York: Holt, Rinehart and Winston, 1951; Paul H. Gebhard et al., *Pregnancy, Birth, and Abortion*. New York: Harper & Row, Publishers, 1958; Calvin C. Hernton, *Sex and Racism in America*. New York: Grove Press, 1965; Abram Kardiner and Lionel Ovesey, *The Mark of Oppression*. New York: Meridian Books, 1962; Albert J. Lott and Bernice E. Lott, *Negro and White Youth*. New York: Rinehart and Winston, 1963; Gunnar Myrdal, *An American Dilemma*. New York: Harper & Row, Publishers, 1944; John H. Rohrer and Munro S. Edmonson, eds., *The Eighth Generation Grows Up*. New York: Harper Torchbooks, 1960; George E. Simpson and J. Milton Yinger, *Racial and Cultural Minorities*. New York: Harper & Row, Publishers, 1953.

Few survey studies covering large regions of the country have been done, although some recent work of this kind is reported by Brink and Harris. Gebhard is an excellent empirical source for data from the Kinsey study comparing white and Negro females (see Chapter 6 of *Pregnancy, Birth, and Abortion*.)

[3] All decks of IBM cards that were used in this study were checked in several ways. First, checks on coding errors were carried out. Marginals and listings on all decks were then made and checked. "Contradictory" punches—such as a male who listed his "husband's" occupation—were researched. It is believed that most errors were removed by this multiphase set of checks.

control but not for the other. For example, it might be found that upper-class people are significantly less permissive than lower-class people when looking at only whites but that when checking Negroes the class difference is not significant with regard to permissiveness. In such a case the conclusion would be that social class relates to permissiveness only for whites. A problem with this approach is that it is possible for one partial table to be just above the level of significance and for another to be just below the level of significance. In such a case, the actual difference is slight, and yet the conclusion would be that the relationship held up in one control category but not in the other. A related second problem revolves around the fact that the number of cases affects the size of the chi-square, so that if there were many more whites than Negroes, the chi-square would tend to be larger for whites. The use of gamma as a measure of the strength of the relationship helps to resolve this second problem in these cases, for it affords a better comparison of tables with unequal numbers of cases. However, the basic problem remains, for it is necessary to have a method of deciding how large a difference in gammas is necessary before it can be said that the two partial tables are significantly different.

In 1964, Leo Goodman published an article that presented a method of solving this problem in the analysis of partial tables.[4] This method yields a figure that enables one to conclude whether the difference between two partial tables is large enough to be significant at the .05 level or at any other level. Simply put, this method affords a way of doing more than just checking the chi-square or gamma in two tables. It affords a more precise way of discerning how likely it is that the difference between two tables is due to chance.

One illustration of the value of this new test for interaction can be seen by looking at Table 3.4. By comparing the two tables for high church-attending females it appears that one is significant at the .05 level and that the other is not. However, a comparison of the gammas shows no difference, and a check using the Goodman technique indicates that the relationship of romantic love to permissiveness is not significantly different for white and Negro females. Thus, the conclusion is something quite different than what a rote use of the chi-square of each partial table would have indicated. This method adds another element of rigor, another check, and thereby affords a sounder base for the interpretation of partial tables. Thus it is used throughout this study as an additional check.

[4] Leo Goodman, "Simple Methods for Analyzing Three-factor Interaction in Contingency Tables," *Journal of the American Statistical Association,* 59 (June 1964), pp. 319–352. Recently, Theodore R. Anderson supervised the programming of this test for the computer used in this study.

Preface to Proposition One

In order to clarify the presentation, the proposition summarizing the findings reported in each of the next seven substantive chapters is informally presented early in each chapter. However, the presentation will make it amply clear that in reality the proposition came last, after the empirical findings were digested.

Basically, the examination of race and sex differences discussed in this chapter indicated that in their degree of permissiveness white females showed a considerable amount of sensitivity to social forces such as re-ligiosity, romantic-love beliefs, and the number of times they had been in love. Negro males showed very little relation between their permissiveness and any of these social forces. Generally speaking, male permissiveness was affected less by such social forces than was female permissiveness, and Negro permissiveness was affected less than was white permissiveness.

These empirical findings led to the proposition that it was the permissive-ness of groups with a tradition of low sexual permissiveness (whites and females) that was more capable of being altered by social forces than was the permissiveness of groups with a tradition of relatively high sexual per-missiveness (Negroes and males). In other words, it seems that the likeli-hood of a change in sexual permissiveness is greater for groups who are low on permissiveness, and this implies that the change would be toward more permissiveness, since these low permissive groups are already quite low on permissiveness. The findings, in detail, and a more formal statement and analysis of the proposition follow.

Race and Permissiveness

The relationship of race to permissiveness by sex is presented in Table 3.1, and it is clearly strong and significant. Although the general level of permissiveness for all groups is lower in the adult sample, race and sex differences are present in the adult sample in slightly stronger form than in the student sample.

The difference in level of permissiveness by sex and race is important, but there are other associated differences that support the position that this is more than just a difference in degree of permissiveness. The relation of several social factors to the level of permissiveness in these sex and race groups differs significantly. The tests concerning these factors were carried out only in the student sample.

Table 3.1

RACE AND PERMISSIVENESS BY SEX
IN THE STUDENT AND ADULT SAMPLES
(PERCENTAGE HIGHLY PERMISSIVE)[a]

	MALE	FEMALE
	Student Sample	
White	61 (287)*	27 (324)
Negro	85 (115)	45 (118)
	$\chi^2 = 21.6$	$\chi^2 = 13.6$
	$P < .001$	$P < .001$
	$Q = .57$**	$Q = .39$
	Adult Sample	
White	30 (607)	6 (649)
Negro	65 (62)	30 (81)
	$\chi^2 = 30.2$	$\chi^2 = 49.6$
	$P < .001$	$P < .001$
	$Q = .62$	$Q = .73$

[a] The permissiveness of each sex is measured by responses to the scale of the same sex; that is, male permissiveness by the answers to the male scale, and female permissiveness by the answers to the female scale.

* In this and all following tables the number in parentheses is the base for the percentage.

** Q is the same as gamma in 2-by-2 tables and is a measure of the strength of the relationship.

Religious Attendance and Permissiveness

Kinsey and others have demonstrated the connection between religious behavior and premarital sexual permissiveness.[5] Accordingly, it was hypothesized for this study that the more religious elements would be lower on permissiveness. No racial differences were hypothesized. The hypothesis was tested only in the student sample, using several measures of religiosity. However, for the purpose of this discussion church-attendance is used as the measure of religiosity, although other measures showed very similar results (Appendix A, Part I, question 5c). High church-attendance was defined as going to church more than once a month. Different cutting points

[5] Alfred C. Kinsey *et al.*, *Sexual Behavior in the Human Female*, Philadelphia: W. B. Saunders Co., 1953, pp. 304–307, 331. Kinsey found that religious devoutness was a better predictor of female than of male sexual behavior. See also Ernest W. Burgess and Paul Wallin, *Engagement and Marriage*. Philadelphia: J. B. Lippincott Co., 1953, p. 339; Rose K. Goldsen *et al.*, *What College Students Think*. New York: D. Van Nostrand Co., 1960, p. 174; Eugene A. Kanin and David H. Howard, "Post-marital Consequences of Premarital Sex Adjustment," *American Sociological Review*, 23 (October 1958), pp. 556–562; and Winston W. Ehrmann, *Premarital Dating Behavior*. New York: Holt, Rinehart and Winston, 1959, p. 94.

showed the same result. It is worth noting that this result, as well as all results on the student sample, were checked in each of the five schools. Thus, there are really five independent samples that test the findings given for the total student sample.[6]

The zero-order relation between church-attendance and permissiveness is negative and significant.[7] Table 3.2 shows that when this relation is

Table 3.2
CHURCH-ATTENDANCE AND PERMISSIVENESS BY RACE AND SEX IN THE STUDENT
SAMPLE (PERCENTAGE HIGHLY PERMISSIVE)

CHURCH-ATTENDANCE	*Male*		*Female*	
	WHITE	NEGRO	WHITE	NEGRO
Low	77 (159)	91 (33)	53 (136)	58 (12)
High	40 (121)	83 (81)	6 (183)	44 (105)
	$\chi^2 = 41.0$	$\chi^2 = 1.2$	$\chi^2 = 92.1$	$\chi^2 = 0.9$
	$P < .001$	NS	$P < .001$	NS
	$Q = .-68$	$Q = -.35$	$Q = -.90$	$Q = -.29$

controlled by race and sex it becomes evident that the relation holds more for whites than for Negroes, and that within the white group it holds more for women than for men. The differences just noted appear valid, for they are sizable, are supported in all schools and are not altered by the use of different check variables. All three white schools in the five-school sample showed the negative relation of permissiveness to church-attendance, while neither of the two Negro schools did so. Since the white New York college is highly permissive, it seems that the racial difference found is not simply due to Negroes being more permissive but most likely reflects some genuine differences in the Negro subculture.

[6] The key measure of the strength of relationships used throughout this study is gamma. Q and gamma are the same for 2-by-2 tables, and since Q is better known, it is listed on the 2-by-2 tables. For a full discussion of gamma see three articles by Leo A. Goodman and William H. Kruskal, all published in the *Journal of the American Statistical Association:* "Measures of Association for Cross Classifications," 49 (December 1954), pp. 732–764; "Measures of Association for Cross Classifications II: Further Discussion and Reference," 54 (March 1959), pp. 123–163; "Measures of Association for Cross Classification III: Approximate Sampling Theory," 58 (June 1963), pp. 310–364. C (coefficient of contingency) will be used in tables where the relation is clearly curvilinear. Note that since Q is a special use of gamma, it will often be referred to as gamma. For a good general discussion of the use of statistics see Leslie Kish, "Some Statistical Problems in Research Design," *American Sociological Review*, 24 (June 1959), pp. 328–338.

[7] For the zero-order association, $\chi^2 = 89.3$ and $Q = -.600$. For all male students, $\chi^2 = 23.4$ and $Q = -.495$; for all female students $\chi^2 = 52.6$ and $Q = -.651$.

The stronger association for white females is congruent with other researchers' findings that religion exerts more control over the female's sexual life than it does over the male's. The culturally less-developed erotic imagery of females may make control of their sexual life easier.

Goodman's test for Interaction generally supports this interpretation of Table 3.2. For example, the differences between white and Negro females in the relationship of church-attendance to permissiveness are significant at the .01 level. However, the differences between white and Negro males are significant only at the .25 level, indicating a weaker male difference. The difference in this relationship between white males and white females is significant at the .01 level,[8] but the difference for Negro males and females is not significant.

The Negro-white difference in the association of church-attendance and permissiveness can be seen another way by shuffling the columns in Table 3.2. If the relation between permissiveness and race is controlled for by

Table 3.3
RACE AND PERMISSIVENESS BY SEX AND CHURCH-ATTENDANCE IN THE STUDENT SAMPLE (PERCENTAGE HIGHLY PERMISSIVE)

	High Church-Attendance		Low Church-Attendance	
RACE	MALE	FEMALE	MALE	FEMALE
White	40 (121)	6 (183)	77 (159)	53 (136)
Negro	83 (81)	44 (105)	91 (33)	58 (12)
	$\chi^2 = 36.7$	$\chi^2 = 62.7$	$\chi^2 = 3.1$	$\chi^2 = 0.1$
	$P < .001$	$P < .001$	$P < .10$	NS
	$Q = .76$	$Q = .86$	$Q = .49$	$Q = .11$

church-attendance, then the racial difference is reduced. In this table the Negro-white difference in permissiveness is accentuated among the high church-attenders but reduced considerably among those who were the low church-attenders. This result is due to the fact that the negative association between church-attendance and permissiveness holds predominantly for whites. Thus, low church-attending whites show a significant increase in permissiveness, while the low church-attending Negroes show relatively little increase in permissiveness; as a result, the racial difference tends to disappear in this group of low church-attenders. Among the high church-attenders, the racial difference is accentuated and strong racial differences become obvious. This result further indicates that church-attendance implies something rather different in Negro culture than it does in white culture.

[8] The Y-square test was used for these measures. Goodman notes that this test is similar to a chi-square test, except it uses logs instead of frequencies.

In the latter it seems to be symbolic of a conservative style of life. It is a key variable in understanding premarital sexual permissiveness and is discussed frequently in this study.

Romantic Love and Permissiveness

Beside the investigation of racial difference in level of permissiveness and the way religion affects permissiveness, an investigation was made of the relation of romantic-love beliefs to permissiveness, using the student sample. An eight-item Guttman scale was employed to measure romantic love.[9] (This is discussed and analyzed in more detail in Chapter 5.) For purposes of this analysis the respondents were divided into the categories high and low, on the basis of whether or not they endorsed item 4: There is only one real love for a person. The results were quite similar even if the entire scale was used with more cuts or with different cuts.

Just as with the previous examination, no racial differences were expected, but they did occur. It was assumed that both races would show that those who were low on romantic love were more permissive sexually. It was reasoned that romantic love was an idealistic, conservative element in our culture, and that the less an individual adhered to this belief the more permissive he would be. Nevertheless, the zero-order relation between romantic love and permissiveness was weak and not significant. Among white students, however, the relationship was significant and negative, as was hypothesized. On the other hand, in the Negro group the association was positive, though slightly short of the .05 level of significance. Both the negative association among white students and the positive association among Negro students were stronger for women than for men.

Since church-attendance had shown itself to be a powerful influence, under certain conditions, it was used here as a control on the relationship of sexual permissiveness to romantic love. It was found that the *positive* association between romantic love and permissiveness among Negro women held largely for those who were *high* on church-attendance, whereas the *negative* association among white women held primarily for those *low* on church-attendance. Males generally showed no effect of this control and

[9] The eight items in scale order are: (1) True love leads to almost perfect happiness; (2) When one is in love, the person whom he loves becomes the only goal in his life. One lives almost solely for the other; (3) True love will last forever; (4) There is only one real love for a person; (5) True love is known at once by the people involved; (6) Doubt may enter into real love; (7) Even though one's past love affair was not as strong as the present one, it may still have been a real love relationship; (8) Conflict can be a part of real love. Answers agreeing with the first five items and disagreeing with the last three produced the highest scale score on romantic love. The coefficient of reproducibility for the scale was .90 and the coefficient of scalability was .65. See Appendix A, Part VI for the full set of questions. Two questions were dropped for reasons discussed in Chapter 5.

continued to exhibit relations that were not significant. However, high church-attending Negro males did show some tendency toward a positive relationship.

Church-attendance proved to be the most powerful control, more powerful than race and much more powerful than sex. This can be seen in Table 3.4. High church-attendance interacts with the relationship between

Table 3.4

ROMANTIC LOVE AND PERMISSIVENESS BY RACE, SEX, AND CHURCH-ATTENDANCE
IN THE STUDENT SAMPLE (PERCENTAGE HIGHLY PERMISSIVE)[a]

	High Church-Attendance		Low Church Attendance	
ROMANTIC LOVE	WHITE	NEGRO	WHITE	NEGRO
Female				
High	9 (57)	58 (45)	30 (27)	50 (2)
Low	3 (124)	33 (55)	58 (106)	60 (10)
	$x^2 = 2.6$	$x^2 = 6.3$	$x^2 = 6.7$	
	NS	$P < .05$	$P < .01$	$P = .85*$
	$Q = .48$	$Q = .48$	$Q = -.53$	$Q = -.20$
Male				
High	42 (36)	93 (27)	70 (30)	90 (10)
Low	40 (78)	79 (47)	80 (123)	94 (18)
	$x^2 = 0.0$	$x^2 = 2.4$	$x^2 = 1.3$	
	NS	NS	NS	$P = .59*$
	$Q = .04$	$Q = .54$	$Q = -.25$	$Q = -.31$

[a] Correction for continuity could be used in the smaller not-significant tables. This would, of course, merely lower the already not-significant chi-square. It is used in other fourfold tables where the correction could make a difference in significance.

* Fisher's "Exact" test was used instead of chi-square because of the small number of low church-attending Negroes.

romantic love and permissiveness in all sex and race groups to produce some sort of positive association of these variables, even though this is significant only for Negro females. Again, low church-attendance interacts with the relationship between romantic love and permissiveness to produce some sort of negative association of these variables, even though this is significant only for white females. It is difficult to throw away all the nonsignificant groups arbitrarily, for the difference between them and the two significant groups is not always great. Instead, it would seem best to conclude that high church-attenders generally tend to display a positive association between romantic love and permissiveness, and low church-attenders generally tend to display a negative association, and that this is generally stronger for females than for males. This is a more reasonable statement than simply to assert that the romantic love–permissiveness relation holds exclusively for certain racial groups of females. Finally, it might be noted that here again a variable—romantic love—has greater effect on females than on males. This might be due to the absence of strong sexual motives among females, which aids variables like romantic love in affecting sexual permissiveness.

Goodman's test for interaction generally supports this interpretation. It is interesting to note that although white and Negro females in both high and low church-attending groups display an interaction effect (with only Negro females significant in the high church-attendance group and only white females significant in the low church-attendance group) the test for interaction shows no significant difference in the relation of romantic love to permissiveness between white and Negro females in the high church-attendance group and no significant difference between the white and Negro females in the low church-attendance group. This agrees with the previously stated interpretation that all females show the same tendencies when in the same church-attendance categories. The low church-attenders seem to define romantic love differently than do the high church-attenders. Most Negroes happen to be high church-attenders and thus display the positive association, but the tendency also is there among white females. One value of this check for interaction is that it affords the opportunity to test for a significant difference between partial tables and thus avoids mere mechanical use of them.[10]

Frequency of Falling in Love and Permissiveness

One additional test was made—it was on the hypothesis that those who have been in love more often are more permissive. This was expected to be particularly true for females, for research has shown that a woman's sexual life is more affected by being in love than is a man's.[11] This was checked in the student sample. The zero-order relationship was significant but weak ($x^2 = 11.6$ and gamma $= .20$), and it held somewhat more strongly among women than men. The association was strongest among white women and just reached the level of significance among white men, whereas in both

[10] The number of cases affects chi-square, and so one should always examine the gamma, or Q, rating in comparing tables. The test for interaction is also valuable as a comparison of tables of different size. Although the .05 level of significance will be used in this study the level of significance for .10 findings will be presented too, since in a one tail test these are actually at the .05 level. Zero cells in a 2 by 2 table affect Q. One zero cell makes $Q = 1$ and two zero cells makes $Q = 0$. For some warnings about pitfalls of tests for significance see Hanan C. Selvin, "A Critique of Tests of Significance in Survey Research," *American Sociological Review*, 22 (October 1957), pp. 519–527.

[11] For recent empirical evidence see Ehrmann, chap. 4.

Negro sexes it was weak and not significant. Once again the data showed a racial difference, and once again such a state of affairs had not been hypothesized.

The relationship among white students of permissiveness to the number of times an individual has been in love differs according to sex, for as the number of times a woman has been in love increases so does her permissiveness; whereas among men the relationship is curvilinear, with those who have been in love only once being less likely to be permissive than those who have never been in love or who have been in love twice or more. A control by church-attendance does not alter these relationships, but romantic love(as can be seen in Table 3.5) does prove to be a condition of the relationship. Women *low* on romantic love and men *high* on romantic love showed a positive relation between the number of times they had been in love and permissiveness. Although the relation was not significant, white men who were low on romantic love showed the curvilinear relation that characterized the entire group of white males. White women showed a posi-

Table 3.5

Number of Times in Love and Permissiveness by Romantic Love, Race, and Sex in the Student Sample (percentage highly permissive)

NUMBER OF TIMES IN LOVE	High Romantic Love		Low Romantic Love	
	WHITE	NEGRO	WHITE	NEGRO
Female				
Never	12 (25)	42 (12)	9 (68)	27 (11)
Once	19 (37)	65 (23)	37 (79)	34 (29)
Twice or more	24 (21)	45 (11)	37 (76)	50 (20)
	$x^2 = 1.1$	$x^2 = 2.2$	$x^2 = 18.2$	$x^2 = 1.8$
	NS	NS	$P < .001$	NS
	$G = .25*$	$G = .38$	$G = .43$	$G = .34$
		$C = .22**$		
Male				
Never	35 (20)	70 (10)	70 (64)	84 (19)
Once	53 (34)	100 (15)	56 (77)	75 (20)
Twice or more	87 (14)	100 (6)	69 (55)	90 (20)
	$x^2 = 8.6$	$x^2 = 5.4***$	$x^2 = 4.0$	$x^2 = 1.8$
	$P < .01$	$P < .10$	NS	NS
	$G = .56$	$G = .0$	$G = -.03$	$G = .37$
			$C = .14$	$C = .17$

* *G* is gamma and is used in all tables larger than 2×2 as a measure of association.

** *C* is the coefficient of contingency and is used in curvilinear tables as an additional measure of association.

*** The small number of cases in this table makes chi-square an inadequate test; but no adequate test of significance exists for such a table.

tive relation regardless of the degree of romantic love, although the relation was stronger for women low on romantic love. Although the Negro groups did not show any significant relation, it was clear from the results of their tests that they showed some tendencies in the same direction as the whites. However, tests using different measures and different cuts in each school substantiated the racial difference.

The Goodman test for interaction as applied to the partial tables in Table 3.5 generally supports the interpretation just given, but it does qualify the strength of the differences noted. Romantic love as a control seems to affect males somewhat more than females in that white males who differ on romantic love are significantly different; so are Negro males. However, females do not show significant differences. This is so despite the fact that on low romantic love white females show a significant relation and Negro females do not. The difference here is not significant, and this demonstrates the point that two partial tables may not be significantly different even though one is significant and the other is not. Finally, the male-female differences in this table generally seem to be stronger than the Negro-white differences.

Summary, Conclusions, and Proposition One

The Negro-white differences found in all the examinations detailed in this chapter were largely unexpected. Of course, they can be explained in a very general sense as the result of different historical backgrounds, which have produced contrasting orientations toward the church, romantic love, falling in love, and sexual permissiveness in general. This explanation is supplemented here with a less abstract and more specific factor—namely, the *traditional* level of premarital sexual permissiveness in a group.

The relationships discussed were checked carefully in order to be sure they were not due to the arbitrary use of a type of cutting point or to a particular way of measuring social forces. Results were also checked whenever possible to ascertain if they held up in each of the five schools. The highly permissive white New York college was compared with the Negro schools to see if equally permissive schools would still show a racial difference. They did. The Negro-white differences were not due to social class, for in tests in which class was controlled for, the differences remained quite strong. Twelve different measures of social class were used to check this result.[12] The Negro-white differences in courtship reported here are but part of a larger set of differences (presented in other chapters) and thus are not a rare finding.

By reading across Table 3.6, which presents the race comparison for

[12] These measures are discussed in the next chapter.

Table 3.6
SOCIAL CLASS AND PERMISSIVENESS BY RACE AND SEX IN ADULT AND STUDENT
SAMPLES (PERCENTAGE HIGHLY PERMISSIVE)

	WHITE MALE		NEGRO MALE		WHITE FEMALE		NEGRO FEMALE	
Adult Sample								
SEI								
Low (0–19)	32	(202)	70	(49)	5	(221)	33	(63)
Middle (20–59)	26	(254)	46	(11)	6	(271)	13	(15)
High (60–100)	32	(136)	50	(2)	8	(154)	33	(3)
Income[a]								
$0–3000	25	(100)	56	(25)	9	(87)	37	(35)
3000–5000	28	(103)	79	(19)	4	(141)	38	(21)
5000–7000	24	(145)	60	(10)	6	(160)	7	(15)
7000–10,000	39	(133)	75	(4)	5	(133)	0	(5)
10,000+	31	(111)	50	(2)	10	(108)	33	(3)
Student Sample								
SEI								
Low (0–49)	56	(96)	86	(88)	17	(109)	42	(90)
Middle (50–69)	64	(87)	82	(11)	23	(83)	38	(8)
High (70–100)	63	(92)	75	(4)	37	(114)	60	(15)
Income[a]								
$0–3500	75	(8)	81	(31)	23	(22)	50	(32)
3500–5000	54	(24)	85	(39)	21	(34)	48	(29)
5000–7500	71	(51)	90	(20)	17	(47)	41	(22)
7500–10,000	34	(53)	93	(14)	20	(70)	45	(11)
10,000+	70	(134)	67	(6)	35	(113)	43	(7)

[a] The income categories are almost the same in both samples. The slight difference is
due to the way the check categories were set up. (See Appendices A and C.)

both the student and adult samples, one can see that with social class
controlled for, Negro-white differences in permissiveness persist in both
samples. Dollar income and Duncan's Socioeconomic Index (SEI) are used
to measure social class. There are few upper-class Negroes, and thus, the
best comparisons with whites can be made at the lower levels. It is clear
that at the lower levels both male and female Negroes are more permissive
than whites. Other checks using different cuts show the same results. All
the relations discussed in this chapter remain unaltered when they are
computed with a control for social class. Despite the popularity of assuming
that social class is the great equalizer of all race differences, this is not the
case in these data.[13]

[13] The "Moynihan Report" was criticized for not using social-class controls to
show how similar lower-class white and Negro families were. The evidence of the
present study indicates that this similarity is illusory. Even with class controls the
Negroes in the student sample came from larger families, with more fathers lower

Negro sexual permissiveness seems to have different sources and different implications. For example, students in the highly permissive white New York college were as permissive as those in the Negro schools, but the majority of these white students were low on church-attendance and romantic-love beliefs, whereas the Negro students generally were high on these variables. It seems that a liberal, or permissive, attitude toward premarital sexual behavior is generated and maintained in a different manner in Negro subcultures than in white subcultures.

In looking over these Negro-white differences and searching for an explanation, the similarity of the differences between men and women *within* each racial group and between Negroes and whites considered as total groups was striking. To illustrate—men are significantly more permissive than women; romantic love does not affect men in the same way it does women; and among white students church-attendance and the number of times the individual has been in love affects female permissiveness more than male permissiveness. Very similar differences were reported between Negroes and whites. This situation reflects a general difference between subcultures in American society that are traditionally more, and traditionally less, permissive. The finding that the social forces examined in this study affected white permissiveness more than Negro permissiveness and female permissiveness more than male permissiveness suggests that an inverse relation exists between the traditional level of permissiveness and the susceptibility of an individual's permissiveness to such social forces.

Proposition One subsumes these sex and race differences as special cases: THE LOWER THE TRADITIONAL LEVEL OF SEXUAL PERMISSIVENESS IN A GROUP, THE GREATER THE LIKELIHOOD THAT SOCIAL FORCES WILL ALTER INDIVIDUAL LEVELS OF SEXUAL PERMISSIVENESS.

The findings fit this theoretical explanation rather well. Studies of the Negro church indicate that it is a source of emotional satisfaction rather than an inhibitory influence on sexual behavior.[14] The church may in fact strive to reduce sexual permissiveness, but the strong tradition of sexual permissiveness among Negroes seems to counteract this effort, whereas the less-permissive white customs do not have this counteracting force. Similarly, church-attendance seems less able to affect the sexual attitudes of

---

educated than mothers, and from more families with only a mother. For the Moynihan Report see *The Negro Family,* Office of Policy Planning and Research, United States Department of Labor, March 1965. For a review of the controversy see Lee Rainwater and William Yancy, "Black Families and the White House," *Transaction* (July–August 1966), pp. 6–11, 48–53. However, the reader should be aware of the difficulties involved in fully matching Negro and white groups. For some discussion of this see Jessie Bernard, "Marital Stability and Patterns of Status Variables," *Journal of Marriage and the Family,* 28 (November 1966), pp. 421–429. See also the discussion of Bernard's article by Rainwater.

[14] See Dollard, especially p. 249. Negro religious participation is higher than white; higher proportions of Negroes go to church, and there are proportionately more Negro churches. See Brink and Harris, chap. 6.

white males as compared to white females; the stronger tradition of sexual permissiveness in males seems more able to counteract the religious efforts at control.

Church attendance also showed its greater effect on females in the relationship of romantic love to permissiveness. High church-attenders showed a positive relation, and low church-attenders showed a negative relation, of romantic love to permissiveness predominantly among females. The males showed no significant relation. The Negro-white differences here were minor and mainly in the female group, where the greater church-attendance adds an emotional quality to the idealistic aspects of romantic love that makes those who are high on both more likely to accept coitus. Perhaps the weaker response of males was due here to the fact that their traditionally high acceptance of permissiveness was sufficient motivation to sexual acceptance, and thus they had no need for such "stimulants" as romantic love.

The relation between permissiveness and the number of times an individual has been in love is affected by the same racial and sexual differences. This relationship held only for white students. It can be argued here too that as a consequence of their traditional acceptance of sexual permissiveness Negroes do not "need" to fall in love as much as whites do in order to promote permissive sexual behavior.[15] The same argument holds for the difference between males and females in the white group, and it explains why the men among whom the relationship between permissiveness and the number of times they have been in love is strongest are a small group of men high on romantic love and somewhat low in sexual permissiveness.

Thus, within traditionally less-permissive groups—women and whites—individual permissiveness is more likely to be affected by such social forces as church-attendance, belief in romantic love, and falling in love.[16] In the traditionally more-permissive groups—men and Negroes—individuals find support and justification for liberal sexual attitudes in the groups' traditions, and their permissiveness is therefore less subject to control by social forces. Highly permissive individuals in traditionally low-permissive social groups are permissive not because they have long-standing traditions to support them, but because they are located in the social structure in such a way as to avoid inhibitory forces (church attendance and the idealistic

[15] Although they are relatively permissive, Negroes in the sample for this study were not generally promiscuous. Table 2.6 shows that they tended to require affectionate relations as a basis for sexual behavior. Others have noted such a requirement (see Myrdal's classic study of the Negro, p. 935). As indicated in Chapter 2, Negroes were less inclined than whites to give high rank to affectionless kissing and petting. Some sex differences in both races are due to other factors, to be discussed in Chapter 5.

[16] Christensen and Carpenter's work on three cultures also showed much smaller variation in male attitudes and behavior than in female attitudes and behavior. See their "Value-Behavior Discrepancies in Premarital Coitus," *American Sociological Review*, 27 (February 1962), pp. 66–74.

version of romantic love for example) and to maximize experiences that promote permissiveness (like falling in love). The best illustration of this is the highly permissive white college students. They were consistently low on church-attendance, tended not to believe in romantic love, and reported falling in love relatively often. The best example of a traditionally high-permissive group is the Negro students. They lacked these characteristics, their permissiveness seeming rather to be a consequence of a long-standing supportive tradition. Thus, there are two distinct paths, both of which lead to high individual levels of permissiveness. The key differentiating factor is the traditional level of premarital sexual permissiveness in the group to which the individuals belong. In this sense, although the white New York college and the Negro college are similar in levels of permissiveness, they are quite distinct in the ways in which these levels were achieved and maintained.

This characterization of the difference between traditionally more- and less-permissive subcultures is further supported by the contrast between two extreme groups—Negro men and white women. The permissiveness of white women is affected by all the variables investigated; that of Negro men, by none of them.

The theory of social change in sexual permissiveness points to several leads for future research and theory. To evaluate the efficacy of any variable on sexual permissiveness it is vital to know the traditional level of permissiveness of the group. A variable may seem relatively impotent in reducing permissiveness in a traditionally high-permissive group, whereas in a traditionally low-permissive group it may have great effect. The theory also suggests that differences in the area of sexual permissiveness between races are analogous to the differences between the sexes—studying one set may well be essential to understanding the other. Finally, Proposition One implies a strong tendency toward long-range, unidirectional change. Once a group becomes highly permissive and stays that way long enough for it to become traditionally so, then it becomes quite difficult for social forces to reduce that permissiveness. On the other hand a group with a tradition of low permissiveness can be altered either way. Since such a group is already low on permissiveness, there is little room to move down, and there is a good chance of increasing the traditional level of permissiveness. The implications are that often it should be possible to find in history a long-range trend in any society toward increased permissiveness. There is some general evidence supporting this historical hypothesis in America.[17]

It may be argued that the twentieth century in America has witnessed precisely this sort of social change regarding sexual beliefs and behaviors. There is consistent evidence from past studies, such as those by Kinsey and Terman, to show trends toward increased permissiveness at all levels

[17] Ira L. Reiss, *Premarital Sexual Standards in America*, New York: The Free Press, 1960, chaps. 2 and 10 contain a large number of references and sources on this point.

of sexual behavior.[18] Chapters 7, 8, and 9 show how permissiveness changes in the various role stages of individuals. It is sufficient to say here that there appears to be arising in America a middle- and upper-class movement toward increased permissiveness, which seems strongly to resemble the Scandinavian sex patterns of the present day.[19] In general, this can be seen in the vast popularity of such standards as "petting with affection," "transitional double standard" and "permissiveness with affection"—all of which accept individual-centered sexual behavior and beliefs. (See Exhibit 2.1 for definitions of all standards.)

In the past, it could be argued that groups with a tradition of high sexual permissiveness were groups that had less to "lose" by being highly permissive. Men and Negroes would be examples, for men cannot become pregnant and Negroes have less social standing to lose. Negroes have a high rate of divorce, desertion, and separation, which tends to reduce the attractiveness of a marital relationship as opposed to a nonmarital relationship. Among both Negroes and whites, the male role in the family institution is somewhat less emphasized socially than is the female role, and this may encourage a preference for the unmarried state and its benefits. Some support for this interpretation comes from a check on personal happiness in the national sample, which indicated that whites were happier than Negroes. Within the white group those who were married were the happiest. Within the Negro group those who were married were the *least* happy. This would indicate the lower relative status of the married state among Negroes and the strains associated with such a state. Generally, in both racial groups males were less happy than females. A control by social class showed that there was less of a difference between the married and single people in the lower and middle classes in terms of happiness than in the upper classes (the top one-third). However, in all race-sex groupings the basic relation of happiness to marriage, although weakened, was still present.

The current movement toward permissiveness among the middle and upper social classes seems to be based differently than it used to be. Rather than permissiveness being the philosophy of a group with less to "lose," it is a philosophy of a group with access to contraceptive controls on pregnancy, ways of combating venereal diseases, an intellectualized philosophy of the importance of ties based on affection and sex, and an integration of

---

[18] Kinsey *et al., Sexual Behavior in the Human Male* and *Sexual Behavior in the Human Female;* Lewis Terman, *Psychological Factors in Marital Happiness.* New York: McGraw-Hill, 1938. For a recent statement see Ira L. Reiss, "The Sexual Renaissance, A Summary and Analysis," *Journal of Social Issues,* 22 (April 1966), pp. 123–137. These articles stress that many recent changes in coitus are in the area of attitudes rather than behavior. This is also discussed in chaps. 7 and 10 of the present study.

[19] For a recent coverage of Scandinavian sex customs see Harold T. Christensen, "Scandinavian and American Sex Norms," *Journal of Social Issues,* 22 (April 1966), pp. 60–75.

this viewpoint with a generally liberal position.[20] The following chapters deal with this general view of sexual permissiveness in America and further test the specific proposition put forth concerning the relation of traditional levels of sexual permissiveness to social forces.[21]

[20] A regression analysis was performed on the tables in this chapter. No changes in interpretation occurred. In addition almost all the tables used in the study were examined by Somers *"d"* and Rosenberg's "standardization" approach. No changes in analysis or interpretation were required. See Robert H. Somers, "A New Asymetric Measure of Association for Ordinal Variables," *American Sociological Review,* 27 (December 1962), pp. 799–811, and Morris Rosenberg, "Test Factor Standardization as a Method of Interpretation," *Social Forces,* 41 (October 1962), pp. 53–61. The technique used to arrive at SEI scores was composed by Donald McTavish. The original deck referred to in his article has some minor errors, which were later removed. See Donald G. McTavish, "A Method for More Reliably Coding Detailed Occupations into Duncan's Socioeconomic Categories," *American Sociological Review,* 29 (June 1964), pp. 402–406.

[21] Such relations as that between the number of times an individual has been in love and permissiveness could be viewed with permissiveness as the independent variable. However, the evidence is interpreted predominantly to support permissiveness as the dependent variable. This does not rule out the other possibility. Such interpretations are made from time to time on other relationships in order to present a particular causal point of view, but this should not be taken to mean the exclusion of all other causal patterns.

4

Social Class and Premarital Sexual Permissiveness: A Reexamination and Reformulation

Preface to Proposition Two

The work explored in this chapter led to some rather surprising findings. No pronounced relation between social class and premarital · sexual permissiveness was found. After extensive checking it was discovered that if either the student or the adult sample was divided into two groups —one basically conservative about religion, politics, and economics, and one basically liberal on these matters— then the conservative group displayed a negative relation of social class to permissiveness and the liberal group displayed a positive relation of social class to permissiveness. It seemed that in a liberal group there was a general tendency toward higher sexual permissiveness and toward a greater tolerance of higher sexual permissiveness. This in essence is Proposition Two. The rest of the chapter examines the evidence and the findings that resulted in this proposition.

Previous Work

American sociologists have long assumed that persons of higher socioeconomic status are relatively low in premarital sexual permissiveness and that persons of low status are rather high on premarital sexual permissiveness.[1]

[1] Some earlier comments on this area are in Ira L. Reiss, "Social Class and Premarital Sexual Permissiveness: A Re-Examination," *American Sociological Review*, 30 (October 1965), pp. 747–756.

The first Kinsey report provided a wealth of empirical data supporting this belief, and community studies tended to add general, impressionistic support.[2] Kinsey found that by the age of twenty-five only 10 percent of the unmarried men with an eighth-grade education were virginal, while 16 percent of those with a high-school education, and 36 percent of those with at least some college education, were virginal.[3] The less-educated men began their coital behavior five or six years earlier than the others. Similarly, the less-educated women started having coitus five or six years earlier than those women with a high-school or college education. Between the ages of sixteen and twenty, 82 percent of the girls who were entering college had not had coitus, compared with 62 percent of the girls who did not enter high school.[4] In comparing those who married at the same age, the difference between education groups is greatly reduced, but only for females. College-educated females differ from their male counterparts also in that they eventually achieve or surpass the coital rates of the less-educated females, whereas the males with a college education never surpass the less-educated males. These are the basic Kinsey findings regarding social-class differences in premarital coital behavior.[5]

Kinsey considered each educational group as a social class with its own sexual mores.[6] Social class, as indicated by education, was for men the most powerful predictor of coital behavior,[7] whereas for women church attendance was even better than education as a predictor.[8] It should be remembered that Kinsey was talking of an individual's own social class and

[2] Alfred C. Kinsey *et al., Sexual Behavior in the Human Male.* Philadelphia: W. B. Saunders Co., 1948. Community studies generally present only impressionistic evidence, if any, on sexual relations in various social classes; See August B. Hollingshead, *Elmtown's Youth.* New York: John Wiley & Sons, 1949, for a good example of evidence based on a community study. Few textbooks on the area of social class have much to say about the relation of class to sexual relationships. One of the longest treatments is is to be found in Reinhard Bendix and Seymour Lipset, eds., *Class, Status and Power.* New York: The Free Press, 1953, pp. 300–316. However, the 1966 edition of this reader dropped these selections.

[3] Kinsey *et al., Sexual Behavior in the Human Male,* p. 550. Kinsey also used occupation as an indicator of social class, but found it to be less useful than education (p. 331).

[4] Kinsey *et al., Sexual Behavior in the Human Female,* p. 337.

[5] It should be noted that Kinsey concludes that women do not vary by social class in their sexual behavior, in spite of the fact that the lower-class women began their coital experience five or six years earlier, married earlier, and had more coitus during their teens than did the upper-class women in his sample. In addition, a slight negative relation between social class and permissiveness is present even when age at marriage is held constant; see Table 79, p. 337, in *Sexual Behavior in the Human Female.*

[6] Kinsey *et al., Sexual Behavior in the Human Male,* pp. 329–335.

[7] Kinsey found that upper-class men had more experience in certain behaviors such as petting to orgasm and masturbation (*Sexual Behavior in the Human Male,* chap. 10).

[8] Kinsey *et al., Sexual Behavior in the Human Male,* pp. 477–479, and *Sexual Behavior in the Human Female,* pp. 304–307.

not of the social class of his parents. Kinsey did not find any strong relation between parental social class and coital behavior.[9] In this sense the National Adult Sample is a better test of Kinsey's notions than is the Five-School Student Sample, for the student sample uses a measure of parental social class.

The Kinsey findings have set the tone for most of the commentaries on social-class differences in premarital coital behavior during the past fifteen years. Many have commented on this negative relation of social class and sexual permissiveness. Whyte describes a "slum sex code"; Hollingshead gives an impression of the high level of permissiveness among his "out of school" group in Elmtown; Ehrmann reports findings moderately similar to Kinsey's, and so forth.[10] Nevertheless, recent studies of the relation between social class and child-rearing have not been so consistent with Kinsey.

A Test of the Relationship of Social Class to Permissiveness

In the present study the hypothesized negative relation of social class to sexual permissiveness was tested for, using Guttman scales, in both the student and adult samples, and no strong relationship in either sample was found. This result was quite unexpected; in order to increase faith in this finding, it was checked by using about a dozen different measures of social class that were available in the data.[11] The permissiveness scale was also

[9] A few studies have reported no relation of coital behavior to social class of parents. See Warren Breed, "Sex, Class and Socialization in Dating," *Marriage and Family Living*, 18 (May 1956), pp. 137–144; Jean Dedman, "The Relationship between Religious Attitude and Attitude toward Premarital Sex Relations," *Marriage and Family Living*, 21 (May 1959), pp. 171–176; Michael Schofield, *The Sexual Behavior of Young People*. New York: Little, Brown & Co., 1965. Also see Kinsey *et al., Sexual Behavior in the Human Male*, pp. 417–447, where it is shown that although parental social class does show some relation to coital behavior, an individual's own social class shows even more of a relation to a variety of sexual behaviors. The third report from the Institute for Sex Research by Paul H. Gebhard, et al., *Pregnancy, Birth, and Abortion*. New York: Harper & Row, 1958, does present contrary data supporting the relevance of parental social class and lower class female sexuality.

[10] William Foote Whyte, "A Slum Sex Code," *The American Journal of Sociology*, 49 (July 1943), pp. 24–31; Hollingshead; Winston W. Ehrmann, *Premarital Dating Behavior*. New York: Holt, Rinehart and Winston, 1959. Eugene A. Kanin and David H. Howard, "Postmarital Consequences of Premarital Sex Adjustments," *American Sociological Review*, 23 (October 1958), pp. 556–562.

[11] The measures of social class were income, education, occupation, Duncan's SEI, Duncan's Decile Scores, white- and blue-collar occupational categories, and the NORC Transform. In the student sample these measures were often applied to both parents. In the adult sample the measures usually applied to the individual himself. The adult sample was checked using only those who were currently married, only those who were single, and so on; the results were not different. Duncan's SEI is used in both samples here for the head of the family. See Duncan's chaps. 6 and 7 in

used, with a wide variety of different cuts and with sexual standards substituted for permissiveness. As usual, a large number of control variables
were also used to search for interaction effects, intervening variables, and
spurious relations. However, no support was found for the expected relationship. Table 4.1 indicates virtually no association in the student sample
and only a very weak curvilinear association in the adult sample.[12] Actually,
the whites in the adult sample did not show any relation. It was the Negro
group that produced what relation does appear in the adult sample of
Table 4.1. Even this weak relation in the adult sample is unusual, for in the

Table 4.1
SOCIAL CLASS AND PERMISSIVENESS IN THE STUDENT
AND ADULT SAMPLES

	Permissiveness	
SEI[a]	STUDENT SAMPLE	ADULT SAMPLE
Low	49 (383)	24 (535)
Middle	46 (189)	16 (551)
High	50 (225)	20 (295)
	$\chi^2 = 0.60$	$\chi^2 = 11.8$
	NS	$P < .01$
	$G = .01$	$G = .13$
	$C = .03$	$C = .09$

[a] For the student sample, low = 0–49, middle = 50–69, high =
70–100. For the adult sample, low = 0–19, middle = 20–59,
high = 60–100.

checks made, almost all of the results were not significant, even at the .05
level. As usual, the five-item universal "same-sex" scale was dichotomized
between scale-types two and three (see Table 2.14), that is, those who
accepted coitus were separated from those who did not. Duncan's SEI was

Albert Reiss, *Occupations and Social Status*. New York: The Free Press, 1963. This
measure includes occupational prestige, education, and income. It allows occupations
to be ranked in terms of the amount of income and education reported by the census
for that occupation. (For a recent report on the stability of occupational prestige in
the U.S., see Robert W. Hodge, Paul M. Siegel, and Peter H. Rossi, "Occupational
Prestige in the United States, 1925–63," *The American Journal of Sociology,* 70
(November 1964), pp. 286–302.

[12] In the National Adult sample the relationship was not significant for whites
($\chi^2 = 1.9$; gamma = .02), but it was stronger and negative for Negroes ($\chi^2 = 5.8$;
gamma = − .32). Even such a weak relation as found in Table 4.1 was a rarity. This
finding for Negroes is in opposition to Proposition One. Negroes should be less sensitive to social forces, such as social class. However, whites do show a stronger
sensitivity under other conditions, discussed later.

selected as one of the better measures of social class and was trichotomized in all computations.[13] SEI uses occupational, educational, and income information in its composition (see footnote 11). It should be kept in mind that even in the National Adult Sample the interviewers probably did not pick up the very bottom or the very top of the SEI hierarchy. What is called low, middle, and high social class in this study is merely a convenient way of dividing the samples. As noted previously, results were constant regardless of cuts used.

The fact that the same results appeared in all five schools within the student sample and in the adult sample, with more than a dozen different measures of social class and with premarital sexual permissiveness scales that met all scaling requirements and had some established validity, forces one to accept these zero-order findings, despite the conflict with Kinsey's findings and with conventional expectations. Nevertheless, it must be noted that the possibility remains that the relation between social class and permissiveness is obscured by other sociocultural factors.

Table 3.6 presented data showing that in the adult sample the Negro group displayed some evidence of a negative relation of SEI to premarital sexual permissiveness. This was not true of the Negroes in the student sample—perhaps because they represent a more homogeneous group. The white group in both samples showed no clear-cut relationship, as has been noted above. The apparent positive relation for white females in the student sample was spurious. It was due to the fact that the highly permissive New York college had a large porportion of white females rating high on SEI. Within each school no relation between social class and permissiveness appeared.

As pointed out in the last chapter, and as found in the work of Kinsey and others, religion has a powerful effect on sexual relations.[14] Thus, it was decided to try this control as one of many that might help clarify the relation of social class to permissiveness. The religious control yielded dramatic results.

Among those high on church-attendance, the *negative* relationship postulated by Kinsey and others did appear, that is, the lower status groups were more permissive. Those who were low on church-attendance displayed a somewhat weaker but *positive* relation between social class and sexual per-

---

[13] SEI scores are divided into ranges called low, middle, and high. For the student sample low $= 0$–49, middle $= 50$–69, and high $= 70$–100. In the adult sample low $= 0$–19, middle $= 20$–59, and high $= 60$–100. The results are the same using different cutting points. "Head of household" SEI is used in both samples. (See fn. 11 for a further explanation of SEI as a measure.) In the student sample, whenever the father's or the male guardian's occupation was given it was used. In other cases the mother's occupation was used.

[14] See Ernest Burgess and Paul Wallin, *Engagement and Marriage*. Philadelphia: J. B. Lippincott Co., 1953, p. 339; Ehrmann, p. 93; Kanin and Howard, p. 557; and Jean Dedman. The effect of religiosity on permissiveness in the samples for the present study held at each class level.

Table 4.2

SOCIAL CLASS AND PERMISSIVENESS BY CHURCH-ATTENDANCE
IN THE STUDENT SAMPLE (PERCENTAGE HIGHLY PERMISSIVE)

	Church Attendance	
SEI	HIGH	LOW
Low (0–49)	42 (262)	64 (113)
Middle (50–69)	26 (98)	67 (89)
High (70–100)	23 (102)	72 (119)
	$\chi^2 = 15.9$	$\chi^2 = 2.0$
	$P < .001$	NS
	$G = -.35$	$G = .14$

missiveness.[15] Using Goodman's test for interaction, the difference between the two partial tables in Table 4.2 was found to be significant at better than the .01 level. Thus, despite the weakness of the "low attendance" partial table there is support for the view that interaction occurred.[16]

The way in which the church-attendance variable interacted with the relation of social class to permissiveness led to the speculation that in a generally "liberal" setting (such as low church-attendance may indicate) the relation of social class to sexual permissiveness may well be fundamentally different than it would be in a generally "conservative" setting (such as high church-attendance may indicate). "Conservative" and "liberal" are not used here in terms of sex attitudes but in terms of a general style of life;[17] that is, a liberal would favor change rather than tradition,

[15] A recent book by Charles Y. Glock and Rodney Stark (*Religion and Society in Tension.* Chicago: Rand McNally & Co., 1965) reports some interesting findings. They note that the higher classes are the highest church-attenders. Table 4.2 indicates just the opposite for our student sample. This information is lacking on the adult sample, and it could well have been different. The student sample is a more homogeneous and age-restricted group and thus may differ. Erich Goode recently reported ("Social Class and Church Participation," *American Journal of Sociology,* 72 [July 1966], pp. 102–111) that church attendance was for white-collar classes more a reflection of general associational participation and that for the working classes more religious meaning was present. In this connection, it should be noted that in the student sample religiosity was measured by answers to questions concerning self-view of devoutness, and this variable was positively correlated to the church-attendance variable. But perhaps Erich Goode's point would be borne out more on an adult sample.

[16] The Y^2 is equal to 12.8. This number is treated as a chi-square would be treated for estimating level of significance. For a full discussion see Leo Goodman, "Simple Methods for Analyzing Three-Factor Interaction in Contingency Tables," *Journal of the American Statistical Association,* 59 (June 1964), pp. 319–352.

[17] As Lipset and Lenski have recently pointed out, a group that is liberal on one issue may not be liberal on another. (Seymour M. Lipset, *Political Man.* New York: Doubleday & Co., 1960, p. 298; Gerhard Lenski, *The Religious Factor.* New York: Doubleday & Co., 1961, pp. 186–191.) Certainly it is an empirical question whether

particularly change that involved use of his intellect. He would emphasize individual expression and a universal ethic that stressed concern for all men, including those unlike himself. A conservative would be more likely to support the traditional social order and would place less value on individual expression and a universal ethic than the liberal would. This conception is, of course, debatable, and others are possible; but it has the virtue of attempting to get at some key underlying factors rather than just at attitudes toward specific issues. The definitions of "liberal" and "conservative" distinguishes between the working man who favors the welfare state because of self-interest and the working man who favors the welfare state because it also fits his general liberal orientation. In this way it affords a general conception that can be used to measure how liberal or conservative an individual is. In this connection it was hypothesized that among generally conservative people those of higher status would be less permissive than those of lower status, whereas among generally liberal individuals the relation would be in the opposite direction.

Unfortunately, this specification of the relationship of social class to sexual permissiveness was not thought of before research had begun and thus a set of questions to measure liberalism and conservatism directly had not been developed.[18] However, a total of thirty-three items in both samples seemed indirectly to reflect such a dimension. But since they were indirect measures, they had other qualities blended with the liberalism dimension and thus could not be expected to show very strong tendencies. Thus, it was decided to test the hypothesis by using a sign test to discern how many of the thirty-three checks would come out in the predicted direction. Of the thirty-three predictions, thirty were in the predicted direction.[19]

those in this study who are called liberal in general are liberal (that is, highly permissive) in their sexual attitudes. Nevertheless, there are some underlying qualities that are less variable than specific issues and that may reasonably be identified as "liberal." For a discussion of liberalism in relation to student populations, see Rose K. Goldsen, Morris Rosenberg, Robin M. Williams, Jr., and Edward A. Suchman, *What College Students Think.* New Jersey: D. Van Nostrand Co., 1960, chap. 5. See also L. W. Milbrath, "Latent Origins of Liberalism-Conservatism and Party Identification," *Journal of Politics,* 24 (November 1962), pp. 679–688.

[18] Glock and Stark, pp. 120–121, suggest a fivefold division of religion along liberal and conservative lines. There were not enough cases to test this out fully in the present study, but some support for their division was found in both the student and adult samples, for Presbyterians and Episcopalians did show less of a negative (conservative) relation of social class and permissiveness than did other Protestant groups. However, it should be added here that no major differences in level of permissiveness were found among the Jewish, Catholic, and Protestant groups. This was so in all samples. Kinsey, too, reports only slight differences among the three major religions.

[19] For several other characteristics no relationship was predicted because of their broad nature: married, living with both parents, Catholic (both samples), living in Northeast region, North Central region, or the West, age thirty-five to fifty, and having both teen and preteen children. Gamma for the class-permissiveness relationship of these characteristics averaged .07. Gamma for the characteristics in Table 4.3 averaged about .21. A few of the thirty-three relations did show some curvilinearity, but they were treated as in the direction shown by a comparison of the upper and lower classes.

Table 4.3

SOCIAL CLASS AND PERMISSIVENESS BY LIBERAL
AND CONSERVATIVE SETTINGS IN THE STUDENT AND ADULT SAMPLES[a]

CHARACTERISTIC	Direction of Observed Relationship	
	STUDENT SAMPLE	ADULT SAMPLE
Liberal Setting: Positive Relationship Predicted		
Divorced	+	+
No religious affiliation	+	+
Jewish	+	+
Lives in town of 100,000 or more	+	−
Lives in New England and/or Middle Atlantic Region	+	
Low church-attendance	+	
Low on romantic-love beliefs	+	
In love twice or more	+	
Believes his standard does not apply to others	+	
Believes sex is not dirty or nasty	+	
Age 21–35	+	
Favors integrated schools[b]		−
Would take part in civil rights march[c]	+	−
Conservative Setting: Negative Relationship Predicted		
Widowed		−
Protestant	−	−
Lives in town of 10,000 or less	−	−
Lives in South Atlantic region	−	
High church-attendance	−	
High on romantic-love beliefs	−	
Believes his standard applies to others	−	
Believes sex is dirty and nasty	−	
Lives in southern region		−
Age 50 or over		−
Has only teen-age children		−
Favors segregated schools[b]		−
Would not take part in civil rights march[c]		−

[a] Only the first four "liberal," and the first three "conservative," items were asked of both samples.

[b] Asked of white respondents only (used by courtesy of Herbert Hyman and Paul Sheatsley).

[c] Asked of Negro respondents only (used by courtesy of Norman Miller).

Both samples in Table 4.3 seem to support the hypothesis that the liberalism or conservatism of the setting is a key condition for the relation of social class to sexual permissiveness.[20] In a liberal setting the upper classes

[20] An additional explanation of Table 4.3 may be helpful. First, the items in Table 4.3 were chosen ahead of time and predictions were made and then later tested. The only exception was "church attendance." The conception of the liberalism-conservatism dimension underlies all of the items selected to measure this dimension. Different and more direct items would have been used if there had been a plan to measure this dimension before doing the research. Thirteen items were chosen as indices of liberalism. "Divorced" was chosen because those willing to get divorced in our society

were the most permissive; but in a conservative setting they were the least permissive. If being high on sexual permissiveness is defined as "liberal," then these results tend to indicate that general liberalism goes with sexual

---

are assumed to be above average in nonconformity and individualism when compared to a matched group of married people. (In the student sample this applied to the parents of the students.) "No religious affiliation" was assumed to indicate a low value on conformity and an individualistic approach. "Jewish" was considered a liberal designation because of the high level of education of this group, its low degree of organized religion, and its political liberality (see Lawrence H. Fuchs, *The Political Behavior of American Jews.* New York: The Free Press, 1956; also Lenski, p. 190.) "Lives in town of 100,000 or more" was assumed to indicate less likelihood of community controls on the behavior and beliefs of the person and thus more nonconformity. "Lives in New England and/or Middle Atlantic region" was used on the student sample because, from personal knowledge, these students were felt to be liberals. "Low church-attendance" was taken to indicate nonconformity and individual expression. "Low on romantic-love beliefs" was taken as a sign of an individualistic break from conformity to the tradition of romantic-love beliefs. "In love twice or more" indicates a free, open approach to love relations, possibly based on a high value on individualistic expression. "Believes his standard does not apply to others" is indicative of a tolerance for others, which fits with a universal concern for others. "Believes sex is not dirty or nasty" was conceived as a measure of general open-mindedness and use of the intellect. "Age 21–35" was the "young" group in the National Adult Sample, and young people were viewed as less conforming, more favorable to change, and so on. "Favors integrated schools" and "would take part in civil rights march" both indicate a favorable attitude toward change in an area that is part of the American liberal position today. All these items showed some positive association with permissiveness.

Thirteen items were also used to measure the conservative setting. "Widowed" was taken as a conservative measure partially because of the age of this group, which, it was felt, would lead to low tendency toward change and partially because the social expectations of the widowed person were felt to promote a more conforming attitude (In the student sample the parental status was used here.) "Protestant" was viewed as the group with the strongest Puritan heritage of dogmas against drinking, dancing, and sex (see Lenski). "Lives in town of 10,000 or less" indicates a high possibility of social pressures toward conformity. "Lives in South Atlantic region" indicates exposure to a region that has been low on many measures of nonconformity and whose approach toward Negroes is conservative. (This is one of the two major areas from which the student sample was obtained.) "High church-attendance" is a conforming attitude toward religion that may reflect a high value on conformity. "High on romantic-love beliefs" reflects a conforming attitude toward a nonintellectual area. "Believes his standard applies to others" indicates a low value on individual expression. "Believes sex is dirty and nasty" indicates an emotional and narrow, conforming approach to one area that may reflect generally conservative attitudes. "Lives in southern region" indicates contact with a region low on nonconformity and tolerance. "Age 50 and over" is the older group of respondents in the National Adult Sample, and it was assumed that older people generally conform to traditional ways of doing things. "Favors segregated schools" and "would not take part in civil rights march" are taken as indices of conservatism since they indicate a lack of endorsement of certain key changes in American society that are central to the current liberal position. Only the first four of the liberal indices, and the first three of the conservative indices, were usable on both samples due to the many different questions asked respondents in these two samples. (See Appendices A and C.) In cases where special cuts were needed these were made. For instance, few Negroes would fit into an upper-class division of the white group, so a separate class cut was made to test the Negro group. Few Jews are lower class, and this too was taken into account. Many of the checks were explored further on the variables involved, even if no special conditions existed.

liberalism. This can be seen in Table 4.2, for only one-third of the high church-attenders accepted coitus, while two-thirds of the low church-attenders did so. Of course, a more direct measure of the liberal-conservative dimension would afford a more conclusive test of the hypothesis, but the present evidence is persuasive.

A check within each school and sex grouping in the student sample and within each race-sex, married and single grouping in the adult sample indicated that, so far as it was possible to check, the liberalism or conservatism of the setting was an important condition for the class-permissiveness relationship in each of these groups. Generally, the liberalism or conservatism of the setting was more crucial in the white groups than in the Negro group in both the student and adult samples. This finding is congruent with Proposition One, that the lower the traditional level of sexual permissiveness in a group, the greater the likelihood that social factors will alter individual levels of sexual permissiveness. Because whites are traditionally less permissive than Negroes, the liberalism or conservatism of the setting may have a stronger effect on their sexual permissiveness.

The same theoretical position helps account for the fact that the upper social classes seemed more "sensitive" to the liberalism or conservatism of the setting. If it is assumed that there is a relatively high permissive tradition among lower-class groups, then, according to the theory, they should be less susceptible to social forces such as the liberalism or conservatism of the setting. This is precisely what appears to occur, in fact the greater susceptibility of the attitudes of high-status individuals is the key reason for the positive relation between social class and permissiveness within the liberal setting. There is a positive correlation between social class and the amount of change in permissiveness produced by a liberal, as opposed to a conservative, setting. (See Table 4.4) In the higher status groups, liberal individuals are much more permissive than conservative individuals, whereas in the middle status groups the difference is less, and in the low status groups it is smallest. This is congruent with the theoretical expectations just discussed.

Comparisons with Kinsey's Findings

The question still remains as to why the results differed from those reported by Kinsey and his associates. The most obvious answer is that the samples used in this study were probability samples and Kinsey's were not. Furthermore, Kinsey's data represents mainly ten states in the northeastern part of the country, with a heavy proportion of college-educated respondents. Almost two-fifths of the national sample used in the present study are in the lower range of Duncan's SEI, and of course the student sample includes high school as well as college students. Kinsey's nonrandom, re-

Table 4.4

PERCENTAGE ACCEPTING COITUS IN EACH SOCIAL CLASS BY LIBERAL
AND CONSERVATIVE SETTINGS IN THE STUDENT AND ADULT SAMPLES[a]

| | *Percentage Accepting Coitus* | | |
	LIBERAL SETTING	CONSERVATIVE SETTING	PERCENTAGE DIFFER- ENCE IN SETTINGS
	Student Sample		
Low (0–49)	58	43	15
Middle (50–69)	60	35	25
High (70–100)	68	27	41
	Adult Sample		
Low (0–19)	32	23	9
Middle (20–59)	29	16	13
High (60–100)	38	14	24

[a] The liberal and conservative characteristics used in Table 4.3 are utilized here to calculate the average percent accepting coitus under these two settings.

stricted sampling was less heterogeneous than the present adult sample, and this may have been responsible for his finding a negative relation between social class and premarital sexual permissiveness.

More specifically, Kinsey's "group sampling" technique was such that his sample, particularly in the upper classes, may have been disproportionately involved in a conservative setting. Respondents were obtained, typically, by contacting a member or leader of a group, through whom it was tried to obtain the cooperation of the entire group. This means that people who belonged to organizations were heavily represented. For example, sorority and fraternity members, and students belonging to religious groups and social clubs are the source of much of the information about college students. For older respondents, groups such as the church, the PTA, and women's cultural organizations were used.[21] This sampling method may have biased the sample in a generally conservative direction, particularly for the upper classes, since members of such organizations are likely to be of high socioeconomic status,[22] thus producing or accentuating a negative relation between social class and sexual permissiveness. Kinsey's sample is also heavily Protestant,[23] which might also have tended to promote a negative relation between social class and permissiveness. In fact, if only the upper-class portion of Kinsey's sample were biased toward a

[21] The types of groups Kinsey contacted are listed in *Sexual Behavior in the Human Female,* p. 38. Most Americans do not belong to voluntary organizations, although they may belong to other organizations. See Charles R. Wright and Herbert H. Hyman, "Voluntary Association Memberships of American Adults: Evidence from National Sample Surveys," *American Sociological Review,* 23 (June 1958), pp. 284–294.

[22] Wright and Hyman.

[23] Kinsey *et al., Sexual Behavior in the Human Female,* p. 36.

conservative setting, that would be enough to produce the negative relationship even if the middle and lower classes were more fairly represented, for upper-class permissiveness is most affected by the liberal-conservative setting.

Finally, it should be noted that Paul Gebhard, the current director of the Institute for Sex Research, will not allow the reprinting of Kinsey's "male volume," one of the major reasons being that the lower classes in this volume were mixed heavily with interviews obtained from men in prison, a highly permissive lower-class element. This fact would also tend to make for a negative relation.[24]

Another important factor that may explain the different findings of the Kinsey study is the fact that Kinsey studied sexual *behavior* and that the present project has been concerned with sexual *attitudes*. It is possible that sexual behavior is related negatively to social class while sexual attitudes are not. Upper-class people may behave *less* permissively than they feel is proper, and lower-class people may behave *more* permissively than they believe is proper.[25]

In their study of Danish, midwestern, and Mormon college students,[26] Christensen and Carpenter found that although the Danish students had the most permissive sexual attitudes, they were less likely to have done as much as they believed proper. The Mormon students had the least-permissive attitudes but were most likely to have done more than they believed proper. However, there was no evidence that persons of high social status are less likely to achieve the behavior their standards permit, so these results, although relevant, are surely not conclusive.

Some limited data on this point has been gathered from 248 unmarried students in the Iowa College Sample. Table 4.5 shows that only 64 percent of those who accepted coitus had actually had coitus. The main reason seems to have been that many students maintained a prerequisite of love or engagement. Upper-class men were least likely to go as far as their sexual standards allowed, but it was the lower-class women who were least likely to go as far as their sexual standards allowed.[27] College women from lower-

---

[24] The information concerning Kinsey's sample was communicated to the author in a letter from Paul Gebhard dated December 14, 1965. Higher sexual permissiveness for the criminal population has been recently reported by Robert Dentler of Columbia University in unpublished form. However, it should be borne in mind that some prisoners would belong in a random sample of lower-class males, but much less than was included in Kinsey's samples.

[25] Although the lower classes may have no higher percent nonvirginal members than the higher classes, they could still have higher frequency rates and may still start sexual activity at an earlier age.

[26] Harold T. Christensen and George R. Carpenter, "Value-Behavior Discrepancies Regarding Premarital Coitus," *American Sociological Review*, 27 (February 1962), pp. 66–74.

[27] It was the more "conservative" students (high church-attenders) in particular who were in this category, and thus one may wonder if this finding would hold in a liberal setting.

Table 4.5

PERCENTAGE HOLDING EACH SEX STANDARD WHO REPORTED
EXPERIENCING EACH OF THE TYPES OF SEX BEHAVIOR
IN THE IOWA COLLEGE SAMPLE

	KISSING STANDARD	PETTING STANDARD	COITAL STANDARD
Kissing behavior	100	100	100
Petting behavior	36	85	95
Coital behavior	4	7	64
N	(25)	(139)	(84)

$$\chi^2 = 137.8$$
$$P < .001$$
$$G = .83$$

class backgrounds are upwardly mobile and may be reluctant to risk sexual behavior that might interfere with their mobility. Kinsey cites evidence that the upwardly mobile are even more restrictive than those in the class they are moving toward.[28] Further, upwardly mobile females may be desirous of giving a clear impression that they do not fit the stereotype of the "loose" lower-class female. Careful testing on larger and more representative samples is needed to determine the extent of such discrepancies between standards and behavior, and to discover whether the Iowa College Sample findings are representative.[29]

There is some evidence from the permissive scales to support the interpretation that upper-class people are generally the last to achieve the behavior that their standards allow. This can be seen most clearly by looking at differences in sexual standards by social class. Patterned differences, although quite small, do exist among the social classes in their sexual standards. Generally speaking, higher-class individuals stressed affection as a

[28] Kinsey *et al., Sexual Behavior in the Human Female,* p. 297, and *Sexual Behavior in the Human Male,* pp. 417–448. Also see Frank Lindenfeld, "A Note on Social Mobility, Religiosity, and Students' Attitudes Towards Premarital Sexual Relations," *American Sociological Review,* 25 (February 1960), pp. 81–84. Lindenfeld reports findings similar to Kinsey's and speculates that perhaps mobility socialization produces both religiosity and low sexual permissiveness. Gebhard (p. 155) reports that lower-class females keep their sex patterns as they move up, and this seems at odds with earlier reports of their research in the "female" volume by Kinsey *et al.*

[29] Other recent research reports indicate similar attitudes may be present among groups who behave quite differently. See Robert A. Gordon, James F. Short, Jr., Desmond S. Cartwright, and Fred L. Strodtbeck, "Values and Gang Delinquency: A Study of Street-Corner Groups," *American Journal of Sociology,* 69 (September 1963), pp. 109–128; Hyman Rodman, "The Lower Class Value Stretch," *Social Forces,* 42 (December 1963), pp. 205–215; John C. Ball and Nell Logan, "Early Sexual Behavior of Lower-Class Delinquent Girls," *Journal of Criminal Law, Criminology and Police Science,* 51 (July–August 1960), pp. 209–214.

prerequisite for coitus more than did lower-class individuals. In a liberal setting, however, those of higher status were more equalitarian and thus also accepted affectionless sexual behavior for both sexes, whereas in a conservative setting those of higher status were less equalitarian and were strong supporters of the orthodox double standard.[30] Emphasis on affection as a prerequisite was generally visible in the upper classes, making it less likely that a person would behave at the level of permissiveness he acknowledged as legitimate if he had difficulties achieving the required state of affection.

A third and final approach to the differences in Kinsey's findings refers to the evidence from studies of social class and child-rearing practices. Recent studies indicate that changes in social-class differences have occurred since 1945. Because most of the Kinsey data were gathered during the 1940s, it might not reflect such changes as clearly as the more recent data in the present study. Some of the researchers in this area, such as Sears, Maccoby, and Levin, suggest that although they found large class differences, ethnic and religious reference groups are also of importance in premarital sexual permissiveness.[31] Lenski concludes from his Detroit study that attitudes in the marriage-and-the-family area are more affected by religion than by social class.[32] These findings fit with the notion that the liberalism or conservatism of the setting is a condition of the relation between social class and permissiveness, for they point to the importance of such nonclass factors in this area.

Urie Bronfenbrenner, in his classic summary of class differences in child-rearing, points out that since the 1940s middle-class parents have become more permissive than lower-class parents in things such as feeding, toilet-training and sex permissiveness.[33] Prior to World War II the evidence suggested a more impulsive, uninhibited lower-class mode of child-rearing,[34] but the more recent studies, such as that by Melvin Kohn, show that lower-

---

[30] For a full description of American sexual standards see Ira L. Reiss, *Premarital Sexual Standards in America.* New York: The Free Press, 1960.

[31] Robert F. Sears, Eleanor E. Maccoby, and Harry Levin, *Patterns of Child Rearing.* New York: Harper & Row, Publishers, 1957, pp. 426, 428, 481.

[32] Lenski, chaps. 5 and 8.

[33] Urie Bronfenbrenner, "Socialization and Social Class Through Time and Space," *Readings in Social Psychology,* Eleanor E. Maccoby, Theodore M. Newcomb, and Eugene L. Hartley, eds. New York: Holt, Rinehart and Winston, 1958, pp. 400–425. Sears, Maccoby, and Levin (*Patterns of Child Rearing,* p. 429) are among the major authorities for this recent middle-class permissiveness. Although they were puzzled by the discrepancy between their findings and Kinsey's, they never questioned the validity of the Kinsey data. Other recent studies supporting the increased permissiveness of middle-class child-rearing include Gerald R. Leslie and Kathryn P. Johnsen, "Changed Perceptions of the Maternal Role," *American Sociological Review,* 28 (December 1963), pp. 919–928; and Donald G. McKinley, *Social Class and Family Life.* New York: The Free Press, 1964.

[34] Middle-class families in many of these child-rearing studies (such as that by Sears, Maccoby, and Levin) would be in the top third of Duncan's SEI and therefore in the upper-class category in this study.

class families have become "middle class" in their stress on respectability, while middle-class families have become much more permissive and stress internalized standards of conduct.[35]

Thus, Kinsey may have found a negative relation between class and permissiveness because his sample was composed of representatives of the "older" social-class system. In the "newer" social classes, a more liberal sexual philosophy may produce a positive relation between class and permissiveness.[36] According to Peter Drucker, the largest occupational groups in the new middle classes are the professionals and the managers,[37] and in the samples in the present study these occupational categories displayed the most prominent high level of permissiveness in a liberal setting. Further, the proportion of the total group who were in professional and managerial occupations was considerably higher in the liberal setting than in the conservative setting.[38] In this sense the liberal setting was a somewhat higher-class setting. Table 4.6 shows this class difference in both the adult and student samples. It seems that in the liberal setting it is the managerial, and particularly the professional, occupational group that is highly permissive, and this is the major reason that upper-class people in that setting are highly permissive.[39] These occupational changes may not have been represented in large enough numbers at the time of the Kinsey studies for them to have affected his findings.

[35] Melvin Kohn, "Social Class and Parental Values," *American Journal of Sociology*, 64 (January 1959), pp. 337–351. The lower-class elements that make the greatest demand for respectability in their children may well be the "conservative" lower-class. Also see Lenski, p. 200.

[36] Numerous references to the "new" classes appear in sociological literature. Daniel R. Miller and Guy E. Swanson designate entrepreneurial and bureaucratic classes (*The Changing American Parent*. New York: John Wiley & Sons, 1958); David Riesman proposes a distinction between the older inner-directed style and the newer other-directed style (*The Lonely Crowd*. New York: Doubleday & Co., 1953), and William H. Whyte, Jr.'s "organization man" is also a member of the new middle class (*The Organization Man*. New York: Doubleday & Co., 1956).

[37] For a discussion of these new occupational groupings see Peter F. Drucker, "The New Majority," pp. 309–317 in Edgar A. Schuler, *et al., Readings in Sociology*, 2d ed. New York: Thomas Y. Crowell Co., 1960. See also U.S. Bureau of the Census, *Trends in the Income of Families and Persons in the United States: 1947–1960*, Technical Paper 8. Washington, D.C.: U.S. Government Printing Office, 1963, especially pp. 1–16.

[38] Using church-attendance in the student sample to divide the group into liberals and conservatives, it was found that 62 percent of the liberal group were in professional and managerial occupations, whereas only 43 percent of the conservatives were in these occupations.

[39] In the student sample, using church-attendance to divide the group into liberals and conservatives, 70 percent of the liberal professional and managerial group accepted coitus, whereas in the conservative setting only 22 percent of this group accepted coitus. Lewis S. Feuer suggests that the scientific intellectual has a hedonist-libertarian ethic. This may in part explain some liberal tendencies in the modern professionals, many of whom are scientists. See Feuer's *The Scientific Intellectual*. New York: Basic Books, 1963.

Table 4.6

PERCENTAGE IN EACH SOCIAL CLASS BY LIBERAL AND CONSERVATIVE SETTING
IN THE STUDENT AND ADULT SAMPLES[a]

SEI	LIBERAL SETTING	CONSERVATIVE SETTING	PERCENT DIFFERENCE
	Student Sample		
Low (0–49)	37	60	+23
Middle (50–69)	29	19	—10
High (70–100)	35	21	—14
	Adult Sample		
Low (0–19)	32	45	+13
Middle (20–59)	42	38	— 4
High (60–100)	25	18	— 7

[a] Based on a mean average of all thirty-three characteristics used to create liberal and conservative controls in Table 4.3.

In the National Adult Sample, few Negroes were professionals and managers, and among Negroes there was a mild negative relation between social class and permissiveness (see Table 3.6). As has been noted, such a relation may be typical of the older class system. Furthermore, the liberal-conservative dimension affects Negro permissiveness less than white permissiveness, possibly due to a smaller "new" class system in child-rearing. Time may be needed for these changes to affect the Negro group more fully.

Summary, Conclusions, and Proposition Two

Neither the adult nor the student sample revealed the expected negative relationship between social class and premarital sexual permissiveness.[40] This was one of the many major surprises that this research project involved. Three reasons have been offered for the difference between these findings and Kinsey's, and each of them seems to have validity; only the future accumulation of data will enable us to delineate this situation more precisely.

A check of many thousands of tables revealed only one dimension that seemed to mask the relation between social class and premarital attitudes— the liberal-conservative dimension. In a generally liberal attitudinal setting, the relation between social class and permissiveness was positive; in a conservative setting it was negative. These two opposed tendencies canceled

[40] Situs (a measure of occupational differences among occupations with similar status) was partially checked for its relation to permissiveness *within* social class. Generally it was found that in the national sample, "manufacturing" was high on permissiveness and "building and maintenance" was low on permissiveness.

each other out in the basic checks made on the class-permissiveness relationship.

Upper-class permissiveness was more sensitive to the liberalism or conservatism of the setting, and it was primarily because liberal persons of higher status displayed a marked gain in level of permissiveness that the relation between class and permissiveness became positive among liberals. (See Tables 4.2 and 4.4 for relevant data.)

These findings are congruent with Proposition One that the lower the traditional level of sexual permissiveness in a group, the greater the likelihood that social factors will alter individual levels of sexual permissiveness. The traditional level of sexual permissiveness is assumed to be lowest in the upper classes, and upper-class permissiveness responds most easily to change in the liberal-conservative dimension. Within each class whites were more affected by this dimension than were Negroes, and this too is consistent with Proposition One.

One result that creates some difficulty in terms of this proposition is the finding that the liberal-conservative differences in the student sample were considerably larger at each class level than were those in the adult sample (see Table 4.4). It could be asserted that this is simply because the student group traditionally has a lower level of sexual permissiveness and therefore, according to the proposition, it should be more sensitive to social forces. The greater sexual permissiveness allowed to adults in our culture would seem to support this, but the argument does not seem so forceful when we remember that adults who are parents are traditionally low on sexual permissiveness. It could also be argued that the student sample is overall higher in socioeconomic status than is the adult sample, and that higher socioeconomic groups tend to have lower permissive traditions and to be more sensitive to social forces. There is little support for this view, however, for generally even when SEI scores are identical, the student sample shows larger differences between liberal and conservative student groups in the acceptance of coitus.

Another explanation here could be that the stronger the level of general liberalism in a group, the greater the likelihood that liberals and conservatives in that group will differ sharply on premarital sexual attitudes. Perhaps it is mainly in a generally liberal context that diversity of belief develops on a controversial area such as sex. The youthfulness of our student sample and their higher status (higher than the adult sample) can be taken as indices of a high level of general liberality.[41]

Perhaps the greater sensitivity to the liberalism or conservatism of the setting in the upper classes in both samples is due, in part, to the presence

---

[41] Females and males did not show very sharp differences. Perhaps the "tradition of low permissiveness" tendencies of the females were counterbalanced by the greater "general liberality" of the males.

of a higher level of general liberality.[42] (See Table 4.6.) The notion of the general level of liberality as an important contextual factor is, in any case, worth checking in future research.[43]

General liberality may indicate a general susceptibility to social forces that maintain sexual permissiveness and not just a setting that accentuates the contrast of liberals and conservatives in such a group. It may be that liberalism emphasizes the type of social forces that maintain high permissiveness, for example, low religious orthodoxy, low value on tradition, high value on autonomy. Young people in the courtship stage may be more favorable toward change, and thus, generally more liberal. This may be particularly true for upper-class youngsters. This is not to say that only liberal groups are high on permissiveness. Other sources of high permissiveness exist, and the high permissiveness of the Negro group and of some conservative lower-class groups testifies to this.[44] But the newer permissiveness in America in the middle classes seems to be associated with general liberalism. The older brands of high permissiveness are supported by tradition and socioeconomic forces and not by liberalism. The concept of liberalism in this regard is similar to the concept of the traditional level of permissiveness; the ideal condition for change, then, is in a group with a tradition of low permissiveness that is coming to accept a general level of high liberality. The liberality notion can be summarized as Proposition Two: THE STRONGER THE AMOUNT OF GENERAL LIBERALITY IN A GROUP, THE GREATER THE LIKELIHOOD THAT SOCIAL FORCES WILL MAINTAIN HIGH LEVELS OF SEXUAL PERMISSIVENESS.

The upper part of the population in America appears to be a group with a relatively high level of general liberality but a tradition of low sexual permissiveness. Thus, it is precisely in this top part of the class system that one would expect to find significant changes—particularly among white females from a generally liberal setting. The urban growth in the last one

---

[42] One test of the "general liberality" thesis was made in the student sample by comparing two colleges, one of which had a reputation for being generally conservative and the other of which had a reputation for being generally liberal. The generally liberal college showed a greater difference in sexual attitudes between its liberals and its conservatives at both the lower and upper social-class levels. This is congruent with the "general liberality" thesis.

[43] A check was made to see if the differences between the student and the adult sample were due to the different measures of liberalism and conservatism used in each. The check used only the seven measures common to both samples and the same difference appeared.

[44] Lee Rainwater of Washington University is currently engaged in a long-term study of lower-class families in a St. Louis housing project. He has reported quite high permissiveness among his lower-class Negro population, which is in line with the findings reported in Table 3.6 in the present study. Much of this fascinating work is available now only in graduate theses. A broad survey, like the present one, often picks up only very small segments of the lower-class, and thus Rainwater's study is of considerable value.

hundred years may well be one key aspect of this new setting. One of the characteristics of present-day liberals would seem to be the increasing acceptance of sexual liberalism as part of a general liberal philosophy, and the liberals in the sample did turn out more permissive than the conservatives (Table 4.4). Thus, both the tradition of low permissiveness" proposition and the "general liberality" proposition reinforce each other as explanations of the findings on the relation of social class to sexual permissiveness. Both make sense of the data, and taken together, they would seem to be the beginning of a middle-range theory concerning sexual relationships (further elaborated later in this study).

City Size and Region of the Country

It is appropriate here to report briefly some findings regarding the relation of urbanism to permissiveness, for these factors are relevant to the class structure in America. The relation of urbanism to permissiveness can be seen in the following data, which show a significant relation between those cities with a population of under 100,000 and those cities with a population of 100,000 or more. Table 4.7 presents this relation for both the student

Table 4.7

CITY SIZE AND PERMISSIVENESS IN STUDENT AND ADULT
SAMPLES (PERCENTAGE HIGHLY PERMISSIVE)

CITY SIZE	ADULT SAMPLE[a]	STUDENT SAMPLE
1–9999	17 (428)	39 (293)
10,000–99,999	12 (361)	47 (255)
100,000 or more	26 (344)	61 (266)
	$\chi^2 = 25.1$	$\chi^2 = 27.4$
	$P < .001$	$P < .001$
	$G = .19$	$G = .29$
	$C = .15$	

[a] Currently married only.

and adult samples. In terms of standards, the big cities (of more than 100,-000) have an excess of double-standard and permissiveness-with-affection adherents. (See Exhibit 2.1 for definitions.) City size appears to operate as a direct determinant of permissiveness, probably due to its encouragement of courtship autonomy. (See Chapters 9 and 10 for discussion of this point.)

Related to city size is region of the country, and here too the most urbanized regions seemed to be the most permissive. The results on the currently married whites in the adult sample are presented in Table 4.8.

Table 4.8
REGION AND PERMISSIVENESS FOR
CURRENTLY MARRIED WHITES IN THE ADULT SAMPLE
(PERCENTAGE HIGHLY PERMISSIVE)

REGION OF THE COUNTRY	PERMISSIVENESS
Northeast	19 (278)
West	17 (171)
North Central	14 (304)
South	11 (277)
	$x^2 = 6.8$
	$P < .10$
	$G = .18$
	$C = .081$

The South is the most rural section in the United States and is lowest on permissiveness. It also has the highest proportion of double-standard adherents. The size of the sample prevented permissiveness checks by many individual states. Only New York and California had sizable numbers of respondents in this study. They both come out relatively high on the permissiveness attitudes of white males and females, but California was considerably higher on those for females. Of course, even this should not be taken as conclusive until checked with larger samples. Negroes were too few to be included in this analysis at all. Among the whites, only those currently married were used, so as to eliminate any variation due to being single or formerly married.

Despite the seeming interrelation, city size and region are independently related to permissiveness, for control by each on the other did not reduce the basic relation each had to permissiveness. Both are indications of the way that broad social forces affect sexual permissiveness. The growth of the new middle classes seems to have been greatest in large cities outside of the South, and thus the high permissiveness of these new classes fits with the high permissiveness of the city and regional areas in which the classes live. The increasing urbanism of rural areas may have made cities and rural areas with a population of under 100,000 more homogeneous.

5

Dating Characteristics and Premarital Sexual Permissiveness

Preface to Proposition Three

One of the major factors presupposed as an influence on premarital sexual standards was the dating experience of the individual. It was reasoned that such aspects of dating experience as the age at which dating began, the number of "steadies" the individual had, the number of times he had been in love, whether he dated one person exclusively, and romantic-love conceptions would all play a part in the development of premarital sexual standards. The student sample was used to check this area.

The empirical results indicated that all of these dating characteristics affected premarital sexual permissiveness, but differently for males and females. For example, romantic love affected permissiveness more for females than for males; the age at which dating began was related to permissiveness mostly for males, and exclusiveness of dates, going steady, and falling in love associated differently with permissiveness for males and females. This led to Proposition Three, which basically asserted that the different courtship roles of males and females in American society made them sensitive to different social factors or to the same social factor in different ways. The tests that led to the formulation of this proposition will now be discussed.

The Romantic-Love Scale

A Guttman scale was used to measure romantic love and examine the relationships that were discovered. Eight statements comprise this scale.[1]

Exhibit 5.1
ROMANTIC-LOVE SCALE[a]

Please circle the degree of agreement or disagreement you have with the following statements concerning love relationships between men and women.[b]
1. True love leads to almost perfect happiness.
   Agree: (1) Strong, (2) Medium, (3) Slight
   Disagree: (1) Strong, (2) Medium, (3) Slight
2. When one is in love, the person whom he loves becomes the only goal in his life. One lives almost solely for the other.
   (The same six-way choice found in statement 1 follows every statement.)
3. True love will last forever.
4. There is only one real love for a person.
5. True love is known at once by the people involved.
6. Doubt may enter into real love.
7. Even though one's past love affair was not as strong as the present one, it may still have been a real love relationship.
8. Conflict can be a part of real love.

---

[a] The scale was constructed by dichotomizing the responses to each statement into "agree" and disagree."

[b] The highest scale type is achieved by agreeing with the first five statements and disagreeing with the last three. The statements are in scale order, so that the lowest scale type would be the individual who disagrees with the first five and agrees with the last three; all other scale types fall in between. The statements have been put into scale order for the sake of simplicity. Actually, they were administered in the questionnaire in mixed order (See Appendix A Part VI). The eight statements were numbered in the questionnaire as follows: 1, 10, 7, 2, 3, 5, 4, 8. Statements 6 and 9 in the questionnaire order were dropped due to excessive error.

---

[1] Statements 6 and 9 from the questionnaire listing were dropped. (See Appendix A, Part VI). These were worded as follows:
   6. True love is mysterious and cannot be understood by reason. It can only be felt, not explained.
   9. It is possible to love two people at the same time.
Statement 6 has two sentences, and each could possibly be taken to have a separate meaning. Statement 9 may be ambiguous because one could say Yes to it due to intense romantic feelings or to a complete lack of romantic feelings. Statement 6 also might be answered Yes both for romantic reasons and for nonromantic reasons.
   It is always difficult to be sure you have not merely rationalized the dropping of the high-error statements even though they are no more ambiguous than any other statements. Further testing of this scale is needed before one can be sure regarding the original ten statements. Beverly Scott Davenport, in her M.A. thesis for the University of Iowa, 1966, "Premarital Sexual Permissiveness and Dating Behavior" (unpublished), found that in one college in the state of Washington it was not statements 6 and 9 that produced the greatest amount of error but rather statements

The Guttman-scale qualities of this scale are not as outstanding as in the premarital sexual permissiveness scale.[2] The romantic-love scale yields a coefficient of reproducibility of .90 and a coefficient of scalability of .65. Both of these measures just meet the minimum requirements. It also has a percent pure scale type of 43 percent and a minimal marginal reproducibility of 64 percent. (See Appendix D for discussion of these measures.) With all ten questions the coefficient of reproducibility was reduced to .87 and the coefficient of scalability to .60. It can be argued that the two questions that were dropped were the most ambiguous in their meaning and therefore could imply both romantic and nonromantic reasons for agreement. Further testing of this scale is needed to validate it fully, although it did "work," as noted above, on all five schools in the student sample.[3]

When examining this scale for differences within race and sex categories as well as among the five schools, patterned differences appear, but they do not seem as radical as the differences noted on the permissiveness scale in Chapter 2. Basic race and sex differences can be seen in Table 5.1.

Turning to specific statements in the scale, there was more relative support for statement 5 among Negroes than among whites and more support among females than among males. (See Tables 5.2, 5.3 and 5.4.) This statement reads, "True love is known at once by the people involved." Similarly, the high-school students seemed to rank statement 5 higher than did

---

4 and 8. In the Five-School Student Sample statement 6 had 18 percent error and statement 9 had 22 percent error. If these items were kept in, the reproducibility would be 87 percent instead of 90 percent. It may be that several of the items are contaminated and that short of a major revision of the scale, it would be just as well to keep all ten even though the scale fell below the 90 percent coefficient-of-reproductibility level. Since this scale has not been tested as carefully as the permissiveness scale, all that can be done is wait for further checks. It was found simple to use only the single statement, "There is only one real love for a person," and this was done in chap. 3. However, it is important to discern whether this one statement stands alone or whether it comes from, and represents, a single scalable dimension.

Two other statements had errors beyond the 10 percent level: statements 5 and 10. Statements 1, 2, 3, 4, 7, and 8 all had 10 percent error or less. (All the statement numbers here refer to the questionnaire numbering. The numbering in Exhibit 5.1 is different. On the bottom of that table the questionnaire numbers are given for comparison.)

[2] One of the earliest investigations in this area is Llewellyn Gross, "A Belief Pattern Scale for Measuring Attitudes Toward Romanticism," *American Sociological Review,* 9 (December 1944), pp. 463–472. See also Charles W. Hobart, "The Incidence of Romanticism During Courtship," *Social Forces,* 36 (May 1958), pp. 362–367. Hobart selected twelve items from Gross for his study. He reported that it was impossible to make a Guttman scale of these or any other items from Gross's list. Also, like most all researchers in this area, he did not examine the relation of love to sex. See also Hobart's analysis of the role of romanticism in freeing men from parents: "Emancipation from Parents and Courtship in Adolescents," *Pacific Sociological Review,* 1 (Spring 1958), pp. 25–29.

[3] For a theory of several types of love, see Ira L. Reiss, "Toward a Sociology of the Heterosexual Love Relationship," *Marriage and Family Living,* 22 (May 1960), pp. 139–145.

Table 5.1

PERCENTAGE DISTRIBUTION OF ROMANTIC-LOVE SCALE TYPES BY RACE
AND SEX FOR THE STUDENT SAMPLE

	Low			*Romantic-Love Scale Types*				*High*		
	0	*1*	*2*	*3*	*4*	*5*	*6*	*7*	*8*	*N*
White male	18	17	21	20	8	8	7	2	1	(252)
White female	15	12	18	27	11	7	6	2	1	(294)
Negro male	12	15	19	17	13	14	9	0	1	(104)
Negro female	10	12	20	16	11	18	9	3	1	(108)
Total	15	14	20	22	10	10	7	2	1	(758)

Table 5.2

PERCENTAGE AGREEING WITH EACH ITEM BY RACE ON THE
ROMANTIC-LOVE SCALES IN THE STUDENT SAMPLE

QUESTION NUMBER	TOTAL STUDENT SAMPLE	TOTAL WHITE	TOTAL NEGRO
1	74.7	74.2	75.9
2	58.7	55.5	67.0
3	52.8	52.0	54.7
4	30.6	26.6	41.0
5	26.5	22.2	37.7
6	23.5	22.5	25.9
7	13.5	12.8	15.1
8	11.7	11.7	11.8
N	(758)	(546)	(212)

Table 5.3

PERCENTAGE AGREEING WITH EACH ITEM BY SEX ON THE
ROMANTIC-LOVE SCALES IN THE STUDENT SAMPLE

QUESTION NUMBER	TOTAL STUDENT SAMPLE	TOTAL MALE	TOTAL FEMALE
1	74.7	71.6	77.4
2	58.7	56.2	60.9
3	52.8	46.6	58.2
4	30.6	29.2	31.8
5	26.5	26.7	26.4
6	23.5	27.5	19.9
7	13.5	13.5	13.4
8	11.7	11.8	11.7
N	(758)	(356)	(402)

Table 5.4

PERCENTAGE AGREEING WITH EACH ITEM BY SCHOOL ON THE ROMANTIC-LOVE SCALES
IN THE STUDENT SAMPLE

QUESTION NUMBER	WHITE VIRGINIA COLLEGE	WHITE VIRGINIA HIGH SCHOOL	WHITE NEW YORK COLLEGE	NEGRO VIRGINIA COLLEGE	NEGRO VIRGINIA HIGH SCHOOL
1	76.7	86.4	61.3	73.2	83.1
2	54.5	73.6	43.5	62.7	78.0
3	54.2	72.0	33.9	45.8	78.0
4	23.3	47.2	16.1	32.7	62.7
5	17.8	39.2	16.1	25.5	69.5
6	18.6	32.0	21.4	22.2	35.6
7	11.9	21.6	11.3	13.7	18.6
8	8.8	18.4	7.7	10.5	15.3
N	(253)	(125)	(168)	(153)	(59)

the college students. Generally speaking, the groups that ranked statement 5 higher were also higher on overall romantic-love beliefs. Negroes, females, and high-school students were relatively high on romantic love. Among the three colleges, the New York college was clearly the lowest on romantic-love beliefs. (See Table 5.4)

The white high-school students were low on permissiveness and high on romantic love; the white college students were higher on permissiveness and lower on romantic love. This negative relation held best for females. The situation was different in the case of Negroes: the higher they were on romantic love, the higher they were on permissiveness. This relation also worked best for the females. The basic Negro-white difference here, however, seems to be due largely to a third factor, church-attendance. (See Table 3.4 for an initial statement on this relationship.) The Negroes were generally high on church-attendance, and such people, whether Negro or white, are more likely to display a positive association of romantic love and permissiveness. The whites are more likely to be low on church-attendance, and both Negro and white groups that are low on church-attendance tend to display a negative association between romantic love and permissiveness. Thus church-attendance is a key condition of the romantic-love–permissiveness relationship; there is no simple unconditional relation between these two variables. This interaction affect held up in all five schools.

Students from both high schools were high on romantic love, but one group was low on permissiveness and the other was high on permissiveness. The reason for this is that the Negro high-school students were also high on church-attendance, encouraging those high on romantic love to be high on permissiveness, whereas the white high-school students were relatively low on church-attendance, encouraging an overall negative relation of romantic love to permissiveness.

The much weaker relation of romantic love to permissiveness in the male groups fits with Proposition One, that groups with higher traditions of permissiveness will be less affected by social forces. The relation holds up much stronger for females, but in opposite ways, depending on the church-attendance of the female.

The reasons for such findings are not clear, but it is reasonable to speculate that the high church-attenders are a group with both an emotional and a low-permissive tendency. Romantic love can reinforce the emotional tendency and thereby overcome the low-permissive emphasis, whereas a lack of this strengthens the purely low-permissive forces. The low church-attenders can be viewed as a group with both an idealistic and a high-permissive orientation. High romantic-love beliefs reinforce the idealistic forces at the expense of the high-permissive orientation, whereas low romantic-love beliefs give freer rein to the high-permissive tendencies. Thus, the high church-attenders would emotionalize romantic love, while the low church-attenders would idealize romantic love, and this different emphasis leads to different consequences of romantic love. The emotional conception of romantic love would seem to be more common for the high church-attending females. They are almost twice as likely to be high on romantic love as the low church-attending females. But when the low church-attenders do accept romantic love, they seem to accept a less emotionalized and more idealistic version of it. The data collected in this study indicate that such low church-attending romantic females tend to accept abstinence, while the high church-attending females tend to accept permissiveness with affection.

It is important to stress that whether romantic-love beliefs promote or discourage sexual permissiveness seems strongly to depend on whether the individual is a high church-attender or a low church-attender. The popular notion that romantic love encourages sexual intimacies seems true largely for those who are high church-attenders. It may be that the parents of these youngsters—high church-attenders themselves—are more likely to become disturbed by this and to verbalize their feelings, thereby establishing the myth that romantic love has such permissive effects in general.[4]

Once again the importance of the religious factor makes itself known. If religion is measured by reported degree of religious devoutness (see Appendix A, Part I, question 5c) instead of by church attendance, the same results are obtained. Religion does indeed seem to be, as Lenski said, a key factor in human behavior.[5] The measure of religiosity that was employed in this study may well be a general measure of the conservative-liberal balance in a group and thereby may well reflect a general style of life and not simply attendance at church. The causal importance of religiosity supports such an interpretation.

[4] For a broad coverage of love see Lee G. Burchinal, "The Premarital Dyad and Love Involvement," pp. 623–674 in *Handbook of Marriage and the Family,* Harold T. Christensen, ed. Chicago: Rand McNally & Co., 1964, pp. 623–674.

[5] Gerhard Lenski, *The Religious Factor.* New York: Doubleday & Co., 1961, chap. 8. He distinguishes associational and communal religious behavior.

Age at Which Dating Began and Permissiveness

A widespread belief among American parents is that the earlier an individual starts to date the more permissive he is likely to be.[6] Data on this hypothesis were obtained from the student sample, and once again the complexities of social life are found to be elusive when put into unqualified common-sense statements. First, it is well to note that Negroes and whites were not alike in this relationship. The Negro fits more closely into the commonly believed supposition that the earlier an individual begins dating, the higher his sexual permissiveness. This negative relation of permissiveness to an individual's age at the time of his first date held up in both Negro schools and for both sexes within each school. A control by social class did not make any difference in these findings on Negroes (nor did it make any difference in the white results, discussed next).

Table 5.5

AGE AT FIRST DATE AND PERMISSIVENESS BY RACE AND SEX IN THE STUDENT SAMPLE
(PERCENTAGE HIGHLY PERMISSIVE)

AGE AT FIRST DATE	Female		Male	
	WHITE	NEGRO	WHITE	NEGRO
Twelve or less	36 (69)	67 (9)	73 (51)	88 (8)
Thirteen to fifteen	22 (207)	47 (68)	56 (176)	90 (62)
Sixteen or more	31 (35)	42 (33)	68 (44)	72 (25)
	$\chi^2 = 5.8$	$\chi^2 = 1.7$	$\chi^2 = 5.9$	$\chi^2 = 4.8$
	$P < .05$	NS	$P < .05$	$P < .10*$
	$G = -.15$	$G = -.19$	$G = -.07$	$G = -.45$
	$C = .14$	$C = .12$	$C = .15$	$C = .22$

* Some of the cells in the Negro tables are low, and the chi-square should be interpreted with this in mind.

The results for the white males and females indicate that the age of an individual at the time of his first date shows a curvilinear relationship to permissiveness, with the results again being weak but statistically significant at the .05 level. In the group of white males, it seems that early dating (at twelve years or less) is no more likely to lead to sexual permissiveness than is late dating (at sixteen years or more). Those who begin dating at ages thirteen to fifteen seem to be the least permissive. Actually, a check by school indicated that for females, the three white schools

[6] For a description of modern dating characteristics among ten to seventeen-year-old children see the study by Carlfred B. Broderick, "Socio-Sexual Development in a Suburban Community," *The Journal of Sex Research,* 2 (April 1966), pp. 1–24.

displayed different patterns, with the white Virginia college showing a positive relation, the white high school a high-middle curvilinear relation, and the white New York college a slight negative relation. None of the relations were significant. Thus the overall curvilinear relation for white females is merely the result of combining the schools, and in reality, white females show no consistent pattern. The curvilinear relation for white males is valid for all white schools except the Virginia college and thus is more reliable. The Negro male relation can be considered at the .05 level, since a direction was predicted, and thus a one-tail test would be suitable. However, the reader should be aware of the few cases in the "at twelve years or less" category. The Negro female relation is not significant.

Overall then, the male results show some pattern, whereas the female results are too weak to depend upon. The difference between white and Negro males is significant at the .05 level using the Goodman test for interaction. Here is one of the few instances where males seem to show more of a relationship than females. Ehrmann, interestingly enough, also found that males displayed a stronger relation between their age at their first date and permissiveness than did females.[7]

Perhaps the male Negro-white difference indicates that in a high-permissive setting, those who begin to date early will tend to have more permissive attitudes toward sex, but in a relatively low permissive setting a curvilinear relation appears. Females at the New York college and all the Negroes fit the high permissive pattern. *The key differences among all schools were in the relative position of the late-starters.* It may be that in a high-permissive setting those who start dating late are strongly oriented against fitting in with high permissiveness and thus postpone dating, whereas in a low-permissive setting those who postpone dating are likely to be unwilling respondents to the restrictive pressures enforced by the group.[8] Thus, when they finally do start to date, they may try to make up for lost time.[9] Perhaps

[7] Ehrmann, however, found that the men who started to date before the age fifteen were the most permissive. All of his males were white, but they fit the Negro pattern found in the present study. See Winston Ehrmann, *Premarital Dating Behavior.* New York: Holt, Rinehart and Winston, 1959, p. 83.

[8] The data in Table 5.5 indicate that a higher percentage of whites start dating by twelve years of age. The percentages are 8.5 percent of the Negroes and 20 percent of the whites. This is surprising, in the sense that one might have expected the high-permissive Negro group to start earlier. In this connection, the high-permissive white New York college did display the highest percent of individuals who started dating by age twelve. Perhaps this is a difference between an established permissive environment and a new permissive environment. Lowrie found that the children of wealthier and better-educated parents started to date earlier, and this would fit with the findings here. See Samuel H. Lowrie, "Early and Late Dating: Some Conditions Associated With Them," *Marriage and Family Living,* 23 (August 1961), pp. 284–291. Lowrie also found that those who started to date late started to go steady in less time than did the early daters.

[9] Michael Schofield found that those who started dating before age fourteen (in England) were more likely to have coitus. However, he did not use a control for the permissiveness of their peer environment. See his *The Sexual Behavior of Young People.* New York: Little, Brown & Co., 1965, p. 69.

the relation does not hold for females because they are more concerned than men about the type of dating (such as whether or not affection is involved). This becomes apparent in the other checks in this chapter.

Exclusiveness of Dating and Permissiveness

One of the most significant findings of Ehrmann's study of Florida College students was the greater tendency of his female respondents to associate their sexual behavior with the degree of seriousness and affection in the dating relationship.[10] For the purpose of this study it was decided to test one aspect of this in relation to sexual attitudes. The respondents were asked the following question: "Would you say that most of your dating activities were restricted to playing the field, dating particular individuals regularly, or about half and half? (Appendix A, Part V, question 8e). The hypothesis was that the female students would show greater permissiveness in their sexual attitudes to the extent that their dating was more restricted to particular individuals. It was expected that the males would show a curvilinear relation, with "half and half" highest on permissiveness and with "dating particular individuals" lowest. This would be similar to the type of findings Ehrmann reported.[11]

Table 5.6 shows that there was a modest amount of support for the female part of this hypothesis. The females, both Negro and white, generally showed the least permissiveness if their dates involved largely "playing the field" and the most permissiveness if their dates were mostly "regular." The Negro females did not display a significant relation. However, they were in the same direction, and if both white and Negro females are combined, a significant chi-square of 11 and a gamma of .30 are obtained. The Goodman test for interaction shows no significant difference between white and Negro females. No significant differences appeared among the males in the various schools. The percentage of all females who accepted coitus doubled when going from those who played the field to those who dated regularly. These results held up in all five schools but were very weak among female Negro college students. The attitude evidence here is in accord with Ehrmann's behavioral evidence for females, and is additional support for the close relation of attitude and behavior reports.

Once again the data indicates that the ways in which social forces affect sexual permissiveness are not uniform for all social groups. Clearly in the case of the exclusiveness of dating, the female group's permissiveness is affected, while the male's permissiveness is relatively immune to such fac-

---

[10] Winston W. Ehrmann, *Premarital Dating Behavior*. New York: Holt, Rinehart and Winston, 1959, chap. 4. Schofield reports some similar findings in *The Sexual Behavior of Young People*.

[11] Ehrmann, p. 134.

Table 5.6

EXCLUSIVENESS OF DATING AND PERMISSIVENESS BY RACE AND SEX
IN THE STUDENT SAMPLE (PERCENTAGE HIGHLY PERMISSIVE)

EXCLUSIVENESS OF DATING	*Female*		*Male*	
	WHITE	NEGRO	WHITE	NEGRO
Play the field	17 (54)	39 (13)	60 (62)	80 (25)
Half and half	22 (135)	45 (40)	64 (104)	91 (42)
Regular	36 (120)	50 (56)	62 (99)	88 (25)
	$x^2 = 9.3$	$x^2 = 0.65$	$x^2 = 0.24$	$x^2 = 1.5$
	$P < .01$	NS	NS	NS
	$G = .33$	$G = .13$	$G = .02$	$G = .21$
	$C = .17$	$C = .08$	$C = .03$	$C = .13$

tors. Males have sufficient motivations in their cultural heritage, and they do not depend on affectionate and individualized relationships to encourage their sexuality. A significant difference between males and females appears only for the white group.

Number of Steadies and Permissiveness

In line with the above hypothesis, it was expected that females who went steady would be more permissive than those who did not. The effect on males was expected to be curvilinear, with those with only one steady the lowest on permissiveness, for they were pictured as being limited to a single steady due to their conservatism and to their not being promiscuous enough to avoid going steady altogether. Since females value affection more than do males, their sexual behavior would be promoted by a close emotional relation such as going steady.

The results were basically in line with this hypothesis. Both Negro and white females showed a positive relation between sexual permissiveness and the number of times they had gone steady. The relation was not very strong, but it was evident, for when all females were combined, a chi-square of 6.6 is produced that is significant at the .05 level. The Negro males showed no association; but the white males showed a curvilinear one, with those males who had gone steady only once being lowest on permissiveness. This finding for white males is similar to that of Ehrmann's study, wherein he reported that those males who were currently dating a steady exclusively had the lowest sexual behavior as compared to those males who were not going steady or who were going steady but also dating other girls. The finding for girls was also similar to Ehrmann's study, which reported the greatest amount of sexual behavior if they were dating only their steady date and the least amount if they were not going steady. Thus, the findings in the present study differ from Ehrmann's mainly for the Negro males.

Table 5.7

NUMBER OF STEADIES AND PERMISSIVENESS BY RACE AND SEX
IN THE STUDENT SAMPLE (PERCENTAGE HIGHLY PERMISSIVE)

	Female		*Male*	
NUMBER OF STEADIES	WHITE	NEGRO	WHITE	NEGRO
None	21 (120)	38 (32)	67 (92)	87 (31)
One	22 (73)	50 (30)	46 (78)	83 (23)
Two or more	33 (114)	50 (48)	68 (102)	85 (41)
	$\chi^2 = 4.8$	$\chi^2 = 1.4$	$\chi^2 = 10.7$	$\chi^2 = 0.21$
	$P < .10$	NS	$P < .01$	NS
	$G = .22$	$G = .16$	$G = .02$	$G = -.04$
			$C = .20$	$C = .05$

Once again the findings indicate that dating experiences affect females differently than they do males, and in this case, Negro males differently than white males. However, the test for interaction reveals that the white and Negro sex differences are not significant. The check also shows that within the races, only the whites came close to showing a significant difference between males and females. It does not seem likely that Proposition One, regarding the effect of differences in traditional levels of sexual permissiveness, fully accounts for all these findings. However, this theory helps initially in making sense of this repetitive finding regarding the relation of sexual and racial differences to the ways in which social forces affect sexual permissiveness. The results also seem to reflect the different courtship roles of the sexes and to show that the sexes in some areas may be equally sensitive but in different ways.

There is a connection between the findings of the number of steadies an individual had and the findings on the exclusiveness of the dating relationship. Both showed positive association for females. This seems to indicate that it is not simply the custom of going steady that encourages permissiveness, but that it is the general custom of getting involved emotionally with a boy that is the causal factor. Social criticism of the going steady custom has often ignored the fact that it is but one custom of a generic type of intimate-dating relationship. It is quite unlikely that we shall ever be rid of all emotional intimacy in our relatively free, participant-run courtship system.[12] The factor that promotes permissiveness on the part of females is emotional involvement, which is an expected consequence of our type of courtship system and which tends to lead eventually to marriage. This interpretation is supported by the findings on the relationship of permissiveness to the number of times an individual has been in love.

[12] Ira L. Reiss, "Social Class and Campus Dating," *Social Problems*, 13 (Fall 1965), pp. 193–205. This article contains a report on an empirical study of our current college dating system, both Greek (sorority and fraternity organizations) and independent.

Number of Love Relationships
and Permissiveness

Concerning the relationship of permissiveness to the number of times an individual has been in love, a male-female difference was posited; the females were expected to show a postive relationship to permissiveness and the males a curvilinear relation, with those having been in love only once being the lowest. The basic results of this check can be seen in Table 3.5. In Table 5.8 the results for each race-sex group are presented. The white

Table 5.8
NUMBER OF LOVE RELATIONSHIPS AND PERMISSIVENESS BY RACE AND SEX
IN THE STUDENT SAMPLE (PERCENTAGE HIGHLY PERMISSIVE)

NUMBER OF LOVE RELATIONSHIPS	*Female*		*Male*	
	WHITE	NEGRO	WHITE	NEGRO
None	10 (93)	38 (24)	61 (85)	79 (29)
One	31 (117)	47 (53)	54 (115)	86 (35)
Two or more	35 (98)	48 (31)	73 (71)	$x^2 = 2.5$
	$x^2 = 18.3$	$x^2 = 0.78$	$x^2 = 6.9$	93 (30)
	$P < .001$	NS	$P < .05$	NS
	$G = .41$	$G = .12$	$G = .14$	$G = .38$
			$C = .16$	

and Negro females show a positive relationship, although it is weaker for the Negro females. The white males show a type of curvilinear relation similar to that which they displayed in the "going steady" checks, and the Negro males indicate a positive relation similar to that of the females. This Negro male pattern was the least expected result of the study, but it is more understandable when we realize the way romantic love affects the relationship under examination. Males who are high on romantic love are in the minority, but they do display the positive association of sexual permissiveness with the number of times they have been in love, which is characteristic of females. A higher percentage of Negro males fall into the high romantic-love groups, and thus the positive relation shows up more in the overall Negro group. However, in their display of a curvilinear relationship Negro males who are low on romantic love are just like white males who are low on romantic love. (See Table 3.5). The reason for the association of permissiveness with the number of times the individual has been in love in a highly romantic group of males may be that romantic love encourages males to view the love relation as of great importance and thereby encourages them to make their sex life agree with their love relationships.

Careful analysis of the relationship for whites reveals a basic male-female difference: the largest difference in permissiveness among females occurs between those who have never been in love and those who have been; the largest difference in permissiveness among males is between those who have been in love two or more times and those who have been in love only once or never. For females the number of times having been in love does not seem as crucial as the fact that love has occurred. For males there is relatively little difference between those who have never been in love and those who have been in love only once. Whatever difference there is in these two categories seems to lead to slightly less permissiveness for those who have been in love only once. It seems, then, that the *repeated* experience of falling in love encourages permissiveness on the part of the males, whereas the *single* experience of falling in love encourages permissiveness on the part of females, and this is not greatly surpassed by repeating the experience.

Perhaps females place such a heavy importance on falling in love that their full capacities for permissiveness are released by the first occurrence of love. Men, on the other hand, tend not to associate love with permissiveness as strongly, and thus it takes repeated experiences to develop this association and thereby to raise their permissive level.

Once again, the Goodman test for interaction revealed little difference *between* the races by sex, and *within* the races only the white males and females showed a significant difference in the way permissiveness relates to the number of times an individual has been in love. So this discussion of male-female differences may be more applicable to whites.

Summary, Conclusions, and Proposition Three

Five dating characteristics were examined in the student sample to test hypotheses concerning their role in the development of sexual permissiveness.[13] Key differences in the way these factors affected permissiveness seemed most strongly related to sex and race groupings, with the sex differences most relevant. Romantic love affected permissiveness most for females and was dependent on church-attendance as a condition. The effects of the age of the individual at his first date seemed to vary somewhat by race and to be strongest for males. Exclusiveness of dating affected females predominately, with exclusive dating corresponding with increased permissiveness. The number of steadies and the number of times the individual had been in love were positively associated to permissiveness for females, but for males the relation was curvilinear. On these last three measures, the

---

[13] Other characteristics were not important enough theoretically to bother with. For example, the number of times an individual dates is quite secondary to the *type* of dating he does. Checks reveal no significant relation to permissiveness.

significant differences were present only for white males and white females. In general, all these findings indicate that females are sensitive to social forces in different ways than are males.

It should be clear by now that all the relationships found in the student sample were examined within each school to be sure that the relation was not spurious. In addition, other key control variables were used, such as social class, romantic love, age, class in school, city size, and church-attendance. Where these controls made any differences, the findings are reported. The one type of control that seemed to have an effect was age and the year in school. Although the results were not always sharp, it did seem that the older students (and upperclassmen) manifested the discovered relationships better than did the younger ones.[14] This makes sense, since they would have more time for the effects to make themselves known. In one sense, the findings given throughout this chapter have more support than they appear to have in the few tables presented here. This is so because they held up in five separate samples of the schools and because the same checks were made with many different measures of the variables involved and with many different cutting points of each variable. Since most of these other checks yielded the same type of findings, the weakness of the relation is not as likely to indicate a chance finding as to indicate that the relation really exists but is weak.[15]

The sexual standards (see Chapter 2) were run against each of the independent variables in place of Guttman-scale measures of permissiveness. The results were generally the same. Finally, the comparison of the four race-sex tables were analyzed in accord with Goodman's test for interaction. The results of these checks were generally incorporated into the analysis in this chapter.

On all factors it was found that males and females differed in the way these factors related to permissiveness. Here, then, is an additional set of data indicating that not only do sex and race groups differ in their sensitivity to social forces, but they also differ in the way these forces affect them. This was shown here for male-female differences; so it might be said that beside there being differences in sensitivity to social forces, groups with different courtship roles will tend to be sensitive to different types of social forces. Thus, Proposition Three is, TO THE EXTENT THAT INDIVIDUAL TIES TO THE MARITAL AND FAMILY INSTITUTIONS DIFFER, INDIVIDUALS WILL TEND TO DISPLAY A DIFFERENT TYPE OF SENSITIVITY OF PERMISSIVENESS TO SOCIAL FORCES. Thus, since the female courtship conception is more marriage-oriented and less free from family influences, affection will be stressed more, and females would be expected to be more sensitive to

[14] Similar results were found by Beverly Davenport in her M.A. thesis.

[15] One can total the separate chi-squares for each of the five samples and judge the relation that way. For the sake of simplicity, and because it does not make much difference, it was chosen not to do this.

affection as a permissiveness-producing force. Males would be expected to be equally or more permissive when not exclusively involved with affection-related forces. This, basically, was what was found in the data. Romantic love was associated with permissiveness predominantly for females; age at the time of an individual's first date was important mostly for males; and exclusive dating, steady dating, and love dating associated differently with permissiveness for males and females. Several other similar dating factors were also examined, with almost identical results. It was found that those females who experienced many serious dating relationships, such as going steady, were more likely to be adherents of permissiveness with affection. This further demonstrates the importance of affection to this group.

It should be kept in mind that, in general, the relation discussed held up more for whites than for Negroes, and thus Proposition Three seems to fit the white group better. Perhaps this is so because the courtship roles of male and female Negroes are more similar. Some evidence for this is the fact that the permissive levels of the sexes are more similar for Negroes than for whites.

Actually, the differences here between whites and Negroes, though supported by tests for significance, should not be over-emphasized. It should be remembered that for such aspects of dating behavior as exclusive dating, steady dating, and the number of times an individual has been in love, the Negro and white males were not significantly different, and neither were the Negro and white females. Nevertheless, the male-female differences in the white group were significant, while those in the Negro group were not. These data represent relations that could be graphed as follows:

The differences are present for Negroes, but only in the case of the white males and white females do they become great enough to be called statistically significant. This weaker relation for a high-permissive group such as Negroes is congruent with Proposition One. However, the primary concern here is not with differences in *strength* of sensitivity—for that is the domain of Proposition One—but rather with differences in *type* of sensitivity, particularly with those related to courtship roles, such as the female's greater sensitivity to affection. There is some evidence that this sex difference in type of sensitivity exists for Negroes, but in this sample it was not often strong enough to reach statistical significance.

This is a good place to reemphasize the difficulty involved in establishing a causal relationship, and to state that there is no pretense that it has been done in this study. After all, the study involved cross-sectional data gathered at one point in time, and therefore the time sequence is difficult to establish. It is possible that the level of sexual permissiveness affects dating characteristics rather than vice versa. Further, it might be that these factors have a two-way causal relationship. Evidence regarding this issue is presented in Chapter 7 in the discussion of the sexual life histories given by almost three hundred students. But it should be made clear that the use of causal terminology in this study is mainly for purposes of presenting a point of view clearly and not in order to eliminate any questions regarding causality.

6

Equalitarianism

Preface to Proposition Four

The concept of permissiveness on the male and female
scales is used as a measure of the extent to which the individual will allow those of his own sex and of the opposite
sex to engage in various types of sexual behaviors. The
measure used to compare the response to these two scales
is equalitarianism, which is computed by noting the similarity or difference in the scale type of a respondent on
the male and female scales. Since Americans have a double-
standard heritage, it was important to check further into
this area.

The check for equalitarianism revealed interesting differences *within* the double-standard and abstinence classifications. Within these two standards it was found that
equalitarianism would increase when the double-standard
and abstinence adherents were members of a high-permissive group (such as males, low church-attenders, or Negroes) rather than of a low-permissive group (such as
females, high church-attenders, or whites). This, basically,
is Proposition Four. Equalitarianism was checked by various measures, and its relation to sociocultural factors was
also investigated before arriving at this proposition, which
implies that the context of permissiveness that the group
possesses can affect equalitarianism within the double-
standard and abstinence classification.

Specifically, a more equalitarian position within the
double-standard classification would be the acceptance of
intercourse for females when they are in love, rather than

the orthodox double-standard position that all coitus for females is forbidden. This more equalitarian double-standard position, it will be remembered (see Exhibit 2.1), is the transitional double-standard subtype, so called because by allowing females to have coitus when in love it is a step in the direction of full equalitarianism. Nonequalitarianism within the abstinence standard would most typically be the acceptance of petting as permissible for males but not for females. Equalitarian-abstinent adherents would accept the same amount of petting and kissing for both sexes. (For the distribution of these and all other standards see Tables 2.5, 2.6 and 2.7.)

Student and Adult Equalitarianism

Table 6.1 shows the distribution of equalitarianism in the student and adult samples. An oddity in this table (previously commented on in Chapter 2) is the presence of "reverse" nonequalitarian responses, that is, of answers indicating that females should be given more sexual rights than males. As noted in Chapter 2, these were taken to be "error" responses; that is, it was assumed that the respondents did not mean to imply "reverse" nonequalitarianism, but that because they had not thought out their position clearly on both scales, they unintentionally gave that impression.

Table 6.1

PERCENT EQUALITARIAN BY RACE AND SEX IN THE STUDENT AND ADULT SAMPLES[a]

| | Traditional Nonequalitarian | | | | | | Reverse Nonequalitarian | | | | | |
	+5	+4	+3	+2	+1	E	−1	−2	−3	−4	−5	N
	Student Sample											
White male	0	0	3	10	14	64	6	2	1	0	0	(272)
Negro male	2	1	2	5	23	56	9	1	1	0	0	(110)
White female	0	1	3	12	16	63	6	1	0	0	0	(320)
Negro female	2	2	5	13	15	55	5	3	2	0	0	(110)
Total	0	1	3	10	16	61	6	1	1	0	0	(812)
	Adult Sample											
White male	1	0	2	8	14	68	5	2	0	0	0	(594)
Negro male	4	0	0	7	7	74	7	0	2	0	0	(57)
White female	0	0	1	7	9	76	4	1	0	0	0	(622)
Negro female	0	1	0	6	14	67	10	1	1	0	0	(72)
Total	1	0	1	8	12	72	5	2	0	0	0	(1345)

[a] A plus sign (+) indicates that males obtained a higher scale score, and the number indicates how many scale types the difference amounts to. For example, a person under "+1" would have answered the scale questions in such a way as to give males greater sexual freedom by approving one more question for them. A "+2" person would have approved two more questions for males than for females, and so on. A minus sign (−) indicates that females obtained a higher scale type. *E* indicates that males and females are equalitarian.

In both the student and adult samples equalitarianism received a majority of supporters. It is quite possible, however, that the percentages in Table 6.1 do not present an entirely true picture, for nonequalitarianism may have been understated by the permissiveness scales. (For additional data on equalitarianism see Table D.1 in Appendix D.) This may not be simply a matter of the kind of measure used, but a matter of nonequalitarianism having permeated American culture to the extent that even those who are intellectually and emotionally equalitarian will have traces of it that are difficult to detect except when they are interviewed in depth. For example, a man may be equalitarian but still feel that men may have more petting partners than women, even though women have just as much right to pet. Or a woman may feel she has just as much right as do men to have coitus when affection is present, but will excuse a male who has coitus without affection more easily than she will a female. These subtle elements of nonequalitarianism are not easily detected by standard measures. Support of strong nonequalitarianism does appear on the scale measure but weaker nonequalitarian elements are absorbed into the equalitarian group, giving the impression of less nonequalitarianism than really exists. What seems to exist in reality is a small, hard core of nonequalitarians and a much larger group only partially affected by nonequalitarianism.

A reflection of nonequalitarianism can be seen in the fact that males are much more permissive than females. Thus, while equalitarian pressures may have an effect, it is still true that American females are much less permissive than American males. This may be due to parents who allow permissiveness for both male and female children but less for female. The paradox may well be explained by unintended signs that the parents give and by differential pressures from other elements of society. For example, parents may respond to permissive behavior reported in the newspapers with different degrees of criticism for males and females.

Tests were run to see if the relation of equalitarianism to other factors would differ when only those who were at least two scale types in the nonequalitarianism direction were used. This did not make a difference. An entirely separate measure of nonequalitarianism also was used. The individuals in the student sample were asked whether men should be allowed more sexual freedom before marriage than women (see Appendix A, Part II, question 15). In some ways this single question seems to have been superior, as a general equalitarian index, to the equalitarian measure of responses to the male and female scales, and it has the advantage of having been independently computed. It was used as an additional check on all the tests discussed in this chapter.[1]

---

[1] All equalitarian checks were made in four ways: (1) reverse nonequalitarian was included in nonequalitarian; (2) all reverse nonequalitarian respondents were dropped; (3) question 15 was used instead of the scale measure of equalitarianism; and (4) the official double-standard was used.

That the equalitarian measure of responses to the male and female scales underestimates the amount of nonequalitarianism present is suggested by the fact that about half the respondents are classified as nonequalitarian on the basis of the single question, while only one-third are so classified by the scale method.[2] As can be seen in Table 6.2, a little over half of those classi-

Table 6.2
RELATION OF EQUALITARIANISM AS MEASURED BY SCALES
AND BY SINGLE QUESTION IN STUDENT SAMPLE

GENERAL EQUALITARIANISM MEASURED BY QUESTION 15	PERCENT EQUALITARIAN ON SCALES
Nonequalitarian	54 (377)
Equalitarian	79 (364)
	$x^2 = 49.7$
	$P < .001$
	$Q = .52$

fied as nonequalitarian by the single question are classified as equalitarian by the scale measure. But about eight of every ten of those classified as equalitarian by the single question are similarly classified by the scale measure. Thus, many individuals who have some nonequalitarian aspects (by their own direct admission) do not show up in the nonequalitarian measure of the scales. This may well be because the type of nonequalitarianism these people feel is too weak to make them give a sufficiently different response for the two sexes on the scale measure.[3] The scales may measure equalitarianism accurately in terms of their design but still miss the more subtle varieties of nonequalitarianism, which, as previously noted, may allow males greater frequency of, and greater access to, certain types of sexual behavior but not exclusive access; thus they do not show up on the scale measures.[4] The single-question approach takes a different cut of the nonequalitarian pie, and although it comes out with a larger "piece," it has drawbacks of its own, for there are many different types of nonequali-

[2] The scale method of computing nonequalitarianism does yield *more* nonequalitarianism than does the checklist-of-standards method. This was tested in the Iowa College Sample. See Appendix B, Part III.

[3] In support of this, those who agreed strongly with question 15 came out 54 percent nonequalitarian on the scale measure, whereas those who agreed slightly with question 15 came out only 35 percent nonequalitarian. Thus the strong nonequalitarian adherents on question 15 were more likely to be called nonequalitarian on the scale measure, and the weaker ones were more likely to be lost in the scale measure.

[4] The male and female scales can increase the amount of nonequalitarianism they reveal by using the full six-way response to each question. If a person differs by sex in any degree in his support, he can be listed as nonequalitarian. Such usage is more complicated, but it would afford a closer measure to that given by question 15.

tarianism included under such a question that may not fundamentally affect sexual standards. Also, there are other aspects of nonequalitarianism that such a single question does *not* encompass. In short, nonequalitarianism seems to be a much more complex variable to measure than was anticipated, and although the two ways used to measure it here are valuable, other approaches should be tried and the aforementioned methods checked out carefully.[5]

Equalitarianism and Permissiveness

The basic relationship between equalitarianism and permissiveness appears to be that a higher percent of low permissives than of high permissives are equalitarian. This can be seen, in part, in Table 6.1, where the more-conservative adult sample is slightly more equalitarian. However, it does not hold up *within* each sample, for at times those who are more permissive seem to be more equalitarian. It is quite important to qualify this by saying that if one examines only those who accept coitus in each race-sex group, then there is more acceptance of the double standard in low-permissive groups, such as females and whites, than in high-permissive groups, such as males and Negroes.[6] Further, those people from low-permissive groups who are abstinent are more likely to be nonequalitarian. This paradoxical situation is simply the result of the fact that a high-permissive group will often have a higher percent of its total group who accept the double standard, and this makes the total group less equalitarian. However, the high-permissive group will have a lower percent of those who accept coitus being double standard, whereas the low-permissive group will have a very high percent of those who accept coitus being double standard. This is particularly true of low-permissive female groups, where the majority of those females who do not believe in abstinence are adherents of the orthodox double standard. In a similar vein, within the abstinence standard the low-permissive individual seems more willing to accept greater sexual liberties for men only. (See Tables 2.6 and 2.7 for the relevant data showing these relations.) The clearest way to investigate this area further is to look at the abstinent and permissive groups separately. A comparison of white males and females in the student sample illustrates the high percent who are equalitarian for both sexes *within* the abstinence standard (87 per-

[5] Although there is frequent comment on nonequalitarianism, very little in the way of precise empirical research exists on this dimension. Usually all that is found are lists of the percent accepting the double-standard on a checklist. See Tables 2.1, 2.2, and 2.3 for relevant data. See Tables 2.6 and 2.7 for indication of the nonequalitarianism in the greater acceptance for males of affectionless sexual behavior. See also Table D.1 in Appendix D for relevant data.

[6] Michael Schofield reports English females to be more double-standard than English males. See *The Sexual Behavior of Young People*. Boston: Little, Brown & Co., 1965, p. 131.

cent for males; 80 percent for females). Looking only at those who are not abstinent, a greater percent of a high-permissive group like males are equalitarian (55 percent) than of a low-permissive group like females (38 percent). Further, of the 45 percent of the nonabstinent white males who were double-standard adherents, only 38 percent were orthodox double standard, and the remaining 62 percent were transitional double standard. For white females 57 percent of the double-standard adherents were orthodox, and only 43 percent were transitional. Since the transitional double standard subtype is more equalitarian, this is further evidence of the greater equalitarianism of those who reject abstinence and are also part of a high-permissive group.

It will be instructive to look within the double-standard classification to see if the percent supporting the more equalitarian subtype called "transitional" will vary. This is done in much of the analysis of the student sample that follows. (The definitions from Exhibit 2.1 should be kept in mind: abstinence forbids coitus to both sexes; orthodox double standard forbids coitus to females; transitional double standard forbids coitus to females unless they are in love or engaged, and nonequalitarian abstinence would typically allow males greater access to petting.)

Age and Equalitarianism

It was hypothesized that age would correlate positively with equalitarianism, because the increased heterosexual experience that age brings would yield more understanding and appreciation of the opposite sex and of oneself, and this would tend to encourage the individual to treat both sexes equally. The zero-order relation of equalitarianism to age was neither significant nor strong.[7] Even in the percent of double-standard adherents among those who were not abstinent there was little difference in this relation. However, a closer examination revealed some rather interesting information.

A check was made *within* the double standard to see if there was a change with increased age from the orthodox to the transitional subtype of the double standard. (This particular check had helped in the analysis of the relation of equalitarianism to permissiveness.) There was support for this change, particularly among white males. Overall, older individuals were slightly more transitional than younger individuals, averaging 54 percent as opposed to 46 percent. Although the relation held up among all four race-sex groups, it was strongest for white males. There was some indication that the relation was stronger for high church-attending white males. Low church-attending white males started out in their youth as high equalitarians and increased only slightly. At a later age, high and low church-

---

[7] Age for the high-school students was divided so that eighteen or more was called old, whereas for college students twenty or more was called old. The adult sample had too few single people to make this sort of comparison effective.

attending white males were quite similar to each other, but this result seemed to involve more change for high church-attenders. However, the relationships here are quite weak and should only be taken as suggestive. Some support for this change among high church-attenders is presented in the next chapter, which discusses several hundred student reports regarding changes in sexual standards from approximately age ten to twenty.

A similar search *within* the abstinence standard was also made. Here too it was found that white males showed a change; but this time it was toward *more* nonequalitarianism (see Table 6.3). The older abstinent males were

Table 6.3

Age and Equalitarianism by Race and Sex in the Student Sample

AGE	WHITE MALES	NEGRO MALES	WHITE FEMALES	NEGRO FEMALES
	Percentage Transitional of Double-Standard Adherents			
Young	56 (36)	75 (4)	35 (26)	38 (13)
Old	74 (34)	81 (26)	44 (34)	44 (18)
	$x^2 = 2.46$	$x^2 = 0.07$	$x^2 = 0.04$	$x^2 = 0.12$
	NS	NS	NS	NS
	$Q = .38$	$Q = .17$	$Q = .20$	$Q = .11$
	Percentage Equalitarian of Abstinent Adherents			
Young	97 (36)	100 (2)	80 (99)	87 (23)
Old	79 (47)	50 (8)	79 (87)	79 (14)
	$x^2 = 4.7**$		$x^2 = 0.02$	$x^2 = 0.45$
	$P < .05$	$P = .33*$	NS	NS
	$Q = .81$	$Q = 1.0$	$Q = .02$	$Q = .29$

* Fisher's "Exact" test is used where the number of cases is very small.
** Corrected for continuity.

more nonequalitarian; for example, they would allow petting for themselves but not for females. No such change appeared for females, but those in the younger group, compared to white males, began relatively high on nonequalitarianism. The Goodman test for interaction showed that support for the white males was different from that for white females in this relationship. The small number of Negroes who were sampled precluded much analysis of their data. Church-attendance had no effect on this relation. The relation was difficult to check in the adult sample, since respondents were all twenty-one years old and over, and most had been or were married. However, the available evidence supported the student sample findings.[8]

[8] In the adult sample, the percent of double-standard white males who were transitional double-standard increased from 44 percent to 50 percent, going from males under thirty to those thirty and over. Similarly the percent of abstinent males

These two changes on the part of white males may well be part of a general growth of permissiveness for abstinent and double-standard males. The abstinent male becomes more permissive as he grows older, particularly for himself, whereas the double-standard male becomes more permissive for his female partner and therefore more equalitarian. Thus, in both cases, the move toward greater permissiveness encourages a change in equalitarianism. On this basis, the key determinant of equalitarianism would seem to be permissiveness. In this sense the original hypothesis should be modified here, for it is not sympathy and understanding that primarily affect changes in equalitarianism but a growth in the individual's desire for permissiveness. However, the few number of cases available for these checks makes this conclusion quite tentative.

Religiosity and Equalitarianism

Table 6.4 shows that church-attendance is related to equalitarianism within the double standard, particularly for whites. Those double-standard adherents who are high church-attenders are less likely to be transitional

Table 6.4
CHURCH-ATTENDANCE AND EQUALITARIANISM BY RACE AND SEX
IN THE STUDENT SAMPLE

CHURCH-ATTENDANCE	WHITE MALES	NEGRO MALES	WHITE FEMALES	NEGRO FEMALES
	Percentage Transitional of Double-Standard Adherents			
High	50 (26)	82 (17)	4 (35)	36 (25)
Low	73 (45)	73 (15)	64 (39)	60 (5)
	$x^2 = 3.9$	$x^2 = 0.04$**	$x^2 = 21.5$	$x^2 = 0.25$**
	$P < .05$	NS	$P < .001$	NS
	$Q = -.47$	$Q = .26$	$Q = -.95$	$Q = -.45$
	Percentage Equalitarian of Abstinent Adherents			
High	85 (55)	63 (8)	77 (140)	83 (36)
Low	93 (27)	50 (2)	87 (47)	100 (1)
	$x^2 = 0.32$**		$x^2 = 2.2$	$x^2 = 0.91$**
	NS	$P = .66$*	NS	NS
	$Q = -.36$	$Q = .25$	$Q = -.34$	$Q = -1.0$

* Fisher's "Exact" test is used instead of chi-square where the number of cases is very small.
** Corrected for continuity.

who were equalitarian decreased from 93 percent to 75 percent for the same age groups. However, there were only thirteen double-standard males and twenty-six abstinent males available for this comparison. This was so because there were only 121 single individuals in the entire adult sample.

double standard than those who are low church-attenders. (As noted in the preceding section, females do not show sharp changes with age in this regard.) Within the abstinence standard no relation is significant, but there is a tendency, particularly for white males and white females, to display an association between being equalitarian and being low on church-attendance. The Goodman test for interaction generally but not fully supports these interpretations.

Once again, then, although the total overall percent of those who are nonequalitarian *in all standards* does not vary by church-attendance, the distribution within the double-standard and abstinent classifications shows some variation. Religion seems to have an effect on males, as noted in the discussion regarding age, mainly by slowing down the acceptance of the transitional double standard. Among females it seems that religion has a rather permanent effect, making them more likely to be adherents of the orthodox double standard and of nonequalitarian abstinence. One can speculate that the stronger tradition of permissiveness among males leads to this eventual breakthrough, whereas females remain contained by their religiousness. This interpretation is in line with Proposition One.

The general tendency, shown to some extent by all race-sex groups, for high church-attenders to be low on equalitarianism *within* the double-standard and abstinence classifications is supported by other checks. For example, a check of the proportion of each standard who are equalitarian shows that the high church-attenders have a lower proportion of adherents who are equalitarian in all standards. By definition, permissiveness with affection and permissiveness without affection should not have any non-equalitarianism. Empirically, there is a small amount present in these two standards, however. Finally, the findings in Chapter 3 generally showed church-attendance to affect white females the most and Negro males the least. Roughly speaking, the findings here are congruent.

Romantic Love and Equalitarianism

Table 6.5 shows two measures of equalitarianism and generally gives a rather weak support to the hypothesized relation of low romantic love to equalitarianism. It was thought that those who were low on romantic love would be less conservative in general and thus more likely to give females greater equality. However, there is only very weak support for this notion, and there is some contradiction among males. Note particularly that the percent of males who are transitional *increases* as the strength of their belief in romantic love increases. This is not a significant relation, but it held up under various checks. This is opposed to the hypothesis, and although it does not occur in the test using believers in abstinence, it may indicate that among double-standard males, romantic love liberates equali-

Table 6.5
ROMANTIC LOVE AND EQUALITARIANISM BY RACE AND SEX IN THE STUDENT SAMPLE

ROMANTIC LOVE[a]	WHITE MALES	NEGRO MALES	WHITE FEMALES	NEGRO FEMALES
	Percentage Transitional of Double-Standard Adherents			
Low	60 (50)	72 (25)	49 (45)	45 (20)
High	79 (14)	100 (5)	21 (14)	38 (8)
	$x^2 = 1.6$	$x^2 = 0.59**$	$x^2 = 3.3**$	$x^2 = 0.003$
	NS	NS	$P = .10$	NS
	$Q = .42$	$Q = 1.0$	$Q = -.56$	$Q = -.15$
	Percentage Equalitarian of Abstinent Adherents			
Low	90 (49)	57 (7)	82 (119)	91 (22)
High	74 (19)	50 (2)	75 (52)	70 (10)
	$x^2 = 1.7$		$x^2 = 0.94**$	$x^2 = 0.97**$
	NS	$P = .42*$	NS	NS
	$Q = -.52$	$Q = -.14$	$Q = -.19$	$Q = -.62$

[a] Low romantic love includes scale-types zero to three.
* Fisher's "Exact" test is used instead of chi-square where the number of cases is very small.
** Corrected for continuity.

tarianism. For double-standard white females, high romantic love worked the other way, lowering the percent who accepted the transitional double standard. A control on church-attendance revealed that these opposed relations hold only for double-standard individuals and mainly for males with rather high church-attendance and females with relatively low church-attendance. For such females, high romantic-love beliefs may support the feeling that the woman must remain chaste in the interests of the formal, idealistic, romantic tradition. (This is compatible with the discussion of romantic love in Chapter 5.) For such males, high romantic-love feelings may be used as a justification for being more liberal toward females.[9] The white male and female difference is almost significant, and it may be worthwhile to note that double-standard males and females who have similar romantic-love feelings may have opposite views regarding the correctness of the transitional double standard. Such people would be more compatible regarding equalitarianism if their romantic-love views were *not* alike. One way of testing this finding empirically would be to test such selected dating couples.

Among adherents of the abstinence standard, although the direction was as predicted for all groups (low romantic love goes with equalitarianism), it was not significant.

[9] Winston Ehrmann, *Premarital Dating Behavior*. New York: Holt, Rinehart and Winston, 1959, chap. 7.

Social Class and Equalitarianism

It was hypothesized that those from a higher social class would also be higher on equalitarianism. The data from both the student and adult samples did not support this hypothesis. This should not be surprising after discussing the results in Chapter 4, which indicated that social class per se was related to premarital sexual permissiveness only under certain conditions. Quite a few controls were applied to see if a relationship could be found, but nothing was discovered. It appears, then, that social class is related to equalitarianism only in rather remote and complicated ways if at all.

Dating Background and Equalitarianism

It was hypothesized that the same dating factors that promoted permissiveness would also promote equalitarianism. It seemed that more regular-dating, more love relationships, more steady partners, and just more dating would all tend to encourage greater equalitarianism. The data did not fully support these contentions. Weak tendencies for males to be more equalitarian appeared if they were dating regularly rather than playing the field and if they had started to date relatively late. But even this support was weak, and it is hard to explain why regular-dating of one person would encourage equalitarianism but exclusive steady-dating and love affairs would not. It is possible that even the few significant findings for males are simply chance results. In any case, the support is very slight, and the nature of the relationship in this area needs further checking.

Summary, Conclusions, and Proposition Four

Basically, as a result of tests, the several hypotheses discussed in this chapter had to be qualified using the existing measures of equalitarianism. It is necessary to test them further to be able to define more precisely what is being measured in these different approaches and hopefully to obtain better insight into equalitarianism per se. However, the different ways of measuring equalitarianism discussed in this chapter did not yield conflicting results[10] regarding the relation of equalitarianism to other factors. Chapter 7

---

[10] Footnote one describes the various measures employed. In effect a general level of permissiveness is being related to a type of permissiveness, namely, equalitarian permissiveness. In this sense the dependent variable is still an aspect of permissiveness.

presents data on changes in sexual standards that strengthen some of the findings of this chapter. These data rely on the memory of the respondent. Such data have advantages over the cross-sectional data of this chapter for cross-sectional data assume that the younger respondents will eventually become like the older ones.

Overall, changes in permissiveness seem most crucial as causes of changes in equalitarianism, and thus factors that affect one should indirectly affect the other. The ways in which age, religiosity, romantic love, and dating background relate to equalitarianism lend some support to this thesis. This is as it should be, for it is only by the individual's increasing or decreasing his own or the other sex's permissiveness level that equalitarianism can be altered. The Goodman tests for interaction, in general, fit the interpretations of the data in this chapter.

The basic reason that high-permissive groups appear to be less equalitarian than low-permissive groups is that nonequalitarianism is a much smaller part of the abstinence standard than the double standard is of the permissive standards. Thus, overall there is really a smaller percentage of nonequalitarians within a low-permissive group. However, when controlled for by standard, the abstinent group indicates that the low permissives are more likely to be nonequalitarian. Looking only at those who accept coitus, the low permissives are more double standard, and within the double standard classification they are more orthodox. Thus, when we compare low- and high-permissive groups (such as males and females, Negroes and whites, low church-attenders and high church-attenders) *and* when abstinence and the double standard are controlled for (so that we look only at abstinence adherents or at double-standard adherents), then the lower the permissiveness, the greater the nonequalitarianism.[11] This is not surprising, for nonequalitarianism is a means of increasing permissiveness only halfway and such a control on permissiveness is more likely to be desired in a low-permissive group. Here is further evidence of the ways in which the level of permissiveness relates to the level of equalitarianism. These data can be summarized as Proposition Four: THE HIGHER THE GENERAL LEVEL OF PERMISSIVENESS IN A GROUP, THE GREATER THE EXTENT OF EQUALITARIANISM WITHIN THE ABSTINENCE AND DOUBLE-STANDARD CLASSIFICATIONS. Some of the data in the next chapter lend support to this proposition, for in the Iowa College Sample it was found that, using memory reports, changes

---

[11] It is true that older abstinent males are less equalitarian than younger abstinent males, and this could be taken to mean that as permissiveness increases, equalitarianism will *decrease*. However, this is not a valid conclusion, because the older abstinent males belong to *lower* permissive groups than do the younger abstinent males. Many of the younger abstinent males accept coitus as they age, and thus the younger abstinent group from which the older abstinent males come is a generally more potentially permissive group. The older abstinent males do fit the proposition, for they are in a hard core low-permissive group and are less equalitarian within the abstinence standard.

in permissiveness were most often remembered to be in the direction of more permissiveness being associated with more equalitarianism. The trend was toward more permissiveness and equalitarianism as the individual grew older.[12]

put as

Support for Nonequalitarianism

One fundamental support for nonequalitarianism is the closer normative tie of the female to the family institution. As the next few chapters show, the family institution is a conservative force supporting low premarital permissiveness. As long as the female is more oriented toward child-rearing and marriage than is the male, she will probably exhibit less permissiveness than he will. Both female participation in the labor force and male participation in family activities have increased, and no doubt they have promoted equalitarian tendencies. It is conceivable that males and females could be raised to be equally interested in child-rearing, but they have not yet reached that stage.[13]

It is the closer family tie for women that gives the fundamental undertone of nonequalitarianism to American premarital sex life. (This is in accord with both Proposition Three and Four.) The lessening of the risk of premarital pregnancy, venereal diseases, social condemnation and such has aided equalitarianism, but it is not likely that such equality can be fully achieved without a more radical alteration in the male and female roles in the family. The family sets the tone for the individual's orientation toward sexuality, and that which is valued in marital sex often comes to be valued in premarital sexuality. Thus, as marital sexuality has become more equalitarian and involved with affection, so has premarital sexuality. It remains to be seen how far family, marital, and premarital roles will proceed toward these equalitarian goals.

[12] Of ten girls who were once orthodox double-standard, not one accepted this at the time of the study. Six of the ten later accepted coitus for themselves, and the other four changed to a petting-with-affection standard. A much larger sample is needed to check out these findings more fully. For a study of male-female role differences that is relevant to understanding the double-standard cross-culturally see Herbert Barry, Margaret K. Bacon, and Irvin L. Child, "A Cross-Cultural Survey of Some Sex Differences in Socialization," *Journal of Abnormal and Social Psychology,* 55 (November 1957), pp. 327–332.

[13] Melford Spiro, *Kibbutz: Venture in Utopia.* Cambridge, Mass.: Harvard University Press, 1956; and *Children of the Kibbutz.* Cambridge, Mass.: Harvard University Press, 1958.

7

Changes in Sexual Standards, Behavior, and Guilt Feelings in Adolescence

Preface to Proposition Five

There is virtually nothing in the sociological research literature concerning the related changes of sexual standards, behavior, and guilt feelings during adolescence.[1] This chapter is the first real inquiry into such an area. A check of changes in sexual behavior, standards, and guilt feelings that relied on the respondent's memory was made predominantly on the Iowa College Sample. (See questionnaire in Appendix B.) Although this was not a probability sample, it was believed to be fairly representative of the college from which it was drawn, and recent checks have indicated that similar results would have been obtained on a more random sample.[2] The limitations of these findings are those of any study that relies on memory as a source of data. A longitudinal study would have been preferable, but this was not practical.

[1] There is a psychiatric account in: Group for the Advancement of Psychiatry, *Sex and the College Student.* New York: Atheneum Publishers, 1966. See also Erik H. Erikson, *Childhood and Society,* rev. ed. New York: W. W. Norton & Co., 1963.

[2] A check was made with a sample of over six hundred students who were taking Introductory Sociology. This is a large and diverse group of students. On the five-item "same sex" scale, this larger sample had 23 percent of the girls and 63 percent of the boys accepting coitus, whereas in the Iowa College Sample 32 percent of the girls and 64 percent of the boys accepted coitus. The girls in the Iowa College Sample were over a year older than the girls in the larger sample. The larger sample was gathered by Gary Hampe as part of his M.A. thesis, "Mixed Faith Dating," University of Iowa, 1967. Nevertheless, the Iowa Sample was not a probability sample, and thus probability statistics are used in this chapter mainly as a convenience.

An examination of the data discussed in this chapter revealed that there were marked differences within the female group and between males and females in the nature of the changes involved in the growth of permissiveness that occurs after age ten. Females felt more guilt, and their level of permissiveness changed more often. Females who changed reported that a relationship with the opposite sex, such as falling in love, was the most important factor. Male sexual standards seemed to start at an earlier age with the acceptance of petting, whereas almost all female standards started with the acceptance of kissing. The summarization of these findings resulted in the proposition that the key determinant of the number, rate, and direction of changes in an individual's premarital sexual standard and behavior was the potential for permissiveness in his basic set of parentally derived values. In short, the sexual changes during adolescence are in good measure an actualization of the potential permissiveness in the individual's basic values. Falling in love, contact with peer groups, and other factors more often help merely to actualize these potentials rather than to create new values.

Changes in Sexual Standards

The major hypothesis in this phase of the study was that there would be an overall trend for increased age to go with increased permissiveness. The Iowa College Sample was composed very largely of juniors and seniors, three quarters of whom were within a year of the age of twenty-one, and thus there was little use in checking the hypothesis by *current* age. Instead, each respondent was asked to choose from a checklist the standards he had from age ten to the present time. The results supported the hypothesis and indicated a rather sharp trend toward increased permissiveness with increased age. The steps by which this increase occurred can be seen by examining Table 7.1. Among females who had never changed their standards, 47 percent accepted kissing. (For purposes of simplicity, all standards have been combined into those that allow the adherent to kiss, to pet, or to have coitus.)[3] Among females who had changed standards once or more, virtually no one accepted such a restricted standard as kissing. Similarly, whereas 6 percent of the females who had never changed their standard accepted coitus, between 14 and 53 percent of the females who had changed their standards once or more accepted coitus (these usually were permissiveness-

---

[3] Where important, mention will be made of the specific standard involved. Since classification is by self-permissiveness, an orthodox-double-standard female would not be classified under the coital standard but would usually be put under the petting standard, which is what she accepts sexually for herself. Only single undergraduate students are used.

Table 7.1

PERCENT IN EACH CURRENT STANDARD BY THE NUMBER OF
STANDARDS EVER HELD BY SEX IN THE IOWA COLLEGE SAMPLE

	Number of Standards Ever Held		
CURRENT STANDARD	ONE	TWO	THREE OR MORE
	Female		
Kissing	47	7	0
Petting	47	79	47
Coitus	6	14	53
N	(32)	(91)	(83)
		$x^2 = 89.8$	
		$P < .001$	
		$G = .79$	
	Male		
Kissing	16	0	0
Petting	36	36	0
Coitus	48	64	100
N	(25)	(11)	(6)
		$x^2 = 7.1$	
		NS	
		$G = .63$	

with-affection adherents).[4] The double-standard adherents changed from orthodox to transitional subtypes. This and other comparisons make it apparent that changes in sex standards occur and that they lead to increased acceptance of the more permissive sexual standards. The increased equalitarianism within the double-standard classification is in accord with Proposition Four. Equally congruent was the finding that equalitarianism within the abstinence standard was highest among those high-permissives who had changed three or more times.[5]

These findings were checked by examining each respondent separately to determine what proportion of the respondents actually increased their sexual permissiveness and what proportion stayed the same or decreased their sexual permissiveness. Of 206 females there were 2 who decreased their level of permissiveness, 5 who were irregular, 32 who stayed the same, and 167 who increased their level of permissiveness. Thus 81 percent increased permissiveness, 1 percent decreased permissiveness, 2 percent were

[4] Of females who changed their standards three times or more (had four or more standards), about eighty percent accepted coitus.

[5] The memory approach may be a better method of checking for change over time on equalitarianism or permissiveness than is the cross-sectional sample. This is so because cross-sectional samples often misrepresent time changes due to the older respondents being a select group of the younger respondents.

irregular, and 16 percent stayed the samed. From Table 7.1 it can be seen that having two or three standards is the norm for the females.[6]

The males, although few in number, illustrated a clear-cut pattern. There was an upward shift, although not as marked as the female shift. Forty percent of all the males (compared to 81 percent of the females) showed an increase in permissiveness in their sexual standards. The other 60 percent showed no change. There were no cases of downward change or irregular patterning. The males seemed to change less than the females in total percentages and even in number of changes. The males, however, started at a higher level of permissiveness, with 48 percent of those who never changed standards accepting coitus for themselves as compared to 6 percent of the females. The greater likelihood to change on the part of females is congruent with Proposition One, regarding groups with traditions of low permissiveness being most changeable. Many males may start out with more permissive standards because when they first start to think about sex, they become aware of the male group's support for permissiveness. This does not mean that their first sexual act is coitus. Most likely it is kissing, but they are willing to accept more than kissing. The female's beginnings lack such group support, so she proceeds slower in her behavior and standards, and gradually changes.

These results reveal a certain regularity in the movement from one standard to another. It seems that having two standards (that is, changing once) leads to a heavy concentration in petting (mostly petting-with-affection subtypes) for females. Almost eighty percent of the females who had changed their standard once currently accepted petting. Similarly, those females who had had three or more standards (had changed twice or more) were heavily concentrated in the acceptance of coitus (mostly permissiveness-with-affection adherents). Fifty-three percent of these females accepted coitus. The pattern for males was harder to substantiate because of the small number of cases, but a clear movement toward greater permissiveness could be seen in the male standards also. Further specification of this pattern is in Table 7.2. It is worth noting that 90 percent of the females who accepted kissing (mostly kissing-with-affection subtypes) as their immediate former standard currently accepted petting. Also, 81 percent of all the females who in their previous standard accepted petting currently accepted coitus. The sexes were similar in this steplike movement; but since there

[6] The standards used in the tables in this chapter are not derived from the permissiveness scales but rather from responses to a checklist of standards (see Appendix B, Parts III and V). The respondent checked his or her current standard. Previous standards were indicated by giving the number of the standard and the ages during which it was held. It was not deemed practical to ask the full set of twenty-four questions for all past standards, so to compare present and past standards fairly the checklist method was used in all tables. This way of measuring standards is used throughout this chapter. It should be noted that, where possible, comparisons were made using the permissiveness scales, and the same general findings appeared. However, the checklist does give a somewhat lower estimate of permissiveness than do the scales.

Table 7.2

PERCENT IN EACH CURRENT STANDARD BY PREVIOUS
STANDARD FOR FEMALES IN THE IOWA COLLEGE SAMPLE

CURRENT STANDARD	Previous Standard		
	KISSING	PETTING	COITUS
Kissing	3	2	13
Petting	90	18	0
Coitus	7	81	88
N	(116)	(68)	(8)

$$\chi^2 = 115.1$$
$$P < .001$$
$$G = .89$$

were so few males who had changed, their data are not presented. Thus, here is further evidence indicating the systematic quality of changes in standards and the predictability of such changes. This knowledge has a practical value, for the researcher can ask how often a person has changed sexual standards and then can predict with good accuracy that the more frequent the change has been, the more permissive the person will be. Such indirect measures may be useful research tools in an area as controversial as sex.[7] It might be useful to add here that the people who had changed in the past were those most likely to say that they expected to change in the future. This further supports the notion of the progressive nature of these changes.

Another indication of the change of standards can be obtained by noting that although about eighty-five percent of all females start out by accepting either kissing with affection or kissing without affection, about nine out of every 10 of these girls accept either petting (65 percent) or coitus (25 percent) by about the age of twenty-one. The exact age at which various sexual behaviors are first performed appears to depend on the type of attitude changes in which a person is involved. This was borne out by a check of 160 females, all of whom had increased their permissiveness with age. Table 7.3 shows that those changing their standard from kissing to petting and then to coitus started accepting petting at the average age of 16.3, which is 1.5 years earlier than those females who had not yet increased their permissiveness beyond petting.[8] The earliest group of females

[7] Another indirect measure was suggested in Chapter 2. Statements 4 and 8 in the scale are ways of checking permissiveness without asking about coitus. For a discussion of such measures in other areas see Eugene J. Webb, Donald T. Campbell, Richard D. Schwartz, and Lee Sechrest, *Unobtrusive Measures.* Chicago: Rand, McNally & Co., 1966.

[8] For information showing increased permissiveness with age for English teen-agers see Michael Schofield, *The Sexual Behavior of Young People.* Boston: Little, Brown & Co., 1965, Chaps. 3 and 4. Schofield deals here mostly with behavior.

Table 7.3

Average Age at First Acceptance of Various Sexual Behaviors by Pattern
of Change for Females in the Iowa College Sample

PATTERN OF CHANGE	KISSING	PETTING	COITUS	N
	Age When Behavior Was First Accepted			
Kissing to petting to coitus	12.0	16.3	19.3	(37)
Kissing to petting	12.1	17.8		(107)
Kissing to coitus	11.4		17.9	(8)
Petting to coitus		13.6	18.5	(8)
	Standard Deviations for Each Calculation			
Kissing to petting to coitus	1.57	1.76	1.12	
Kissing to petting	1.62	1.14		
Kissing to coitus	1.51		2.12	
Petting to coitus		0.74	0.76	

to start accepting petting are those whose first standard is petting and who
eventually accept premarital coitus; they start accepting petting at age 13.6.
As might be expected, coital acceptance is achieved earlier by those who
have only one previous standard—kissing or petting—rather than by those
who previously have accepted kissing and then petting. Those who go
through all three steps seem to go more quickly from stage to stage than
do the others. (Three or four years per move instead of five or six years.)

In sum, it may be noted that petting is accepted shortly after the sixteenth
birthday by the average female who is eventually going to accept premarital coitus and shortly before the eighteenth birthday by the average
female who is not going to accept premarital coitus. Perhaps many of these
"slower" females will eventually accept premarital coitus at an older age
after leaving college. They seem to represent a slower moving, more cautious
group; for example, about a third of these females who had only changed
from the acceptance of kissing to the acceptance of petting did so with the
aid of a minor in-between step. Only a sixth of those changing from kissing
to petting *and* to coitus had any minor in-between steps. This further supports the "cautious" label for those females who only move from kissing to
petting and helps to explain the older age at which they accept petting.
Note that the starting age for acceptance of kissing for the two most popular patterns is almost identical, indicating that perhaps the initial potentiali-
ties differ and that this accounts for the difference in the rate of change.
Males who change standards are distinguished from females mainly by the
earlier age at which they accept petting and by the fact that the "petting
to coitus" change was the most common. These findings are compatible with
the assumption that the male's initial potential for permissiveness is higher
than the females.

It would appear that at about the age of eighteen and nineteen a major change in sexual standards occurs for most females. Table 7.3 shows that all the changes involving the acceptance of coitus, and most of those involving the acceptance of petting, occur at this time. This is the time when these females leave high school and go to college, and in the process they change peer groups and increase their autonomy.[9] Under such conditions, basic tendencies toward increased permissiveness are likely to occur. There may well be another period of increased permisiveness for these females— around the ages of twenty-two and twenty-three—when they move into the world of business and of the professions. Kinsey and others have shown that the female's greatest period of permissiveness occurs in the year or two before marriage, and for college graduates that would be about the ages of twenty-two and twenty-three. Unfortunately, this notion cannot be checked with the present sample.

Guilt Feelings and Changing Standards

The role of guilt feelings in changes of attitudes toward permissiveness is important to investigate. Tables 7.4 and 7.5 give some valuable data regarding this. All the respondents in the Iowa College Sample were asked to state which sexual behavior that once made them feel guilty, they had come to accept and which they had stopped performing.[10] (Appendix B,

Table 7.4

PERCENT OF THOSE WHO ACCEPTED GUILTY BEHAVIOR
IN EACH CURRENT STANDARD IN THE IOWA COLLEGE SAMPLE

	Type of Guilty Behavior Accepted (If Any)			
CURRENT STANDARD	KISSING	PETTING	COITUS	NEVER ACCEPTED GUILTY BEHAVIOR
Kissing	47	2	0	19
Petting	53	78	3	51
Coitus	0	20	97	30
N	(17)	(123)	(36)	(37)

$$\chi^2 = 116.2$$
$$P < .001$$
$$G = .49$$

[9] Theodore M. Newcomb and Everett K. Wilson, eds., *College Peer Groups.* Chicago: Aldine Publishing Co., 1966.

[10] One possible reason for more respondents answering the question used on Table 7.4 than on Table 7.5 is that those who could not answer either question by naming a specific behavior that had been accepted or stopped were more prone not to write anything. The question on Table 7.5 may have received a much greater proportion of such responses.

Table 7.5

PERCENT OF THOSE WHO STOPPED GUILTY BEHAVIOR
IN EACH CURRENT STANDARD IN THE IOWA COLLEGE SAMPLE

| | Type of Guilty Behavior Stopped (If Any) | | | |
| | | | | |
CURRENT STANDARD	KISSING	PETTING	COITUS	NEVER STOPPED GUILTY BEHAVIOR
Kissing	0	29	20	6
Petting	83	65	40	55
Coitus	17	6	40	39
N	(6)	(17)	(15)	(135)

$$\chi^2 = 18.7$$
$$P < .001$$
$$G = .43$$

Part VII, questions 1 and 2). It is interesting to note that eighty-seven percent of the females and 58 percent of the males had come to accept sexual behavior that once made them feel guilty. The difference between the male and the female responses may well indicate that males already accepted a great deal and thus there was a lower percent who would be able to accept more. The females started lower in permissiveness, changed more, and had more guilt barriers to cross. Note that on Table 7.4 the acts that were accepted correlated with the standards the individual held. Thus, it seems that most individuals come to accept the "guilty" behavior they practice. It should be clear that accepting or stopping a form of sexual behavior does not necessarily mean accepting or stopping all forms of that behavior under all conditions; for example, one can stop kissing except when in love.[11]

There appears to be a differential sensitivity to guilt based on past and present standards and reflecting parental values. Comparing petting and coital adherents, it can be noted that whereas many more of the former originally felt guilty about kissing and petting but later came to accept them, a much smaller proportion of the latter ever felt guilty about such behavior. This seems to indicate (particularly for females) that although most individuals start by accepting only kissing, they vary considerably in their likelihood of feeling guilt. A check on past guilt feelings lends further support to this notion, for those who currently accepted coitus were least likely to have ever felt guilty about kissing or petting. The females who eventually came to accept coitus were those who responded with less guilt and thus could move easily through the gradations of sexual practices until

[11] In Table 7.5, 83 percent of those who stopped kissing because of guilt feelings were in the petting standards. This is not a contradiction. It simply means that they stopped a certain type of kissing under certain conditions, but did not stop all kissing.

they reached coitus.[12] Although very few females stop engaging in sexual activities because of guilt feelings, it may be that those most prone to strong guilt feelings are least likely to engage in such behavior.

Only one male (2 percent) in the sample reported having stopped behavior that made him feel guilty, and only 26 percent of the females reported the same. The percent who did not stop their "guilty" behavior was somewhat low for those who currently accepted kissing (50 percent); but for those who accepted petting and those who accepted coitus it was found to be rather similar (77 percent and 87 percent). Thus, if not many more petting-standard individuals than coital-standard individuals stop behavior about which they feel guilty, then it follows that the former must *start* less such "guilty" behavior or else they too would accept coitus. This, then, is further evidence of the greater initial permissive tendencies in some people.

The key determinant of how permissive a female is sexually and what she will eventually accept, then, seems to involve her basic values, to the extent that these values must prevent certain sexual behavior from occurring if she is to remain low on permissiveness, for three out of every four females continue to engage in behavior that makes them feel guilty, and almost nine out of every ten of these eventually come to accept it.[13] The figures for males are comparable. But the question still remains as to why individuals change their standards. What are the immediate reasons that promote the continuance of behavior that so often yield guilt feelings? Pleasure alone cannot be the answer, for this would not explain the differences among large groups of individuals. Basic values may be a general sort of answer, but it would be desirable to find more specific factors. The individuals in the Iowa College Sample were asked for such reasons, and Table 7.6 contains a breakdown of the answers by sex.

The major reason cited for change in the female group appears to be relationships with the opposite sex. This was particularly true for those females who accept coitus. This fit with the previous findings that female permissiveness is affected by such factors as falling in love. For example, among females in the Iowa Sample who were engaged during the time of their standard, 61 percent accepted coitus for themselves, whereas 25 percent of the females who were not involved emotionally accepted coitus. For males the situation was reversed, with 14 percent of those engaged accepting coitus for themselves, compared to 69 percent of those not emotionally involved accepting coitus. Ehrmann and others have long pointed out the association of sexual behavior with close interpersonal relationships

[12] Sexual behavior does seem to fit a Guttman-scale pattern just as sexual attitudes do. See Lawrence Podell and John C. Perkins, "A Guttman Scale for Sexual Experience—A Methodological Note," *Journal of Abnormal and Social Psychology,* 34 (May 1957), pp. 420–422.

[13] It is possible to develop the relation of this area of guilt to cognitive dissonance. See Leon Festinger, *Theory of Cognitive Dissonance.* New York: Harper & Row, Publishers, 1957.

Table 7.6

PERCENTAGE CITING KEY FACTORS IN THE DEVELOPMENT OF CURRENT STANDARDS
BY CURRENT STANDARD AND SEX IN THE IOWA COLLEGE SAMPLE

| | *Current Standard* | | | |
KEY FACTOR	KISSING	PETTING	COITUS	TOTAL
	Females			
Relationships with opposite sex	19	35	62	41
Parental guidance	38	27	5	21
Religious or moral reasons	38	8	3	10
Peer-group influence	0	10	7	8
Maturation in college	0	9	10	8
Other	5	12	12	12
N	(21)	(117)	(58)	(196)
	Males			
Relationships with opposite sex	25	17	25	22
Parental guidance	0	42	20	25
Religious or moral reasons	75	25	10	22
Peer-group influence	0	8	10	8
Maturation in college	0	0	10	6
Other	0	8	25	17
N	(4)	(12)	(20)	(36)

for females but not for males, and support for this was found in Chapter 5.[14]
Only 40 percent of those females who only accepted kissing had been in
love during the time of their currently held standard. The percent of petting
adherents was 60 percent, and of coital adherents 78 percent. It is interesting to note in Table 7.6 that "parental guidance" and "religious or moral
reasons" together account for 31 percent of the female reasons given for
changing standards. However, those who accept kissing are much more
likely to say this than are those who accept coitus (76 to 8 percent). For
the male the results are similar except that relationships with the opposite
sex are not so important a factor. Also, the boys who accept coitus do not
seem to be quite as low on parental and religious influence as the girls who
accept coitus. The double standard may be part of the explanation here.[15]

[14] Winston W. Ehrmann, *Premarital Dating Behavior*. New York: Holt, Rinehart
and Winston, 1959, Chap. 4. For another report on male-female differences, with
data on guilt, see Robert R. Bell and Leonard Blumberg, "Courtship Stages and
Intimacy Attitudes," *Family Life Coordinator*, 8 (March 1960), pp. 61–63.

[15] Schofield, pp. 206–213, reports a similar difference in those males and females
in his sample who accepted coitus. Such reasons help establish the direction of
causality and support the use of permissiveness as a dependent variable. However,
as has been mentioned before, this does not preclude the possibility of feedback.
Also, in some relationships other causal directions are possible. This is so despite the
fact that the hypotheses tested view permissiveness as the dependent variable, since

It is not being suggested here that age causes increased permissiveness. Rather, it would seems that the types of relationships with the opposite sex and the basic values of an individual are the key determinants.[16] The basic values may well make one more or less prone to achieve affectionate ties with the opposite sex. While there is general support for this view, there is considerable need for further testing and specification. For example, what specific basic values make one girl who is in love accept coitus and another not? Or what values encourage one girl who is not in love to accept coitus and another not to do so?

There was a general association for both sexes between having experienced guilt about a previous standard and experiencing guilt about the currently held standard. Sixty-nine percent of those who had previously had guilt feelings, and only 52 percent of those without previous guilt feelings, experienced current guilt. There was a small tendency for guilt feelings to be more common regarding the current standard than regarding the previous standard, particularly for females. Table 7.7 shows that there was no

Table 7.7

PERCENT FEELING CURRENT GUILT IN EACH CURRENT
STANDARD IN THE IOWA COLLEGE SAMPLE

CURRENT STANDARD	TOTAL PERCENT FEELING GUILTY
Kissing	52 (25)
Petting	55 (134)
Coitus	49 (84)
	$\chi^2 = 0.86$
	NS
	$G = .08$
	$C = .02$

greater tendency for guilt feelings in any one standard. The wide range of reference groups held by people in various standards is supported by this finding. Those who are more permissive may well be more likely to have significant others who accept this.

One basic hypothesis tested was that those who experience a gap between behavior and standard will experience guilt feelings. The results of

it is that which is being explained. A full causal analysis would reveal many complicated causal relationships, and it is hoped that such additional analysis will be undertaken by other researchers.

[16] That factual information is not as crucial as basic values is borne out by a test made of the effects of the Kinsey volumes on students: Clifford Kirkpatrick, Sheldon Stryker, and Philip Buell, "An Experimental Study of Attitudes Toward Male Sex Behavior with Reference to Kinsey's Findings," *American Sociological Review,* 17 (October 1952), pp. 580–587.

Table 7.8

PERCENT IN EACH CURRENT STANDARD BY MOST EXTREME
CURRENT BEHAVIOR FOR THOSE WHO DO AND DO NOT
FEEL GUILT IN THE IOWA COLLEGE SAMPLE

	Current Standard		
MOST EXTREME CURRENT BEHAVIOR	KISSING	PETTING	COITUS
Has Current Guilt			
Kissing	31	1	0
Petting	62	89	27
Coitus	7	10	73
N	(13)	(74)	(41)
		$\chi^2 = 80.8$	
		$P < .001$	
		$G = .89$	
Has No Current Guilt			
Kissing	100	34	9
Petting	0	66	35
Coitus	0	0	56
N	(12)	(59)	(43)
		$\chi^2 = 75.7$	
		$P < .001$	
		$G = .89$	

testing this hypothesis are in Table 7.8. They indicate that about the same percent of those who felt guilty and those who did not feel guilty failed to meet their standards, but that those who did not feel guilty more often failed by doing *less* than their standard allowed. Further, there was no major difference in level of permissiveness between those who felt guilty and those who did not feel guilty. The key difference was in the way the standard was lived up to. Finally, it is important to note that the majority of those who felt guilty about their behavior did so concerning behavior that was on the same level as their standard; for example, those who accepted petting felt guilty about petting too loosely, not about coitus. Some of the guilt was for a "lower" level of behavior; for example, an individual who accepted coitus but petted with someone he did not care for may well have felt guilty about petting. The cases in the kissing standard were patterned, but the few cases involved impose a limit on generalizations.

Table 7.9 shows that although there was a close relation between standard and behavior, there was a sizable gap between them for those who accepted coitus before marriage, with behavior being *less* extreme than the standard allowed.[17] This seemed to be particularly true for those who ac-

[17] Males belonging to the kissing and petting standards did not perform behaviors on "higher" behavior levels (petting and/or coitus), whereas females were much

Table 7.9

PERCENT IN EACH CURRENT STANDARD BY MOST EXTREME
CURRENT BEHAVIOR IN THE IOWA COLLEGE SAMPLE

MOST EXTREME CURRENT BEHAVIOR	*Current Standard*		
	KISSING	PETTING	COITUS
Kissing	64	15	5
Petting	32	78	31
Coitus	4	7	64
N	(25)	(139)	(84)
		$\chi^2 = 137.8$	
		$P < .001$	
		$G = .83$	

cepted permissiveness with affection and required love and/or engagement to be present. Here, then, are respondents who were willing to accept coitus under certain circumstances, which had not yet occurred. This interpretation was checked by seeing if among those who accepted premarital coitus, persons likely not to have experienced it were also those most likely not to have experienced love and/or engagement. The results supported this interpretation. Among females who accepted coitus and had engaged in it, 70 percent had been in love, whereas among females who accepted coitus but had *not* engaged in it, only 44 per cent had been in love. The figures for males were 33 percent and 10 percent. A similar, and even stronger, comparison can be made among those who accept petting. This fits with the previously cited finding in Table 7.6 that relations with the opposite sex were one key motivating factor for change in sexual standards. Even for males (although males who are in love are not more likely to accept coitus), those who are in love and *do* accept coitus are more likely to *have* coitus.

Table 7.10 presents further evidence regarding the way standards and behavior relate. It should be noticed that, generally, feelings of guilt are most likely to occur on the level of the individual's own standard for those who accept petting and coitus. Thus, although Table 7.7 shows that there are no differences in overall guilt reactions by standards, it can be seen here that looking only at those who actually experience behavior on the level of their standard, there are differences indicating that petting behavior promotes the most guilt and kissing behavior the least (61 percent as opposed to 25 percent).

more likely to do this. On the coital level an individual can violate his standard by having coitus under unacceptable conditions (without love, and so on). Current behavior refers to all behavior one has performed during the time he has held his current standard.

Table 7.10

PERCENT IN EACH CURRENT STANDARD FEELING GUILT ABOUT THEIR MOST EXTREME CURRENT BEHAVIOR IN THE IOWA COLLEGE SAMPLE

MOST EXTREME CURRENT BEHAVIOR	*Current Standard*		
	KISSING	PETTING	COITUS
Kissing	25 (16)	5 (21)	0 (4)
Petting	100 (8)	61 (105)	42 (26)
Coitus	100 (1)	83 (7)	54 (54)
	$\chi^2 = 13.0$	$\chi^2 = 25.3$	$\chi^2 = 4.7$
	$P < .01$	$P < .001$	$P < .10$
	$G = 1.0$	$G = .88$	$G = .37$

Of equal interest in Table 7.10 is the finding that there are differences in the sensitivity to guilt. For example, none of those who accepted coitus felt guilty about kissing, whereas 25 percent of those who accepted only kissing felt guilty about this. This finding fits with those reported in Table 7.4 to indicate further that those who currently accept coitus have less guilt feelings regarding kissing and petting than those who currently do not accept coitus.

Thus, it would seem that even when behavior is in line with the individual's standards, there is a gradual process of coming to accept it. Those who have accepted their standards for a longer length of time feel less guilt.[18] This probably means that often emotional acceptance follows intellectual acceptance. This point is illustrated in Table 7.11, where it can be seen that even those who do not do as much as their standard allows feel guilty about their behavior; those who equal their standard's permissive level feel more guilty and those who exceed their standard feel the most guilty.[19] Both Tables 7.10 and 7.11 have cells with quite low frequencies. However, inspection of these tables reveals that all the subtables show identical direction, and this lends support to their meaningfulness.

Guilt is a more complicated emotion than one might assume. It is not simply the result of the violation of the individual's standard—although clearly that promotes the greatest amount of guilt—but it also seems to result from behavior that is not emotionally accepted though it may be intellectually accepted. Females are generally more likely to feel guilt than

[18] Sixty-one percent of those who had held their standards for three years or less felt guilty about them. Only 45 percent of those who had held their standards for four years or more felt guilty about them.

[19] The direction in all subtables of 7.11 is the same, although the few number of cases in some subtables prevents a statistically significant relation. But one can see from the gammas that the relation is generally strong.

Table 7.11

PERCENT FEELING GUILT ABOUT VARIOUS BEHAVIORS ACCORDING
TO STANDARDS-BEHAVIOR GAP IN THE IOWA COLLEGE SAMPLE BY SEX

THIS BEHAVIOR COMPARED TO STANDARD IS	*Percent Feeling Guilt about the Following Behavior*		
	KISSING	PETTING	COITUS
	Females		
Not as much as is allowed	47 (34)	51 (35)	60 (10)
Equal to what is allowed	59 (138)	60 (101)	71 (24)
More than is allowed	85 (26)	92 (39)	93 (14)
	$x^2 = 9.0$	$x^2 = 16.7$	$x^2 = 3.8$
	$P < .05$	$P < .001$	NS
	$G = .41$	$G = .54$	$G = .56$
	Males		
Not as much as is allowed	14 (14)	25 (12)	8 (12)
Equal to what is allowed	30 (23)	24 (21)	20 (10)
More than is allowed	33 (3)	67 (3)	100 (2)
	$x^2 = 1.3$	$x^2 = 2.5$	$x^2 = 8.7$
	NS	NS	$P < .05$
	$G = .38$	$G = .28$	$G = .76$

males and also are generally more likely to exceed the limits of their standards.
They begin on a lower permissiveness level, change more during their youth, and in so doing, experience more guilt. Overall, 58 percent of the females and only 24 percent of the males reported feeling guilty.[20] No doubt the less-permissive general values of the female culture also relate to this propensity toward guilt. These results support a general theory of increasing permissiveness, of the relation between behavior and standards, and of guilt being slowly overcome and replaced with new guilt. However, this occurs within a framework of the different male and female subcultures, so that despite the faster rate of change, the female level of permissiveness never catches up to the male level. It is contact of the female's basic values with the demands of the male culture, and most importantly with particular males for whom there is deep affection, that is proposed here as being the most important *current* factor affecting the change in female permissiveness. The influence of peers and parents is further dealt with in later chapters.

[20] Others have also reported sex differences in guilt feelings. See Kinsey *et al.*, *Sexual Behavior in the Human Female*. Philadelphia: W. B. Saunders Co., 1953, p. 332; Ernest Burgess and Paul Wallin, *Enagement and Marriage*. New York: J. B. Lippincott Co., 1953, p. 375.

Which Comes First, Attitude or Behavior?

The question is often asked, Which comes first, the behavior or the standard?[21] The results discussed in this chapter offer some insights into the answer to this question.[22] The fact that behavior that evokes guilt feelings usually comes to be accepted might tempt one to say that behavior precedes standards. However, it is necessary to explain why some individuals practice behavior that evokes guilt feelings and others do not, and why some individuals go on to behavior that evokes even more guilt feelings. Falling in love cannot be accepted as the full causal factor for it is still necessary to explain the individual's greater tendency to fall in love and her association of permissiveness with love. Not all females who fall in love accept coitus, and not all who accept coitus are in love; for example, 40 percent of the females who only accepted kissing were in love. Also, males are affected differently by love than females. How do we explain their changes in sexuality? Clearly other factors are at work.

It is true that of those who accept a standard, those who fall in love are more likely to perform the full range of behavior connected with their standard. Love seems to motivate sexual behavior within the already accepted limits of the individual's sexual standard. In this sense it may promote change by helping fulfill the current standard and thereby preparing the individual for an advance in permissiveness. Although love is a key factor in permissiveness in this and other ways, additional causes are still necessary to account for the level of an individual's standard when he falls in love and for his willingness to extend this level.

It is known from Table 7.4 and 7.10 that those who accept a more permissive standard are less likely to have been as sensitive to experiencing guilt as those who are less permissive. This would indicate that those who become the most permissive have more acceptant attitudes to begin with. To be sure, they may at ten years of age, if female, only accept kissing, but they have a more open and pliable orientation and less likelihood of feeling guilty, so they are more likely to practice petting and either not experience guilt or come to accept it. Thus, there is here an attitudinal dimension that, in one sense, precedes the behavioral dimension. However, the question of how that attitudinal dimension was accepted may be asked, and this may well involve some previous behavior, which in turn

[21] Although Ehrmann does not deal with whether behavior or standards is most important, he does report a close relation of the two. See *Premarital Dating Behavior,* Chap. 5. Also, Harold T. Christensen and George R. Carpenter, in "Value-Behavior Discrepancies in Premarital Coitus," *American Sociological Review,* 27 (February 1962), pp. 66–74, report a similar finding.

[22] The relation between discrimination and prejudice in the field of race relations is similar to the relation of sexual attitudes and behaviors. Similar kinds of controversies have ensued.

involves some previous attitude, and so on, ad infinitum. In short, there is no point to the question of whether attitude or behavior comes first, for both are always involved and are really two expressions of the same thing—of the basic human personality and its fundamental social values.

An added complication to the issue of whether attitude or behavior comes first is pointed up by the fact that those who have held their current standard a shorter length of time are more likely to feel guilty. This would seem to indicate that it takes time to accept "emotionally" what may be initially accepted "intellectually." An individual may accept coitus intellectually when in love but still, for a time, feel guilty about engaging in it. In this sense the intellectual attitude precedes the behavior, and the behavior precedes the emotional attitude, or full acceptance. How common this sequence is, is not certain. Possibly it is quite common; but by no means is it universal. One may fully accept a behavior before it occurs or not at all accept it before it occurs. The intellectual-emotional case is a halfway house between these two extremes and further illustrates the complex intertwining of attitudes and behavior in the human situation.

The complexity of the attitude-behavior situation is further delineated by noting that attitudes from nonsexual spheres may lead to sexual behavior and that nonsexual behavior may lead to changes in sexual attitudes. In the former case the female who has coitus in order to keep her boy friend interested may be cited; in the latter case, the greater sexual permissiveness that may result unintentionally from nonsexual activities between the sexes, such as studying together, talking, and so forth. For purposes of analysis and theorizing it may be best to speak of an ideal, relatively closed system of sexual relationships, but the real world always forces such closed systems "open."

Summary, Conclusions, and Proposition Five

To summarize the findings concerning changes in sexual standards, behavior, and guilt feelings in adolescents—females exhibit greater changes than males and greater feelings of guilt, and they show the general tendency to continue guilty behavior until it becomes accepted. This result is, in part, congruent with Proposition Three, regarding differential sensitivity for males and females. Also, sexual behavior generally reflects sexual attitudes rather closely. This can be seen more directly in Table 7.9, but it has also been suggested by much of the other data in this chapter. The reverse of this statement is equally true—sexual attitudes generally reflect sexual behavior rather closely. The tendency shown in Table 7.4 and elsewhere for behavior to become accepted indicates support for this contention. It might further be contended that in most cases the basic values accepted from parents and from peers during the first ten years of life manifest themselves in this interaction of behavior and standards. As the adolescent ages there is a tendency toward increased permissiveness, which is regulated by the potential for permissiveness in his basic values.[23] Thus, Proposition Five is DIFFERENCES IN THE POTENTIAL FOR PERMISSIVENESS IN ONE'S BASIC SET OF PARENTALLY DERIVED VALUES IS A KEY DETERMINANT OF THE NUMBER, RATE, AND DIRECTION OF CHANGES IN ONE'S PREMARITAL SEXUAL STANDARDS AND BEHAVIOR.

Proposition Five relates to the first four propositions, but it does not subsume them, for they deal with group factors occurring at the time of dating, such as the amount of equalitarianism, courtship roles, liberality, and sexual traditions. It focuses on differences in parental values that distinguish people even before dating begins, and refers to a wider set of values. In short, Proposition Five states that when the social factors covered in Propositions One to Four are the same, then basic parental values are the key determinant of sexual behavior and standards. These parental values can be strengthened or weakened by the social setting. The sample used in this chapter was homogeneous enough so that differences in the social background of the respondents were minimized, and the basic parental values were of more relevance to explain changes. These values can, of course, be partially accounted for by reference to the differences in the social background of the grandparents. How much the structure of the situations to which the individual is exposed helps or hinders such value changes must also be taken into account. But the stronger the tendency, the more likely the individual is to seek for situations that promote their values.[24]

The path of development of sexual standards may be determined by such basic values as autonomy, pleasure, responsibility, risk-taking, psychic needs, conformity, love, adventurousness, liberality, and heterosexuality.

---

[23] For an interesting article on the childhood development of sexuality from a psychological point of view, but one that is compatible with the notion of adolescence being the actualization of earlier values, see John Gagnon, "Sexuality and Sexual Learning in the Child," *Psychiatry,* 28 (August 1965), pp. 212–228. For another speculative article in this area see Miriam M. Johnson, "Sex Role Learning in the Nuclear Family," *Child Development,* 34 (June 1963), pp. 319–333. This very important area of early sex-role learning is not dealt with in the present study, but this is surely an area in which the research reported here should be helpful. For a good summary see Jerome Kagan, "Acquisition and Significance of Sex Typing and Sex Role Identity," *Review of Child Development Research,* Martin L. Hoffman and Lois W. Hoffman, eds. New York: Russell Sage Foundation, 1964, pp. 137–168. See also the work of Carlfred Broderick, "Sexual Behavior Among Pre-Adolescents," *The Journal of Social Issues,* 22 (April 1966), pp. 6–21.

[24] Biology is not likely to be the crucial causal factor, for if it were, there would be little reason to find such congruence between attitude, behavior, and guilt feelings. Those who were stronger in biological motivation (if this dominated) should be most permissive in behavior regardless of the basic social attitudes of their groups.

Some evidence for this view is available in the research literature.[25] The search for a sexual standard during the teen-age years is a search for the ways in which the individual can actualize these basic values in his sexual life, and in this sense the actualization of values is in many ways more a fulfillment than a change. These basic values, of course, usually reflect the nature of the individual's group or of his social existence. The evidence is congruent with this thesis, but more testing is needed. Indirect checks, such as those using low church-attendance as an index of a potential set of high-permissive values, support the notion by showing more rapid growth of permissiveness for low church-attenders. Other data on parental influence is presented in later chapters and bears on this thesis. However, again more direct tests are needed.

Some qualifications are in order. There are many factors—such as falling in love—outside the system of sexual behavior and attitudes that affect the rate at which an individual's basic values are realized. Further, an individual's basic values may not be fixed by the age of ten in a fashion definite enough to rule out at least some significant changes in the future.

It is worth noting that the findings in this chapter show the futility of the partisan view that either attitudes or behavior is *the* most important area to study.[26] They are closely intertwined and are predictive of each other

[25] A recent M.A. thesis using three hundred volunteer students at the University of Utah examined the relation of premarital sexual attitudes to traits measured by the California Personality Inventory (CPI). The author reports, ". . . the results of the study seem to suggest that liberal premarital sexual attitudes, values and behaviors tend to be associated with high scores on such CPI scales as "capacity for status," "sociability," "social spontaneity," "self-acceptance," and "flexibility," while more traditionally oriented premarital sexual attitudes, values and behaviors tend to be associated with high scores on "socialization," "self-control," "responsibility," and "communality." See Brian G. Gilmartin, "Relationship of Traits Measured by the California Psychological Inventory to Premarital Sexual Standards and Behaviors." M.S. thesis, University of Utah, 1964, pp. 223–224. The author cautions that perhaps at a more "liberal" school the results would differ. In any case, this sort of association of personality traits with permissiveness would indicate support for the view in this study that particular basic values of certain social groups form the early roots of permissiveness in adolescence. See also Clark Vincent, *Unmarried Mothers.* New York: The Free Press, 1961; M. F. DeMartino, ed., *Sexual Behavior and Personality Characteristics.* New York: Citadel Press, 1963, pp. 113–143; Abraham A. Maslow, "Self Esteem (Dominance-Feeling) and Sexuality in Women," *Journal of Social Psychology,* 16 (November 1942), pp. 259–294; John Stratton and Stephen Spitzer, "Sexual Permissiveness and Self Evaluation," *Journal of Marriage and the Family,* 29 (in press); Jean W. Butman and Jane A. Kamm, "The Social, Psychological and Behavorial World of the Teen Age Girl." University of Michigan, Institute for Social Research, June 1965 (stencil, 158 pages). Ultimately the sociologist must translate these personality traits into terms of what groups promote relevant values that will produce such traits.

[26] Irwin Deutscher has questioned the assumed connection between attitudes and behavior in a recent article that contains a review of the literature in this area: "Words and Deeds: Social Science and Social Policy," *Social Problems,* 13 (Winter 1966), pp. 235–254. For a view more in line with the author's, see Milton Rokeach, "Attitude Change and Behavior Change," *Public Opinion Quarterly,* 30 (Winter 1966–67), pp. 529–550.

even though there is not a perfect one-to-one relationship. Either one is a legitimate area for research. For problems such as a theory of social change, it is, of course, necessary to study both; for other problems one or the other may be an adequate index. If the researcher is concerned with guilt feelings, then attitudes should be studied; likewise, if he is concerned with qualitative differences in sexual acts, such as engaging in sexual activity with or without affection. If he is going to focus on comparisons of orgasmic output, then behavior is sufficient.[27]

In this chapter *reports* of attitudes are compared with *reports* of behavior. Actual behavior has not been tested, and the question may always be raised as to how validly the attitude and behavior reports reflect such behavior.[28] The question of validity and reliability is dealt with directly in Appendix D, but it is well to add here that the researcher must be aware of the complexities involved. A specific, overt behavior very often results from the balancing of many relevant attitudes, and thus it may be in accord with some and in contradiction with others. A girl may accept coitus when in love and engage in it under such conditions, but with a particular boy that she loves she may abstain because he is a double-standard adherent and would condemn her. The balancing here is of the negative "weight" of avoiding condemnation and the positive "weight" of accepting coitus with love. The resultant overt behavior does not deny either of these attitudes. Despite Irwin Deutscher's view, prediction is not weakened by this, it is just made more complex.[29] Such a situation should not make the researcher say he will only look at overt behavior, for if he did, he would miss the full meaning of the situation; accordingly, he should not look only at attitudes, for he will then miss the complex interaction. In short, behavior, attitude, and their interrelation are all legitimate concerns, but the researcher should know what his theory and problem require and decide on that basis how to carry out the research. As Robin Williams has said, ". . . actions may deceive as well as words and there seems no reason for always giving one precedence over the other."[30]

Most previous studies of sexual behavior reported rather *low* percentages of guilt feelings.[31] The data in this study indicate *high* percentages of guilt

[27] The concept "attitude" is being used here in its usual meaning of a tendency to act a particular way in a certain situation. The concept "behavior" is used to refer to overt physical action. Attitudes can be spoken of as a type of "verbal" behavior, but a distinction must still be made between such verbal behavior and overt physical behavior.

[28] The best-known study of observed human copulatory behavior is primarily a physiological study. See William Masters and Virginia Johnson, *Human Sexual Response*. Boston: Little, Brown & Co., 1966.

[29] Deutscher, "Words and Deeds: Social Science and Social Policy."

[30] Robin M. Williams, Jr., *American Society*. New York: Alfred A. Knopf, 1951, p. 378.

[31] Kinsey *et al.*, *Sexual Behavior in the Human Female*, pp. 316–321; *Sexual Behavior in the Human Male*, p. 562. Burgess and Wallin, p. 374. These studies reported only about five to fifteen percent with strong regrets or guilt feelings about coitus.

feelings on all forms of sexual behavior. This rather sharp difference in findings may be due to differences in the nature of the samples used. An older group of females might well have stabilized their sexual behavior and attitudes so that they had largely resolved what guilt they formerly felt. Kinsey's female respondents were often older and married, and this may account for their low percentages of "regret." The Burgess and Wallin data come from engaged couples, and the data from this study show that engaged couples are less likely to feel guilty about coitus. Also, the measure of guilt used in this study was calculated on the basis of total sexual behavior, not just on sexual behavior between an engaged couple, and thus it would be expected to be higher. Thus, the findings of this study are probably more representative of the general experience of young people during the ages of approximately ten to twenty than are the findings of other studies.

In conclusion, it should be noted that the theory that traditions of low sexual permissiveness change most easily is congruent with the theory that basic values promote permissive changes as the values are actualized. It is in the realization of these basic values that the traditions of low sexual permissiveness are weakened, for these values often realize themselves in such factors as falling in love, low church-attendance, and general liberality, which, as has been shown, will promote sexual permissiveness. Despite their tradition of low permissiveness, females are likely to have some of these values. Males are less involved in this system because their sexual values are more accepted and are allowed to develop early without as much hindrance. Males are involved in this system, however, by the encouragement they offer to females to increase their permissiveness. This male-female difference is compatible with Proposition Three, that differences in the courtship roles affect the type of forces to which males and females are sensitive. The data of this chapter underscore the importance of basic parental values as well as illustrating, in part, the first three propositions. However, there were too few males in the sample, and it was not a probability sample like all the others in this study. Tests, preferably longitudinal ones, using larger and more broadly based samples, are of particular importance to further our understanding of this area.

Relevant Data from Other Samples

Where possible, the student and adult samples were used to check the basic findings of the Iowa College Sample. The adult sample was not very useful in this regard, for only a small proportion of the group was single, and all of these were twenty-one years of age and over and thus not a comparable group. The student sample, however, was a better test of some of the findings.

Generally speaking, there was a trend toward greater permissiveness with an increase in age in the student sample. Fifty-two percent of the older students and only 45 percent of the younger students accepted coitus for themselves.[32] This difference is just significant at the .10 level (.05 for a one-tail test) and is rather weak, with a gamma of only .13.

Table 7.12
AGE AND PERMISSIVENESS IN THE STUDENT SAMPLE

AGE	PERCENT HIGHLY PERMISSIVE
Young	45 (386)
Old	52 (437)
	$\chi^2 = 3.65$
	$P < .10$
	$Q = .13$

The weakness was not entirely unexpected. Students in their last year of high school and their last two years of college are a select group of those who started the freshman year. Less than half the students who enter college receive a degree from that college.[33] This fact detracts from the value of cross-sectional studies of changes in time. (A similar qualification applies to the analysis of data in Chapter 6.) The more basic question here is why the more permissive individuals seem to drop out in higher proportions; for if the Iowa college data are correct, then the direction of change is almost invariably toward increased permissiveness, and thus the weakness of the findings in the student sample must be due to the greater staying power of the nonchanging low-permissive elements in the student body. That the Iowa college findings on trends are correct is borne out by the finding in the student sample that in answer to a direct question (Appendix A, Part VII, question 6) the vast majority of students reported increasing the permissiveness of their attitudes since they had begun to date. Despite this fact the older students did not seem to have increased their permissiveness as much as they would have if this were a longitudinal study.[34]

The ability of the higher permissive individuals to stay in college is perhaps lessened by the greater amount of time, energy, and money they spend on dating. Further, the higher permissive individuals may be from families

[32] For the colleges "young" was nineteen years or younger and "old" was twenty years or older; for the high schools, "young" was seventeen years or younger, and "old" was eighteen or older.

[33] U.S. Department of Agriculture, *Characteristics of School Dropouts and High School Graduates: Farm and Non Farm 1960*, Report 65 (December 1965), Washington, D.C.; U.S. Department of Health, Education, and Welfare, *Retention and Withdrawal of College Students*. (1957), Washington, D.C.

[34] There were a larger percent in the student sample than in the Iowa sample who reported becoming *less* permissive since they began to date. However, it was still a small minority, 14 percent.

that generally are more geographically mobile, and thus they are likely to finish school at some other location. Support for this notion comes from the finding that in the four Virginia schools the most highly permissive individuals were those most likely to have parents who came from an area outside of Virginia.[35] Perhaps the generally liberal individuals are more mobile and more permissive.

Another possible reason for high-permissive students dropping out of school is their greater marital potential. High permissiveness may indicate a deeper courtship involvement (particularly for females) and a greater likelihood of dropping out of college in order to marry. For males there may be an additional "restlessness" factor at work, which also may lead to poor schoolwork and to dropping out or both or to transferring to another school.

The positive relation of age and permissiveness shows up most sharply in those groups that are exposed to social factors that have been shown to be related to high permissiveness, for example, low church-attendance, high number of love affairs, dissimilar sexual standards from parents', high number of changes in sexual standards. The strength of these findings is not particularly impressive, but the consistency is suggestive. Thus, it would seem that being chronologically older is not as crucial as being exposed, through time, to certain social factors. To be sure, the high drop-out rate and the large number of factors make this judgment somewhat less than final, and the need for a true longitudinal study cannot be overemphasized. The findings on equalitarianism are relevant here. (See Chap. 6.) It may well be that cross-sectional data reduced the strength of the relation between permissiveness and equalitarianism as a result of the high drop-out rate of the most permissive individuals.

One further check of the data from the Iowa college is found in the relation of permissiveness to the number of times the individual has changed his standard. It was found that the greater the number of changes, the higher the level of permissiveness. According to Proposition One whites would be

Table 7.13
PERCENT WHO NEVER CHANGED STANDARDS
BY RACE AND SEX IN THE STUDENT SAMPLE

White male	29 (237)
Negro male	59 (90)
White female	26 (286)
Negro female	63 (106)

[35] The fifth school, the New York college, showed the strongest relation between age and permissiveness, and those students from the New York region were the *most* permissive. The white Virginia high school showed the weakest relation.

expected to change more than Negroes, and this too is supported by the student data. The male-female differences that were expected did appear, particularly in the two white colleges; but they are not apparent in the total figures in Table 7.13 because no sex differences occurred in the high schools regarding the percent who never changed standards. This is assumed to be due to the youthfulness of these students.

It is hoped that the findings presented in this chapter are the beginning of a theory of attitude change in general and of a theory of changes in sexual standards in particular, and that it will not be long before others test and elaborate these ideas further.[36]

[36] The reader may wish to compare the breakdown by sexual standards as derived from the male and female scales in the Iowa College Sample with those given in Chapter 2 for the other schools, and therefore they are included here. Using the permissiveness scales, the four major standards for females showed the following breakdowns: abstinence, 56 percent; double-standard, 20 percent; permissiveness with affection, 18 percent; permissiveness without affection, 1 percent; and reverse double-standard, 5 percent. The breakdowns for males were as follows: abstinence, 38 percent; double-standard, 31 percent; permissiveness with affection, 15 percent; permissiveness without affection, 17 percent; and reverse double-standard, 0 percent.

8

Self-Permissiveness and Perceived Permissiveness of Parents, Peers, and Close Friends

Preface to Proposition Six

Three key sources of attitude formation in any area, sexual or otherwise, are the attitudes of parents, peers, and close friends. It would be far too much to explore this area in its totality, so the focus here is on finding out what the respondent's perception is of how his own sexual standards compare to those of his parents, his peers and his "very close friends."

The basic hypothesis in this area was that those who saw themselves as similar to *any* of these three reference groups would be more likely to be low on sexual permissiveness than would those who saw themselves as dissimilar to these three reference groups; for it was held that a "conformist" self-image, even toward peer and friendship groups, would be compatible with a relatively low degree of sexual permissiveness. It was felt that the relative impact of these three groups could be initially gauged and that any patterned relationship could be grasped by this approach. These tests were done only in the Five-School Student Sample.

The findings here, as so often in this study, were somewhat out of line with the initial expectations. The hypothesis concerning similarity to reference groups being associated with low permissiveness held mainly for parents, and the reverse held for peers and close friends. Those who saw themselves as similar to peers and close friends were *more* permissive than those who did not. Basically it seemed that parents were viewed by many respondents as

129

relatively low on permissiveness, and peers and close friends as high on permissiveness. The respondent generally viewed himself as closer to his peers and close friends than to his parents in terms of his sexual standards. This became the basis of Proposition Six. One of the surprises in this work was the high percentage (about two-thirds) who saw their sexual standards as similar to those of their parents. This parental influence lends support to Proposition Five. However, despite parental influence, the influence of the individual's very close friends seemed even greater; yet it would seem reasonable that the choice of close friends should reflect parental values to some extent at least.

Table 8.1

PERCEPTION OF MOTHER'S STANDARDS AND PERMISSIVENESS FOR TOTAL GROUPS AND RACE-SEX GROUPS IN STUDENT SAMPLE

Standards Similar to Mother's		*Percent Highly Permissive*		
		Total Group		
Yes		38 (497)		
No		66 (297)		
		$\chi^2 = 55.99$		
		$P < .001$		
		$Q = .51$		
		Race-Sex Groups		
	WHITE MALE	NEGRO MALE	WHITE FEMALE	NEGRO FEMALE
Yes	50 (139)	79 (62)	18 (213)	40 (83)
No	76 (129)	95 (38)	42 (99)	61 (31)
	$\chi^2 = 18.76$	$\chi^2 = 4.5$	$\chi^2 = 21.4$	$\chi^2 = 4.2$
	$P < .001$	$P < .05$	$P < .001$	$P < .05$
	$Q = .51$	$Q = .65$	$Q = .54$	$Q = .41$

Similarity to Parental Sexual Standards

Table 8.1 gives the overall results for the student sample on the individual's perceived similarities to his mother's standards. Generally, the findings supported the hypothesis and showed a much lower amount of permissiveness for those who perceived their standards as similar to their mother's. Sixty-three percent felt there was such a similarity (497 of 794)—a rather strong testimony to the powerful effects of parental attitudes, and evidence that the highly permissive youngsters were probably from homes that were perceived of as highly permissive. This finding is similar to the findings from other studies regarding the similarity of political attitudes in parents and children.[1] However, there seems to be some evidence of a trend away from similarity as the individual ages; for example, 40 percent of the older students as opposed to 34 percent of the younger students, had different standards than their mothers. The relation also was stronger for the older students, indicating that not only were they more different than their parents, but that the difference was more likely to go with high permissiveness. This is compatible with the finding in Chapter 7 that as the individual ages, parental guidance becomes less important as a determinant of sexual standards.

A relatively high percentage of Negroes expressed a feeling of similarity to their mothers' standards, despite their high degree of permissiveness as a group.[2] Females—a rather low-permissive group—also expressed the feeling of a high degree of similarity to their mothers' standards. Males—particularly white males—had the lowest percent who expressed a feeling of similarity to their mothers. However, in each race-sex group it was the most permissive individuals who were dissimilar to their mothers.

Table 8.2 shows the same type of picture regarding perceived standards of the father. There were only small differences in the percent who felt similarity among the race-sex groupings, but Negroes again showed more perceived similarity. A similarity to their fathers' sexual standards was felt by 68 percent of all students. In Tables 8.1 and 8.2 the Negro groups showed relations that were not significant at as high a level as the white group. However, the gammas showed more equality, and there were no significant differences between the races. The fewer number of Negroes may well account for the chi-square results.

In order to delineate further the relationship between perceived similarity to the mother and the father, each variable was used as a control on the other's relationship. This revealed that being similar to the mother was the more crucial variable, for when this was controlled, the relation between being similar to the father and the level of permissiveness was greatly reduced in both the chi-square and gamma measures (see Table 8.3). This indicates that when the individual perceives himself as similar to his mother there is no difference in permissiveness produced by perceived similarity or difference to his father. The converse is not the case, and thus it seems that the relation between similarity to the father and permissiveness is a spurious one, produced by the fact that perceived similarity to the mother relates to

[1] Eugene Burdick and Arthur Brodbeck, eds., *American Voting Behavior*. New York: The Free Press, 1959. See the article in this book by H. H. Remmers, especially p. 58, for a wide set of parent-child attitude correlations.

[2] Negroes generally showed a much stronger attachment to their mothers than did whites. This was even true looking separately at two-parent and one-parent families. It may well be that the Negro father does not play as intimate a role in his family as does the white father. In this connection, it is interesting to note that a higher percentage of Negroes said their fathers were less educated than their mothers.

Table 8.2

PERCEPTION OF FATHER'S STANDARDS AND PERMISSIVENESS
FOR TOTAL GROUP AND RACE-SEX GROUPS IN THE STUDENTS SAMPLE

Standards Similar to Father's	*Percent Highly Permissive*			
	Total Group			
Yes	42 (524)			
No	61 (247)			
	$\chi^2 = 23.14$			
	$P < .001$			
	$Q = .36$			
	Race-Sex Groups			
Yes	WHITE	NEGRO	WHITE	NEGRO
No	MALE	MALE	FEMALE	FEMALE
	56 (171)	82 (74)	18 (204)	37 (75)
	74 (95)	92 (24)	40 (99)	62 (29)
	$\chi^2 = 8.01$	$\chi^2 = 1.19$	$\chi^2 = 18.37$	$\chi^2 = 5.18$
	$P < .01$	NS	$P < .001$	$P < .05$
	$Q = .37$	$Q = .40$	$Q = .52$	$Q = .47$

perceived similarity to the father and to self-permissiveness. The perception of the mother's sexual standards, then, would seem to be the most important relation to the individual's own permissive level, although there is a high degree of similarity in the perceived standards of mothers and fathers.[3] Perhaps this is so because mothers are perceived as lower than fathers on permissiveness, and thus when the individual sees himself as similar to his mother, he is likely to be low on permissiveness regardless of how he perceives his father. Fathers do not have such a well-established low- or high-permissive image.

Table 8.4 examines the permissiveness of those who are *not* similar to one or both parents.[4] The difference is rather slight and is neither significant nor strong.[5] Eighty-three percent of those who differed from their par-

---

[3] The relation of perception of the mother's standards to perception of the father's standards has a chi-square of 360.3 and a gamma of .94. If the interpretation here is correct, this relation is so close because perception of similarity to the mother's standards very largely determines perception of similarity to the father's standards, but not vice versa. The results in Table 8.3 held for all race-sex groups. One could argue that perceived mothers' standards is an intervening variable but this is not the author's position.

[4] There is a slight difference in the cases involved in Table 8.4 and in Tables 8.1 and 8.2, which affects the comparison of exact percents. Not all respondents answered all the necessary questions.

[5] Computing separately for those who perceived themselves as different from mother and those who differed from father does not affect the results. There is no significant difference between the more and the less permissive groups in either of these subtables.

Table 8.3
PERCEIVED SIMILARITY OF MOTHER'S AND FATHER'S
STANDARDS AND PERMISSIVENESS BY ALTERNATE
CONTROLS ON PERCEIVED STANDARDS OF
MOTHER AND FATHER IN THE
STUDENT SAMPLE

Standards Similar to Mother's

STANDARDS SIMILAR TO FATHER'S	PERCENT HIGHLY PERMISSIVE
Yes	36 (442)
No	45 (40)
	$x^2 = 1.6$
	NS
	$Q = .18$

Standards Dissimilar to Mother's

	PERCENT HIGHLY PERMISSIVE
Yes	73 (74)
No	64 (206)
	$x^2 = 2.1$
	NS
	$Q = .21$

Standards Similar to Father's

STANDARDS SIMILAR TO MOTHER'S	PERCENT HIGHLY PERMISSIVE
Yes	36 (442)
No	73 (74)
	$x^2 = 34.8$
	$P < .001$
	$Q = .65$

Standards Dissimilar to Father's

	PERCENT HIGHLY PERMISSIVE
Yes	45 (40)
No	64 (206)
	$x^2 = 4.8$
	$P < .05$
	$Q = .36$

ent(s) were less strict than their parents (321 of 388), but they did not differ sharply from the 17 percent who saw themselves as more strict than their parent(s). Clearly the concept of their parents must differ radically for these two groups for them to be so similar on permissiveness and so different in their relation to their parents. The "less strict" group must have rather low-permissive parents, and the "more strict" group must have rather high-permissive parents. Thus, since their parental reference groups are opposite poles, the two groups tend to meet as they move in opposite di-

Table 8.4

PERCEIVED STRICTNESS OF STANDARDS COMPARED TO PARENTS' STANDARDS
AND PERMISSIVENESS IN TOTAL GROUP AND RACE-SEX GROUPS IN THE STUDENT SAMPLE

Standards Compared to Parents'	*Percent Highly Permissive*			
	Total Group			
More strict	49 (67)			
Less strict	60 (321)			
	$x^2 = 2.69$			
	NS			
	$Q = -.22$			
	Race-Sex Groups			
	WHITE MALE	NEGRO MALE	WHITE FEMALE	NEGRO FEMALE
More strict	60 (25)	90 (10)	20 (25)	57 (7)
Less strict	73 (132)	87 (37)	41 (125)	52 (27)
	$x^2 = 1.64$	$x^2 = 0.08$	$x^2 = 3.85$	$x^2 = 0.06$
	NS	NS	$P < .05$	NS
	$Q = -.28$	$Q = .17$	$Q = -.47$	$Q = .10$

rections from their parents. The predominance of "less strict" responses evidences a widespread low-permissive view of parents.

In this regard it is interesting to note that the sharpest difference between the more- and less-strict groups occurred among the white females, and the weakest among the Negroes. This would support the view that there is more homogeneity of parental attitudes to white females, so that the parental reference groups used by white females would be more stereotyped; thus the "more strict" and "less strict" groups would differ in their permissiveness from such a fixed permissive point. The widest variety of opinions concerning parental sex attitudes would seem to take place in the conception Negroes have of their parents' attitudes.

A further point for thought here is that this finding may well indicate a double standard, for the white females perceive more unanimity of opinion than do the males, and they come from relatively similar homes (particularly within each school). Thus, parents may impress their daughters more with the unanimity of their viewpoint than they do their sons. Of course, it could be argued that the parents treat both with just as much unanimity but that the males perceive their parents' attitudes differently. However, the differences between the white males and females is not significant using the Goodman test for interaction and thus these "explanations" are not really necessary, although in Tables 8.5 and 8.6 there is additional evidence for this double-standard explanation.

Self-Permissiveness and Perceived
Permissiveness of Peers and Close Friends

Table 8.5 presents the relevant data on perceived similarity to the standards of peers. The overall percent who perceived the peers as similar was 77 percent. There was a definite and strong relation indicating that those

Table 8.5
PERCEIVED STANDARDS OF PEERS AND PERMISSIVENESS IN TOTAL GROUP
AND RACE-SEX GROUPS IN THE STUDENT SAMPLE

Standards Compared to Peers'	*Percent Highly Permissive*			
	Total Group			
More strict	30 (146)			
Similar	51 (627)			
Less strict	82 (44)			
	$x^2 = 40.63$			
	$P < .001$			
	$G = -.48$			
	Race-Sex Groups			
	WHITE MALE	NEGRO MALE	WHITE FEMALE	NEGRO FEMALE
More strict	47 (55)	75 (12)	5 (57)	27 (22)
Similar	64 (201)	87 (94)	27 (244)	49 (88)
Less strict	86 (21)	100 (2)	81 (16)	60 (5)
	$x^2 = 10.50$	$x^2 = 1.66$	$x^2 = 38.57$	$x^2 = 3.77$
	$P < .01$	NS	$P < .001$	NS
	$G = -.41$	$G = -.44$	$G = -.80$	$G = -.40$

who saw themselves as more or less strict than their peers were sharply distinguishable. Such a clear distinction implies that these students have a rather consensual definition of the permissiveness of friends of their own age; for without such a similar definition, those with opposing views of their peers' standards would have had a greater tendency to cancel out and eliminate a significant association, such as that found in Table 8.5. The basic relation in this and all tables in this chapter was checked out for all five schools and within each sex group, and the findings held up quite well. If it is assumed that females are the most clearly defined group (most stereotyped) regarding standards (as proposed in the discussion of Table 8.4), then the relationship in Table 8.5 should hold up strongest for them. This was the case, and the difference was modestly supported by the Goodman test for interaction.

Table 8.6

PERCEIVED STANDARDS OF CLOSE FRIENDS AND PERMISSIVENESS IN TOTAL GROUP
AND RACE-SEX GROUPS IN STUDENT SAMPLE

Standards Compared to Close Friends'	Percent Highly Permissive			
	Total Group			
More strict	44 (59)			
Similar	48 (728)			
Less strict	80 (30)			
	$\chi^2 = 12.43$			
	$P < .01$			
	$G = -.28$			
	Race-Sex Groups			
	WHITE MALE	NEGRO MALE	WHITE FEMALE	NEGRO FEMALE
More strict	50 (28)	88 (8)	9 (11)	33 (12)
Similar	62 (237)	86 (98)	24 (293)	47 (100)
Less strict	90 (10)	100 (3)	73 (15)	50 (2)
	$\chi^2 = 5.06$	$\chi^2 = .51$	$\chi^2 = 19.91$	$\chi^2 = .82$
	NS	NS	$P < .001$	NS
	$G = -.36$	$G = -.14$	$G = -.73$	$G = -.25$

Table 8.6 shows the relation between permissiveness and an individual's conception of his similarity to "very close friends." It is interesting to note that 89 percent of the respondents saw themselves as similar to their very close friends. This is considerably higher than the 63 percent who saw themselves as similar to their mothers and the 77 percent who saw themselves as similar to their peers, and is further evidence for the position that peers, and close friends in particular, are crucial in shaping the individual's sexual standards. This does not rule out the importance of parental, particularly maternal, influence. Maternal influence occurs first, and no doubt it helps shape the choice of close friends; but in time at least, the perceived similarity comes to be higher for friends than for parents. This suggests that the priority and importance may have shifted toward peers, particularly toward close friends. Here too we can test to see if the female definition of "close friend's permissiveness" is also clearest by observing whether or not the relationship holds up best for their group. Again the findings support this interpretation. Overall, it would seem that the contrast of the categories "more strict" and "similar" is less with close friends than with peers (see Tables 8.5 and 8.6). This probably indicates the greater variation in standards with specific groups like "very close friends" as compared to more general groups such as peer groups. Such lack of a uniform group for comparison leads to the blurring of relative differences.

Summary, Conclusions, and Proposition Six

The findings reported in this chapter do not fully confirm any one conception of attitude formation and change in the sexual area. Nevertheless, they are congruent with the findings of the previous chapter. For example, they indicate that although parental influence is considerable, there are other forces that are of great importance. More specifically, *within* each race-sex grouping those dissimilar to parents are the most permissive individuals. This may well be a result of the weakening of the initial congruence of a person with his parents as he increases his permissiveness. Accordingly, similarity to peers and close friends indicates higher permissiveness than similarity to parents. Forty percent of those similar to their parents were highly permissive, whereas about fifty percent of those similar to their peers and close friends were highly permissive. Many of these latter persons are part of the relatively high permissive group who are dissimilar to their parents.

It appears that, in general, there is a tension between parents on the low-permissive side and peers on the high-permissive side. Most individuals feel they are similar to their parents, but the more-permissive individuals feel more similar to their peers and friends. Although there is evidence of stereotyping in conceptions of parents, peers, and friends, it is most marked among peers and thereby produces the sharpest differences between "more strict" and "less strict" individuals. Note that although 83 percent of those who differed from their parents were *less* strict, from 66 to 77 percent of those who differed from their peers or close friends were *more* strict.[6] This contradicts the hypothesized expectation that all "similars" would be lower on permissiveness. However, these findings do support the view that, regardless of the individual's own individual level of permissiveness, he tends to view his parents as low on permissiveness and his peers as high on permissiveness. In point of fact this cannot be true for all individuals, but it does seem to reify the institutional reality for society-at-large, where parents generally are considered to be low on permissiveness and peers to be high on permissiveness.

It was noted in Chapter 7 that the influence of parents on the standard held by their offspring was least for those offsprings who were most permissive. Relatedly, more of those who considered themselves as more strict than their close friends felt a similarity to their mothers (57 percent) than of those who felt themselves to be less strict than their close friends (17

---

[6] Michael Schofield did find that English teen-agers assumed that their friends were having as much, if not more, sex than they themselves were having. This fits with the generally high permissive view of friends found in the present study. See *The Sexual Behavior of Young People*. Boston: Little, Brown & Co., 1965, p. 162.

percent). Also, the older students differed more from their parents and were more likely to be highly permissive when they differed. Again this shows the move away from parents as permissiveness increases. These data support the theory of the opposite pull of these two reference groups.[7] The tendency seems to be for people to conceive of themselves as most similar to their close friends but also to conceive of themselves as close to their parents. So there is no total disregard of parental influence, rather an increase of permissiveness, which may return to its original form after marriage, as shall be seen in the next chapter. In addition, it would seem likely, since so many students professed a similarity to both their parents and their peers, that the conception of these two groups is one of mild, rather than drastic, permissive differences. Further, the individual's feeling that the peer group is more permissive than himself may encourage him to feel that he really is not so different from his parents. The agreement with parents is not as great as the raw percentages indicate. Thirty-four percent of those who saw their standards as similar to their mothers' said they were only somewhat similar, whereas only 18 percent of those who saw their standards as similar to their close friends' reported such a weak degree of similarity.

There is one important possibility that should be discussed. It is conceivable that those individuals who perceive themselves as different in premarital sexual standards from their parents are revolting against their parents and are consequently a highly permissive group. No direct index of "revolt" was available, so this was tested by seeing if "family happiness" was correlated with permissiveness and with perceived parental differences in sexual standards. A relationship did exist between permissiveness and family happiness. Fifty-nine percent of those who were unhappy in their family relationships were highly permissive, whereas only 44 percent of those who were happy in their family relationships were highly permissive. This relationship held up best at the white Virginia college and worst for Negro college males, but there were elements of it in all schools. A control by social class showed no differences. It was also found that unhappy family relationships go with perceived parental difference in premarital sexual standards. Thus, there is some support for the "revolt" theory of high permissiveness.[8] However, only 30 percent of the total group of high permissives were unhappy in their family relationships, and although this is higher than the 17 percent of low permissives who were similarly unhappy, it clearly indicates that at least for the 70 percent who were happy, revolt against parents was not the basic reason for high permissiveness. In these more typical cases it was probably place in the social structure,

---

[7] Ehrmann does give information on tolerance for other people's sex standards and for sex education received and so on. For example, he found that females were more likely to allow their peers to have coitus than to allow themselves to do this. See *Premarital Dating Behavior*. New York: Holt, Rinehart and Winston, 1959, p. 179.

[8] For a report on the effect of the quality of the home on deviance see Robert A. Dentler and Lawrence J. Monroe, "The Family and Early Adolescent Conformity and Deviance," *Marriage and Family Living*, 23 (August 1961), pp. 241–247.

types of social and cultural pressures, that would be most important in explaining the high permissiveness. Finally, among both the high-permissive and low-permissive youngsters, parental values are generally perceived of as similar to one's own and thus probably help promote permissivenesss.

Proposition Six summarizes these findings as follows: THERE IS A GEN-ERAL TENDENCY FOR THE INDIVIDUAL TO PERCEIVE OF HIS PARENTS' PERMISSIVENESS AS A LOW POINT ON A PERMISSIVE CONTINUUM AND HIS PEERS' PERMISSIVENESS AS A HIGH POINT, AND TO PLACE HIMSELF SOMEWHAT CLOSER TO HIS PEERS, PARTICULARLY TO THOSE HE REGARDS AS HIS CLOSE FRIENDS.

Granted that there are loose ends not accounted for by the data presented in this chapter, the consistency of these findings at all five schools argues for their validity. It is better to trust consistent findings in several samples than stronger findings in one sample. As in all chapters, many controls were tried on the relations in a search for other key factors. None of these controls revealed any important differences. Also, the usual tests for interaction were performed and incorporated in the comments on the findings. There is virtually nothing in the research literature that can be consulted to compare the findings in this chapter.[9] Much in this chapter has relevance for a general theory of sexual attitude change and reference group behavior.

---

[9] There is a relatively large literature that deals sociologically with the period of adolescence and thus has some relevance to the discussion here. However, little of this literature is of direct relevance, for it does not relate reference-group theory to sexuality through empirical research. Nevertheless, the discussions are relevant to an understanding of the young person, peer culture, parent-child conflicts, and reference-group behavior, and as such it is important. Those books used in this study are listed here, but this is not an exhaustive list: Jessie Bernard, ed., "Teen-Age Culture," *The Annals of the American Academy of Political and Social Science,* 338 (November 1961); Philip Aries, *Centuries of Childhood.* New York: Alfred A. Knopf, 1962; James Coleman, *The Adolescent Society.* New York: The Free Press, 1960; Frederick Elkin, *The Child and Society.* New York: Random House, 1960; John C. Glidewell, ed., *Parental Attitudes and Child Behavior.* Springfield, Ill.: C. C. Thomas, Publisher, 1961; Rose K. Goldsen *et al., What College Students Think.* Princeton, N. J.: D. Van Nostrand Co., 1960; David Gottlieb and Charles Ramsey, *The American Adolescent.* Homewood, Ill.: Dorsey Press, 1964; A. B. Hollingshead, *Elmtown's Youth.* New York: John Wiley & Sons, 1949; Bernice M. Moore and Wayne H. Holtzman, *Tomorrow's Parents.* Austin, Texas: University of Texas Press, 1965; Theodore M. Newcomb, and Everett A. Wilson, eds., *College Peer Groups.* Chicago: Aldine Publishing Co., 1966; H. H. Remmers and D. H. Radler, *The American Teenager.* New York: The Bobbs-Merrill Co., 1957; Morris Rosenberg, *Society and the Adolescent Self-Image.* Princeton, N. J.: Princeton University Press, 1965; Jerome M. Seidman, ed., *The Adolescent.* New York: Holt, Rinehart and Winston, 1960; Ethel Shanas, and Gordon F. Streib, eds., *Social Structure and the Family: Generational Relations.* Englewood Cliffs, N. J.: Prentice-Hall, 1965; Muzafer Sherif and Carolyn W. Sherif, eds., *Problems of Youth: Transition to Adulthood in a Changing World.* Chicago: Aldine Publishing Co., 1965. There are a few books with a psychiatric bent that are relevant too. See for example, Erik H. Erikson, *Childhood and Society.* New York: W. W. Norton Co., 1963; Erik H. Erikson, ed., *The Challenge of Youth.* Garden City, N. Y.: Doubleday & Co., 1965; Group for the Advancement of Psychiatry, *Sex and the College Student.* New York: Atheneum Publishers, 1966.

9

Family-Role Relationships
and Premarital Sexual Attitudes

Preface to Proposition Seven

The last two chapters have dealt with some key findings concerning changes in sexual attitudes over time and with the individual's conceptions of the attitudes of his parents, peers and close friends. The data indicate an increasing acceptance of premarital permissiveness as the individual ages and undergoes certain social experience, and also as he comes more under the influence of his peers and friends. Now the question arises, What happens to the individual's premarital sexual attitudes after marriage? Does he become less permissive, and if so, does this depend on his age or on the number and sex of his children?

The data from the National Adult Sample permit a check of this area. The basic hypothesis here was that although age would show a negative relation to permissiveness, there would be a definite relation between the parental role and premarital permissiveness regardless of age; that is, having children and the aging of these children would decrease permissiveness, particularly if the children were female.

Tests of these hypotheses were made using only those in the adult sample who were currently married. Later on in this chapter a separate examination of those who were divorced, separated, or widowed is presented, and data from the student sample are also introduced. For the present purposes, it can be said that the states of being divorced, separated, and widowed are distinct from that of being currently married, and thus they are treated separately. In addition, it should be clear that the large number of controls used in the checks made it difficult to interpret the Negro results. And although the Negro results seemed to resemble those for whites, it is difficult to be sure because of the small sample size employed. Thus, the results apply with more certainty to whites than to Negroes.

The findings on both two-parent and one-parent families indicate that as the number of children in a family increases, and as the children age, the permissiveness of parents decreases. Thus, parents of teen-age children are relatively low on permissiveness compared to parents of younger children or to married couples without children. Within family groups it was found that the oldest sibling was the least permissive and that the only child was the most permissive. It seemed that the responsibility of caring for younger siblings tended to lower permissiveness. Thus, it appeared that the greater responsibility of parents with teen-age children and the greater responsibility of older siblings fitted together, indicating that as responsibility for other family members increased, the individual's permissiveness decreased. Also, it was noticed that divorced parents were more permissive than married people. This led to the generalization that the closer the individual is to being a participant in the courtship process (rather than responsible for other participants), the more permissive he would be. This fitted into the findings of Chapter 7, which indicated a constant growth in permissiveness as the individual became more involved in courtship. Proposition Seven states, therefore, that low permissiveness goes with being responsible for others in the family, and high permissiveness goes with being involved in courtship. Evidence and a discussion of this last proposition follow.

Children, Aging, and Permissiveness

Table 9.1 shows that there was a weak but noticeable relation between age and permissiveness. The races were quite similar in this relation, but the sexes did differ, with the females showing the sharpest drop in permissiveness between the young and middle-aged categories and the males drop-

Table 9.1

AGE AND PERMISSIVENESS FOR CURRENT MARRIED
INDIVIDUALS IN THE ADULT SAMPLE

AGE	PERCENT HIGHLY PERMISSIVE
Young (21–34)	21 (363)
Middle-aged (35–49)	20 (411)
Old (50 and over)	13 (351)
	$\chi^2 = 7.4$
	$P < .05$
	$G = -.16$

ping the most between the middle-aged and old categories. The true importance of age is difficult to obtain outside of a longitudinal study, but some perspective on this is afforded by the analysis of the effect of children on permissiveness when age is controlled for.

AGE OF CHILDREN AND PERMISSIVENESS   One measure of the effect of children of various ages on parental attitudes toward premarital sexual permissiveness is obtained simply by comparing the permissiveness of individuals in various types of parental roles.[1] Table 9.2 does just this, and in

Table 9.2
MARITAL AND FAMILY STATUS AND PERMISSIVENESS
IN THE ADULT SAMPLE

MARITAL AND FAMILY STATUS	PERCENT HIGHLY PERMISSIVE
Single[a]	44 (108)
Married	
No children	23 (124)
All preteen	22 (384)
Preteen and older	17 (218)
All teen or older	13 (376)
	$\chi^2 = 53.8$
	$P < .001$
	$G = -.32$

[a] Without the "single" category $\chi^2 = 12.7$, $P < .01$, and $G = -.21$.

addition, lists figures for single respondents. A clear decrease in permissiveness begins sharply with the advent of marriage and drops gradually in accord with the proportion of an individual's children who are teen-age or older.[2]

It was thought that perhaps the results in Table 9.2 were due to the relation between age and permissiveness; that older people were more conservative and also happened to have older children. But this was carefully checked out for each race and sex group, and it was found that the relation held up despite controls on race, sex, and age.[3] Here, then, is data supporting the view that the conflict between parents and their children on sexual attitudes does not result from rapid social change of the generations

[1] The greater importance of controlling for the stage of the family life cycle (as opposed to controlling just for age) is well documented by John B. Lansing and Leslie Kish, "Family Life Cycle as an Independent Variable," *American Sociological Review,* 22 (October 1957), pp. 512–519.

[2] Included with the category "teen or older" are married children. It was found that married and unmarried older children had the same effect on the relation of age of children to permissiveness.

[3] Not all control categories had sufficient cases; for example, there were only a few parents of teen-agers who were under thirty-five years of age and only a few parents of pre-teens who were over fifty years of age.

but rather from being in sharply different role positions.[4] Robert Bell and others have alluded to this, but these are the first national data available to test this conception.[5]

The data in Chapter 7 indicated a steady *rise* in permissiveness on the part of young people during their teens and later. The data in the present chapter indicate a steady *drop* in permissiveness on the part of parents, which increases as their children reach their teens and beyond. Thus, in effect, we have a graph of two curves that dissect each other, one of which reaches its highest point at almost precisely the same time as the other reaches its lowest point! Here, then, in bare statistical terms is a key basis for parent-youth conflict regarding sexual standards today. If one were to generalize from this data, it would seem that the conflict is, in part, an inevitable one, due to the different perspectives that such different roles afford. The young person at eighteen or nineteen is exposed to the temptations of being out alone with an attractive member of the opposite sex, with whom he typically engages in suggestive dances, shares alcoholic beverages, and finds some secluded place to spend the last hour or so of the evening. The parent of forty-five or fifty has had a regularly available sexual outlet for a few decades and feels responsible for any undesirable consequences that may result from sexual activity on the part of his or her children. Given such vast differences in role perspective and responsibilities, it is no wonder that sexual attitudes also differ greatly. Life-cycle changes in sexual permissiveness demonstrate further the plasticity and social nature of the sexual relationship and of our attitude toward it. Even though a steady, unchanging societal system might well minimize such role conflict, it would, to some measure, exist owing to the different demands of the roles involved. It would be of considerable sociological value to undertake a longitudinal study of such attitude changes,[6] for it would surely throw light on the entire area of societal and attitudinal changes.[7]

[4] For evidence of how role positions affect behavior see Clark E. Vincent, "Socialization Data in Research on Young Marrieds," *Acta Sociologica*, 8 (Nos. 1 and 2, 1964), pp. 118–127.

[5] Robert Bell, "Parent-Child Conflict in Sexual Values," *Journal of Social Issues,* 22 (April 1966), pp. 34–44.

[6] It is possible that a self-selective factor is operative and that the less-permissive people are more likely to marry and to have children. However, this would not account for the drop in permissiveness as the children age. Also, there is evidence in Paul Gebhard, *Pregnancy, Birth, and Abortion.* New York: Harper & Row, Publishers, 1958, that the less-permissive females are *least* likely to marry. In Chapter 5 he reports finding high postmarital coitus rates (75 percent) for previously married females, most of whom were divorced or separated. The idea of an initial difference in these females is supported by the fact that they were also high on premarital coitus and were unusually independent and aggressive. These traits may have caused them to be oriented to finding a mate but also have made their marriages less likely to last. Additional testing in this area is needed.

[7] For some introductory insights into the area of attitude research and its problems see Paul F. Lazarsfeld *et al., People's Choice: How the Voter Makes up His Mind in a Presidential Campaign.* New York: Columbia University Press, 1948, and Joseph Klapper, *The Effects of Mass Communication.* New York: The Free Press, 1960.

NUMBER OF CHILDREN AND PERMISSIVENESS   What is the effect on permissiveness of the number of children an individual has? As age of children increases, does permissiveness decrease more if the individual has twice as many children as another? Table 9.3 presents data on these questions. The

Table 9.3
NUMBER OF CHILDREN AND PERMISSIVENESS
FOR CURRENTLY MARRIED INDIVIDUALS
IN THE ADULT SAMPLE

NUMBER OF CHILDREN	PERCENT HIGHLY PERMISSIVE
One	21 (197)
Two or three	18 (550)
Four or more	14 (258)
	$\chi^2 = 3.3$
	NS
	$G = .13$

relationship is almost significant ($P < .10$ for a one-tail test) and shows that permissiveness does decrease somewhat as the number of children increases. The relation holds up with controls on race, sex, and age of respondent, which lends further credence to it despite its weakness. The possibility that larger families are formed by less permissive people was checked out partially by seeing if the relation held best for those fifty years old and more who could be assumed to have finished their family growth. The relation did not hold best at that age, thus supporting that permissiveness changes, at least in part, as one adds children.

SEX OF CHILDREN AND PERMISSSVENESS   The findings regarding the relation of the sex of children to the permissiveness of parents do not indicate a very pronounced relationship. Basically, there appears to be only a slight difference between the parents of boys and the parents of girls. Looking at children in their teens or older, it would seem that only the males who are fifty years old or more are less permissive when they have daughters than when they have sons. Looking only at preteen children an interesting but not significant relation is found: fathers, at all ages, are more permissive when they have girls than are fathers who have boys; the mothers are more permissive when they have boys. Thus, the parents of preteen children have a slight tendency to be more permissive when they have children of the opposite sex.

The analysis of the effects of the sex of children is based on rather small but quite consistent differences among families composed of various ages and sexes. Even if one decides that there is no relation, the data are surprising, for the common lay belief is that parents of girls are less permissive.

This is true only for mothers of preteen girls and for fathers over fifty of older girls, and even here the relation is weak. A cautious conclusion based on the above data would simply state that there was no significant difference noted between parents when the sex of their children was varied. Taking this cautious position leads to the conclusion that although there is evidence that as an individual's children age, and probably as the number of children increases, his permissiveness decreases, it would seem that this process is independent of the sex of those children. In short, a parent passes on a less-permissive version of his own permissiveness to his children, and the version is not altered on the basis of the sex of the children. This is not to say that many parents are not double-standard adherents and give male children more sexual freedom. Rather it is to say that the permissive beliefs seem unaltered by the sex of the children, even if the beliefs themselves are sex-specific and males are taught differently than females.

Although the sex of children does not seem very important in relation to permissiveness, there is an interesting relation of this factor to the *intensity* of permissive feelings. (See the end of Appendix D for a full description of this variable.) White males tend to become *less* intense about their permissive feelings as the number of their male children increases, and *more* intense as the number of their female children increases. These changes are significant, in part, for white males and are presented in Table 9.4. Also seen in this table is the tendency of white females to show exactly opposite trends in their intensity and to become more intense as the number of their

Table 9.4
SEX OF CHILDREN AND INTENSITY OF PERMISSIVENESS
FOR CURRENTLY MARRIED WHITES IN THE ADULT SAMPLE

Number of Male Children	Percent High Intensity	Number of Female Children	Percent High Intensity
WHITE MALES			WHITE MALES
One	47 (195)	One	39 (183)
Two	40 (101)	Two	44 (98)
Three or more	26 (58)	Three or more	51 (49)
	$x^2 = 8.6$		$x^2 = 2.5$
	$P < .05$		NS
	$G = -.26$		$G = .15$
WHITE FEMALES			WHITE FEMALES
One	62 (189)	One	64 (162)
Two	62 (109)	Two	62 (119)
Three or More	71 (72)	Three or More	60 (79)
	$x^2 = 1.9$		$x^2 = .48$
	NS		NS
	$G = .10$		$G = -.07$

male children increases. However, this tendency toward increased intensity of permissiveness for children of the opposite sex is not significant. Nevertheless, the white male-female difference regarding male children is significant at the .025 level when tested by the Goodman test for interaction, but on female children the difference is significant at only the .30 level.[8]

Here, then, is some support for the conventional notions about daughters, at least as far as fathers are concerned. The relation seems strongest for the older fathers. The results on mothers are somewhat surprising, for intensity does not rise with the number of daughters but rather with the number of sons. It could be speculated that this finding reflects an increased concern (particularly on the part of fathers) for children of the opposite sex, due perhaps to lack of familiarity with, and increased awareness of, their special sexual problems as the number of children of that sex increases.

SUMMARY OF RELATION OF CHILDREN AND AGING TO PERMISSIVENESS   In order to test the independent relation of parental age, age of children, and number of children to permissiveness, checks were run with each as a control on the other. It was found that there was no strong evidence of interaction among these variables and that they therefore represented independent relations to permissiveness.

Basically, it would seem that permissiveness concerning premarital sexual relations decreases with age and that this occurs regardless of marital status when the individual reaches middle age (but earlier for females). Another largely independent force promoting decreased permissiveness is indicated by the sharp drop in permissiveness that relates to being married and by the continuing drop as one's children reach the teen-age years. Further, as an individual has more children the decrease in permissiveness is accentuated. The sex of the children does not seem terribly important in terms of the permissiveness of parents, but it does seem to affect the intensity with which that permissiveness is felt, particularly by fathers.

The following notion can be deduced from the aforementioned findings: As the relation to the courtship process changes from that of participant to that of responsible observer, one's premarital sexual permissiveness tends to decrease. The converse of this notion has been shown to apply to the findings of Chapter 7, which showed an increase in permissiveness as an individual's participation in the courtship process increased. The observations reported in this chapter are congruent with this proposed theory, for older people do tend to participate less in the process and parents do tend to become more responsible observers as their children age and increase in number.

---

[8] Negroes had too few cases to be used here. Checks were made comparing those who only had male children with those who only had female children and those who had offspring of both sexes. The results were the same as reported in this chapter. Intensity checks were made throughout this study, and where important differences occurred they are reported.

One-Parent Families and Permissiveness

The adult sample was examined to see if widowed, divorced, and separated parents would show different relations to the age, sex, and number of their children. Although not all checks were possible, due to the small number of cases in these "one parent" categories, there was sufficient evidence to indicate that one-parent families showed the same relations as the currently married did in Tables 9.1 to 9.4. However, despite the similarity in the effect of parent-child structures on permissiveness, there was considerable difference in actual *levels* of permissiveness between single parents themselves and between single parents and currently married parents.

Table 9.5 presents the basic comparison, which clearly shows that the divorced and separated groups are significantly higher on permissiveness than are the widowed and currently married groups.[9] This finding is compatible with the notion that the closer an individual is to being a participant in courtship, the more permissive he is. It is also compatible in the sense that, as seen in Table 9.5, permissiveness is slightly more acceptable for

Table 9.5
MARITAL AND PARENTAL STATUS AND PERMISSIVENESS
IN THE ADULT SAMPLE

Type of Parent	*Percent Highly Permissive*	
Currently married	18 (1129)	
Widowed	42 (56)	
Divorced or separated	14 (99)	
	$\chi^2 = 23.7$	
	$P < .001$	
	$G = .17$	
	$C = .13$	
	WITH CHILDREN	WITHOUT CHILDREN
Currently married	17 (1005)	23 (124)
Divorced or separated	40 (43)	54 (13)
Widowed	13 (82)	18 (17)
	$\chi^2 = 15.1$	$\chi^2 = 6.7$
	$P < .001$	$P < .05$
	$G = .13$	$G = .20$
	$C = .11$	$C = .20$

[9] The separated and divorced parents have been combined because of their small number and because they show very little in the way of fundamental differences except that separated are somewhat more permissive. The only area where a possibly important difference appeared was in the student sample, where children of divorced parents were more likely to say their relations with their family was happy. Forty-six percent of the children of separated parents checked "unhappy"; 30 percent of the children of divorced parents, 24 percent of the children of widowed parents, and 21 percent of the children of currently married parents did likewise. In all other respects the divorced and separated groups were quite similar.

those formerly married persons without children. This is compatible with the findings on those who are currently married. However, the difference is not large enough to be significant. An explanation is still wanting as to why the widowed group does not show increased permissiveness, as the "courtship participant" conception might make us expect. The reason is not age, for the difference between those who are widowed and those who are divorced or separated persists even with age controlled. Possibly the reason is the low orientation to remarriage and the different set of societal-role expectations of the widowed individual.

Paul Jacobson and others have demonstrated the lower remarriage rates of widowed individuals as compared to divorced individuals of the same age.[10] For example, a fifty-year-old female whose husband dies has a 20 percent chance of remarrying, while a fifty-year-old divorcée has a 53 percent chance of remarrying.[11] A single female at the age of fifty has only a 10 percent change of marriage. The figures for males are higher, but the relative position remains the same. The likelihood of marriage is roughly related to the level of permissiveness of the various groups. For example, the total group of single persons fifty years old or more in the National Adult Sample had 17 percent who were high on permissiveness; the widowed group at this age range had 14 percent who were highly permissive, and the divorced group at this age range had 35 percent in this category. In all cases the males surpassed the females, and they were also more likely to marry.

The rates of marriage do not fit perfectly with the "courtship participant" conception for those who are fifty years old or more and single have a lower chance of marrying than have the widowed, yet in their level of permissiveness in the adult sample (17 percent) they were about the same as the widowed (14 percent). But the divorced group does show up as distinct (35 percent), and there is a much greater difference in the likelihood of marriage between this group and the widowed and the single groups than there is between the widowed and single groups. Thus, the major distinctions do show up in accord with the thesis. The male-female difference is also congruent with males having a greater chance of marriage and more permissiveness. The important distinction here, however, is that males are different among themselves according to whether they are single, widowed, or divorced in ways that fit the courtship thesis.

[10] Paul H. Jacobson, *American Marriage and Divorce*. New York: Holt, Rinehart and Winston, 1959; Paul C. Glick, *American Families*. New York: John Wiley & Sons, 1957.

[11] Paul Jacobson, pp. 83–85. It should be noted that these figures are for the year 1948. However, the divorce rate and the remarriage rate have not changed in ways that should affect the general relations shown here. More recent figures for 1961–63 show similar remarriage rates. See U. S. Department of Health, Education, and Welfare, *Monthly Vital Statistics Report,* Advance Report Final Marriage Statistics, 1963. Vol. 15, supplement 3, Washington, D. C.: May 31, 1966. For a popular analysis of the formerly married see Morton M. Hunt, *The World of the Formerly Married.* New York: McGraw-Hill, 1966.

The lower permissiveness among widowed individuals may be due to a factor that relates to their low remarriage rate—society's attitude toward widowed persons, which is more somber than the public attitude toward divorced people. There is more of a sense of finality of status, a feeling that the widowed status will be stable. The divorced status, on the other hand, is extremely unstable, with approximately seventy-five percent of the divorced population entering marriage again, and most of these do so within five years. The comparable percent for widowed individuals would be about half of this rate.[12] Perhaps the public attitude of finality is based on the stereotype of the elderly woman who loses her husband and on the notion that the marriage broken by death is more often than not a happy one whereas the one broken by divorce is an unhappy one. Thus, the end of a happy marriage may not produce as much pressure to remarry as does the end of an unhappy marriage. The widowed individual has lived up to the ideal of achieving a happy marriage and thus is less socially pressured to enter into another union.

On the other hand, the attitude toward the divorced person may be based on the stereotype of the young female with small children who "needs" a father in the home, and thus remarriage is more encouraged. In reality two women of the same age and with the same number of children will have different chances of remarriage if one is divorced and the other is widowed; so it would seem to be something other than age and number of children that is responsible for their different remarriage rates. It may well be the public attitude and the internalization of this attitude that contributes to this difference between divorced and widowed individuals.

An alternate explanation of the difference in remarriage rate of divorced and widowed individuals could be that the divorced are a selective group of generally liberal people, and this liberality is the explanation for both the divorce and for the high level of permissiveness. Such an explanation has some validity, but it would have had more force fifty years ago than today. At that time, the public opposition to divorce was much stronger, and accordingly there was more necessity to be strongly motivated and to have strong attitudes favoring divorce before undertaking such an unpopular action. Although today there probably is still a general tendency for divorced individuals to have a somewhat larger proportion of liberals in their group, the proportion of liberals is relatively smaller than it used to be because of the greater general acceptance of divorce by many conservative, as well as many liberal, groups.[13] Thus, this interpretation would seem valid, but only as a partial explanation of the higher sexual permissiveness

[12] Paul C. Glick, pp. 139–140.

[13] In Chapter 4 divorce was used as one of the "rough" indices of "liberality." However, it was admitted that these measures were not the best nor the "purest" ones. The divorced and widowed respondents picked up in a survey such as this may not be typical of all widowed and divorced people. Such a group contains a high percentage of those who are slow to remarry.

of divorced individuals. The basic explanatory factor might well be the greater tendency for this group to have an orientation toward marriage. Of course, it can be argued that this greater tendency is also a result of being in a more liberal group; nevertheless, it is believed by this researcher that the immediate antecedent factor promoting greater sexual permissiveness is the tendency to marry, even if liberal forces are antecedent to this tendency. Liberality alone still seems an insufficient explanation, for one must not underestimate the psychological pressures to remarry and to demonstrate the ability to have a happy marriage, as well as the sociological pressures resulting from the strains of being a divorced person, regardless of the individual's liberality. William Goode has elaborated on this explanation of remarriage pressures on divorcées.[14]

Children in One-Parent Families

The children of divorced, widowed, and separated individuals, as well as of currently married individuals, were examined in the student sample to see if they differed in ways similar to parental differences and if the only child was the most permissive, as were the parents of an only child.[15]

There were some clear similarities in the student sample to the results in the adult sample. For example, the student who was the only child in his family was the most permissive, regardless of whether his parents were married and living together at the time of the study. This result, shown in Table 9.6, was similar to that found in the adult sample (Table 9.3), and was

Table 9.6

NUMBER OF CHILDREN AND PERMISSIVENESS
IN THE STUDENT SAMPLE

NUMBER OF CHILDREN IN FAMILY	PERCENT HIGHLY PERMISSIVE
One	60 (136)
Two	44 (305)
Three	45 (177)
Four or more	53 (205)
	$\chi^2 = 12.6$
	$P < .01$
	$G = .03$
	$C = .12$

[14] William Goode, *After Divorce*. New York: The Free Press, 1956.

[15] Table 9.3 shows this tendency, and it holds up when only fifty-year-old parents are looked at. Such elderly parents would not be planning on having more children.

further similar in that it held up for one-parent, as well as two-parent, families. However, the "four children or more" category shows an upswing that was not characteristic of the adult results. This category is particularly pronounced for the one-parent families. Bossard and others have hypothesized that as the size of the family increases, both parents are likely to be drawn into authority positions to control the group.[16] Perhaps when only one parent is present the difficulty of control leads to lessening of controls and to more permissivenes when four or more children are present.

Table 9.7

TYPE OF PARENT AND PERMISSIVENESS
IN THE STUDENT SAMPLE

TYPE OF PARENT	PERCENT HIGHLY PERMISSIVE
Currently married	47 (680)
Divorced or separated	64 (88)
Widowed	52 (67)
	$\chi^2 = 9.0$
	$P < .05$
	$G = .21$
	$C = .33$

Table 9.7 shows that those students whose parents were divorced or separated were significantly more likely to be highly permissive. Table 9.5 showed that in the adult sample those parents who were divorced were more likely to be highly permissive. The two sets of data confirm each other. However, it should be clear that the student sample is by no means representative of the same population as the adult sample, and so the results can only be taken as suggestive.[17]

The high-permissive character of the children of divorced and separated parents is further supported by findings showing that they were less likely to attend church and less likely to view sex as nasty or dirty than were those whose parents were currently married or those whose parent was widowed.[18] Checks by social class, school, and sex, and by race and sex

---

[16] James H. S. Bossard, *Parent and Child*. Philadelphia: University of Pennsylvania Press, 1953; James H. Bossard and Eleanor Stoker Boll, *The Large Family System*. Philadelphia: University of Pennsylvania Press, 1956.

[17] In the student sample, those with separated parents were more permissive than those with divorced parents. The white females with a widowed parent were the least permissive. In the other race-sex groups those with a widowed parent were closer to those with a divorced parent but still always lower in permissiveness. F. Ivan Nye reports that children in broken homes are more sexually active than those from intact homes. See *Family Relationships and Delinquent Behavior*. New York: John Wiley & Sons, 1958, p. 45.

[18] The percentage in the student sample who said they thought there was something nasty and/or dirty about sex was 20 percent of the children of the currently married

controls, as usual, were employed, and the results supported this interpretation. In addition a wide number of key relationships were checked with a control for marital status. The student sample, as the adult sample, generally showed no difference in the relationships for one-parent families. The key difference associated with a one-parent family, then, is the higher likelihood of permissiveness if divorce or separation is the reason for the single parenthood.

It is important, then, to avoid lumping all one-parent families together, for even when age and number of children are the same, the divorced and separated families are quite distinct from the widowed families. Finally, it may be noted that the similarity of the adult and student samples lends support for the importance of parental attitudes in the development of sexual standards of young people. The more-permissive parents seem likely to have more-permissive children, and although peers and friends may in time take over some of the power to shape sexual attitudes, their very selection is most likely influenced by parental values.

Birth Order and Permissiveness

It has been shown that various aspects of marital and family roles are related to permissiveness. The only remaining question to be treated here concerns the relation of birth order to permissiveness: Does the child's permissiveness relate to his birth order relative to other siblings? This was checked in the student sample. So far in this study evidence has been presented to the effect that if an individual is an only child, there is a likelihood that he and his parents will be high on permissiveness (see Tables 9.3 and 9.6). Now other types of sibling combinations will be examined.

Table 9.8 shows the relationship of sibling order to permissiveness. It was found again that the only child is high on premarital sexual permissiveness. A very large number of controls were investigated to see if the relationship of sibling order to permissiveness could be altered. The basic order remained, regardless of such controls. Other rather interesting relationships appeared in sibling order. For example, it was found that divorced people were significantly more likely to have only one child than were two-parent families. It was also found that divorced people were more permissive than those who were currently married. Thus, it was possible that the higher permissiveness shown by the only child was merely a product of his being more likely to come from a divorced home. However, a control by marital status did not eliminate the higher permissiveness of the only

parents, 11 percent of the children of the divorced and separated parents, and 30 percent of the children of widowed parents. The differences are significant at the .05 level. The response in the widowed parent category can perhaps be taken as evidence for the attitudes of the widowed not being helpful for remarriage.

Table 9.8

SIBLING ORDER AND PERMISSIVENESS
IN THE STUDENT SAMPLE

SIBLING ORDER	PECENT HIGHLY PERMISSIVE
Is only child	58 (129)
Has older sisters	55 (177)
Has older brothers and sisters	48 (106)
Has older brothers	47 (127)
Is oldest	39 (257)
	$\chi^2 = 17.2$
	$P < .01$
	$G = .21$

child. Such a child was highly permissive in both two- and one-parent families. In addition, the social-class factors were controlled for, because one-parent families were somewhat lower in socioeconomic status than were two-parent families. As might be expected from the analysis of class in Chapter 4, this did not change the relationships found. Many other variables were similarly checked, and the basic findings of Table 9.8 held up. This came as somewhat of a surprise, for there were no hypotheses formulated in this area. Perhaps this is simply a chance result or one that is due to some unexamined third factor, but it is persistent enough to warrant some brief comment.

A control on race and sex did show some noticeable differences, but they were not overall statistically significant. The white female group showed the highest level of significance in the relationship between sibling order and permissiveness. Among girls, those with older sisters and those who were an only child were almost twice as permissive as those in other sibling orders. A further check revealed that these two groups of girls had the expected social characteristics that go with high permissiveness, that is, they were low on church-attendance, high on number of love affairs, and so on. These two sibling orders were high on permissiveness in almost all of the race-sex groups, but not as distinctly as in the white female group.

There was little difference in the race-sex groups regarding the low-permissive position of the oldest child. The greatest variation occurred in the rank order of those who had an older brother and those who had an older brother and sister. For males, having an older brother was a high-permissive category, whereas for females it was a low-permissive category. Having an older brother and sister was generally a moderate category for both sexes.

It can be speculated that having an older sibling of the same sex encourages permissiveness because it sets up a role model that the younger sibling can follow and thereby initiates him into sexual sophistication at an earlier age than an individual who is the oldest in the family.[19] The oldest also has the greatest likelihood of responsibility for other children and this may give him more self-discipline and more concern for possible consequences, thereby restricting his permissiveness.

This does not explain why having an older sibling of the opposite sex produces different results for the two sexes. It can be speculated and held, however, that the double standard in American culture makes it likely that older brothers will try to "protect" their sisters and will thereby be restrictive, whereas older sisters generally will not act this way toward their brothers.[20] As a matter of fact, girls with older brothers were more likely to believe in the double standard, whereas girls with older sisters were more likely to believe in permissiveness with affection. Those who have older brothers and sisters hold a middle position, possibly because of the conflicting tendencies such older siblings have among themselves.

The only child is high on permissiveness for a special reason. His solitary position in the family tends to gain him more attention and special privileges, and this promotes permissiveness. In a sense the only child is the exact opposite of the oldest child; the former has no responsibility whatsoever for other siblings, and the latter has the most such responsibility. Table 9.8 shows that these two birth orders are the most distinct. The three other sibling orders are cases of younger siblings with moderate amounts of responsibility in the family. Thus, it may be argued that the findings in Table 9.8 may be explained most simply by the notion that as sibling responsibility decreases, premarital sexual permissiveness increases. This explanation would maintain that girls with older brothers still have responsibility of caring for even younger siblings or helping around the house, whereas girls with older sisters are freer. Boys with older brothers or sisters would be free because the male child's responsibilities in the home are less than those of the female child. This lesser responsibility to care for other siblings or to help around the house would lead to the expectation that males show

---

[19] Orville Brim put forth a similar view. See "Family Structure and Sex Role Learning by Children: A Further Analysis of Helen Koch's Data," *Sociometry*, 21 (March 1958), pp. 1–16. Richard Schmuck, in a separate study, found girls with older sisters less likely to conform; see "Sex of Siblings, Birth Order Position, and Female Disposition to Conform in Two-Child Families," *Child Development*, 34 (December 1963), pp. 913–918. Speculations on the effects of siblings on each other can also be found in much of the literature, although not specifically on sexual relations. For example, see Talcott Parsons *et al., Family, Socialization, and Interaction Process.* New York: The Free Press, 1955. The shortage of research done directly on sibling relationships is ably commented on in Donald P. Irish, "Sibling Interaction: A Neglected Aspect in Family Life Research," *Social Forces,* 42 (March 1964), pp. 279–288.

[20] Some additional support for this is found in the fact that of all white females, about thirty-nine percent of those with older brothers have never been in love, whereas only 27 percent of those with older sisters have never been in love. A check was made to see if the number of children in a family would affect the birth order findings. No important changes occurred.

a weaker relation of sibling order to permissiveness than do females. The difference was found but was significant only at the .15 level.

The notions of role model and responsibility as keys to understanding the relation of birth order to permissiveness are not necessarily mutually exclusive. The role-model, double-standard ideas supplement the responsibility thesis, but the latter has the advantage of simplicity. In particular, the responsibility notion makes sense of the only-child and oldest-child groups, which are the most distinct. Further, the notion of responsibility differences among siblings leading to permissive differences is congruent with the notion put forth earlier in this chapter, namely, that as adult responsibility for offspring who are dating increases, permissiveness decreases. Being responsible for someone else seems to inhibit the individual's own permissiveness. This seems to be so because the individual becomes more aware of the possible pitfalls involved and becomes more imbued with adult, conservative values when he performs adult-like responsibility tasks. Accordingly, a child who is responsible for his siblings and thereby learns adult supervisory values is strengthened against peer-group values and thus grows up more sexually conservative.[21]

This notion has implications for a basic theory of social control as well as practical implications for those who have children of their own. It should be quite clear that it is not being implied here that it is the irresponsible person who is permissive, but that *within one family* it is the person who is mainly answerable only to himself and who has few others for whom he is responsible who is more likely to be sexually permissive. Such a person may still be a reliable and trustworthy person when responsibility is placed upon him. All children cannot fit this role, for there must be a "younger" child for every "older" child and a "less" responsible child for every "more" responsible child. There is a difference between having less responsibilities and being irresponsible.

Summary, Conclusions, and Proposition Seven

The thesis put forth in this chapter concerning parents contends that as an individual's responsibility for the courtship of his children increases, his permissiveness decreases. The thesis regarding siblings contends that as

---

[21] The need for positing some counteracting force such as "responsibility" is apparent in the finding that older children are *low* on permissiveness. Such children are born when their parents are younger and thus *more* permissive. It is posited in this study that the force of sibling responsibility outweighs the higher parental permissiveness. It may also be that although parental values do not become more liberal, parents become more acceptant and resigned and do not control younger children quite as much as older ones.

sibling responsibility increases, permissiveness decreases.[22] The findings on divorcées resulted in the thesis that permissiveness increases as courtship aims increase. These theses can be combined into one general proposition. Proposition Seven will read: THE GREATER THE RESPONSIBILITY FOR OTHER FAMILY MEMBERS AND/OR THE LESS THE COURTSHIP PARTICIPATION, THE GREATER THE LIKELIHOOD THAT THE INDIVIDUAL WILL BE LOW ON PERMISSIVENESS. Thus, the sibling with responsibility for younger siblings is low on permissiveness compared to other siblings; the parent with responsibility for teen-age children is low on permissiveness compared to other parents; and divorcées, by being more involved in courtship, display higher permissiveness than married people. It seems that, in general, responsibility diminishes permissiveness and courtship activities increase permissiveness.[23]

This proposition would seem to imply that a cohesive family in which the responsibilities of the parents for the children and the children for each other are clear-cut would be less permissive than one that has less cohesiveness. It can be generalized that as family responsibility, or role integration, is reduced, permissiveness increases. This thesis has many important implications for a general theory of social change.[24] However, it does *not* imply that all high-permissive groups come from low-responsibility families. Rather, it implies that the lowering of family responsibility raises the existing level of permissiveness in a group. However, even with such an increment of permissiveness the low-responsibility family might still be less permissive than some high-responsibility families that come from a more permissive background. It might be argued that the increased permissiveness among young people in the twentieth century is due in part to the lower level of family responsibility, the lesser responsibilities of parents for children and of children for each other. In place of family responsibilities the ties

[22] Other researchers have indicated that firstborn children are the "conservators of traditional culture." See Kenneth Kammeyer, "Birth Order and the Feminine Sex Role Among College Women," *American Sociological Review,* 31 (August 1966), pp. 508–515; Alice S. Rossi, "Naming Children in Middle-Class Families," *American Sociological Review,* 30 (August 1965), pp. 499–513. However, Kammeyer also states that his "only" children were conservative, and this contradicts the findings in this present study. Sears, Maccoby, and Levin, p. 418, report that the oldest child was more responsible and was quicker to develop a conscience. F. Ivan Nye, p. 37, reports that the oldest child is the least delinquent. However, he also found the only child to be low on delinquency. It was the youngest child who was highest on delinquency.

[23] A recent study found "responsibility" to be a trait present more in low-permissives than in high-permissives. See Brian G. Gilmartin, "Relationship of Traits Measured by the California Psychological Inventory to Premarital Sexual Standards and Behaviors," M.S. thesis, University of Utah, 1964.

[24] David Gottlieb, Jon Reeves, and Warren D. Ten Houten, *The Emergence of Youth Societies: A Cross-Cultural Approach.* New York: The Free Press, 1966, especially pp. 40–47. This section presents an interesting theory of adolescence that fits with the competitive nature of parent and peer groups. See also James S. Coleman, *The Adolescent Society.* New York: The Free Press, 1961.

to peer and friendship groups have been strengthened, and as shown in Chapters 7 and 8, these ties promote permissiveness. Surely, these changes have not "disorganized" the American family system; rather, they have brought about a different type of system—one that is more compatible with premarital sexual permissiveness. But those who are most involved with the care and responsibility for others are still the lowest on permissiveness in this new system.

It might be further argued that this is one factor explaining the female's lower permissiveness vis à vis the male. Throughout her life she is placed in a position of greater family responsibility, and this may bring her more in touch with adult-type low-permissiveness values and insulate her more from peer-group pressures. Evidence supporting this interpretation comes from Table 8.1 and 8.2 in Chapter 8, wherein the female in each race is shown to be more likely to see herself as similar to her parents in her sexual standards.

Family integration can be checked by looking at family happiness reported by the respondents. The student sample showed some slight tendency for the only child to be less happy about his family life, even in a two-parent family. There was also an independent tendency for those who are unhappy in their relations with their parents to be more permissive. Here, then, is some indirect evidence that family integration (or family happiness) is negatively correlated with permissiveness.[25] Some of the higher permissiveness of the Negro group in the samples may be attributed to the low cohesiveness in their family systems,[26] for higher percents of Negroes live in one-parent families.[27] However, in the student sample there was actually a slightly lower percentage of Negro children who said they are unhappy in their family relations (15 percent as opposed to 25 percent), despite the fact that in the adult sample more Negroes expressed personal unhappiness (41 percent as opposed to 14 percent).[28]

[25] The relation of *personal* unhappiness to permissiveness held only for single white males and females and for married white females and married Negro males in the adult sample.

[26] One person who stressed the key role of the family was Patrick Moynihan, *The Negro Family,* Washington, D.C.: U.S. Department of Labor, March, 1965. It should be clear that much of the Negro-white difference persists even when comparing similar family types. Moynihan was aware of the importance of other social factors.

[27] In the student sample 30 percent of the Negroes and 14 percent of the whites came from one-parent families. Negroes particularly exceeded whites in the one-parent family in which the parents were separated. In the adult sample 23 percent of the Negroes and 11 percent of the whites were one-parent families; however, Negro males were not different from whites, but Negro females were—perhaps due to a higher remarriage rate for males. It is also worth noting that Negroes tend to come from considerably larger families than do whites.

[28] The measurement of family integration is a complex thing. The expectation level is an important factor. Key differences appear to exist between Negro and white families. Almost ninety percent of the Negroes in the student sample felt closer to their mother than to their father or to both parents. Less than seventy percent of the

Again, it must be added that much of the high permissiveness that exists is traditional or due to other societal factors and is not explainable by family-responsibility–cohesion factors alone. For example, in the analysis of social class in Chapter 4, the liberal upper-class whites who were highly permissive as compared to liberals in the lower classes, gave no indication of less family responsibility. Nor is the higher Negro permissiveness at all class levels just a matter of lower family responsibility, for it is due to other factors, such as a high-permissive tradition and current social position.[29] The family-responsibility factor is a key factor in explaining why children in the same family differ in permissiveness and why parents and children in one family differ on permissiveness, but it is only one factor among many in the explanation of why the general level of permissiveness for one group of families is higher than for another. The other causes of the general group level of permissiveness—such as the basic values of the group regarding sexual pleasure and interpersonal interaction, and the social pressures the group contains—operate independently of family responsibilities. However, the family-responsibility level sometimes operates as an intervening variable. For example the growth of modern industrial society has encouraged the development of a free courtship system, which lessens parental and sibling responsibilities and may thereby reduce the general level of role integration in the family. This in turn may lead to less inculcation of adult restrictive values and thus more permissiveness. The same broad historical change may lead to increased permissiveness through other causal links, such as those that alter our basic value system regardless of family-responsibility levels. The exact way in which the family-responsibility factor fits

---

whites gave this response, and this difference holds whether the family has one or two parents. Tables 8.1 and 8.2 show that more Negroes perceive themselves as similar to their parents. Both races, however, show that those who feel equally close to both parents also are more likely to say they are happy in their family relations; those closer to their mother are moderately happy in family relations; and those closer to their father are the most likely to be unhappy in family relations. This holds for two-parent families and is not simply the result of the loss of a parent. It seems, then, that when a child becomes closer to his father, it is a possible sign of unhappy family relations. This is particularly true for female children, and perhaps this is so because closeness to the father, particularly for girls, is likely to indicate that the mother is not performing her role adequately. Following this same line of reasoning, perhaps the greater emphasis on the mother role in the Negro family explains the greater closeness to the mother and the greater likelihood of the individual's being happy with his family relations even though on a personal level he may not be happy. For some valuable and compatible findings in the area of happiness see Norman M. Bradburn and David Caplovitz, *Reports on Happiness.* Chicago: Aldine Publishing Co., 1965, especially pp. 56–57.

[29] The National Adult Sample revealed interesting political differences between Negroes and whites. From 80 to 90 percent of the Negroes said they favored Kennedy over Nixon in the 1960 election, whereas only 55 to 60 percent of the whites said this. Of those eligible to vote in the 1960 election, 20 percent of the whites and 40 percent of the Negroes did not vote. Negroes were also more certain of eventual early integration and were more satisfied with President Kennedy on the question of civil rights. These questions were asked in June 1963.

into the network of other causes of sexual permissiveness will have to be worked out empirically.[30] All that need be said here is that one important variable related to premarital sexual permissiveness seems to have been located.[31]

[30] Certainly other types of sibling order and relations can be explored beyond those commented on in Table 9.8. There is a vast literature in this general area of birth order, although there is very little regarding the effect of it on sexual permissiveness. For one recent article with a good bibliography see Glen H. Elder, Jr. and Charles E. Bowerman, "Family Structure and Child Rearing Patterns: The Effect of Family Size and Sex Composition," *American Sociological Review,* 28 (December 1963), pp. 891–905. Also see Robert Sears *et al., Patterns of Child Rearing.* New York: Harper & Row, Publishers, 1957. Those interested in probing the general literature in this area should begin with Kurt H. Wolff, ed., *The Sociology of George Simmel.* New York: The Free Press, 1950.

[31] The Goodman tests for interaction were done on this chapter, as on all chapters, and the comments take their results into account.

10

Final Analysis: Propositions, Theory, and Summation

Review of Propositions

The major reason that the rather massive amounts of data from the samples used in this study could be handled was that they tended to fall into definite patterns, even if they were not always the patterns that had been hypothesized.[1] In this final chapter the basic task is to examine the separate clusters of relationships that have emerged from the analysis of the data so far in order to see what broad, overall relations, if any, exists among them.

First let us briefly review the seven propositions that basically subsume almost all the empirical generalizations reported in this study. In each of seven substantive chapters, one proposition was developed to cover the major findings. Each of these is now reviewed in turn and each is illustrated by reference to *some* of the empirical generalizations from which it was logically derived.

PROPOSITION ONE: THE LOWER THE TRADITIONAL LEVEL OF SEXUAL PERMISSIVENESS IN A GROUP, THE GREATER THE LIKELIHOOD THAT SOCIAL FORCES WILL ALTER INDIVIDUAL LEVELS OF SEXUAL PERMISSIVENESS The fundamental evidence for this proposition is presented in Chapter 3.

[1] Some eighty thousand tables were examined over a period of several years. The number of tables is high because each relation was checked with all the different measures of the variable available. Each relation was checked using different cuts on each variable and always using race, sex, and school controls, plus many others. The fact that these many checks led to patterned results was a source of confidence.

Traditionally high-permissive groups such as Negro males were the least sensitive to social forces such as church-attendance, love affairs, and romantic love; traditionally low-permissive groups such as white females showed the greatest sensitivity to these social forces. The data in Chapter 4 on social classes are also relevant here. If it is assumed that the lower social classes have a tradition of higher sexual permissiveness, then the findings that they are less sensitive to social forces also fits Proposition One.

PROPOSITION TWO: THE STRONGER THE AMOUNT OF GENERAL LIBERALITY IN A GROUP, THE GREATER THE LIKELIHOOD THAT SOCIAL FORCES WILL MAINTAIN HIGH LEVELS OF SEXUAL PERMISSIVENESS   The bulk of the evidence for this proposition is reviewed in Chapter 4. It was found that the student sample (which was more generally liberal) showed more effect of general liberalism on premarital sexual permissiveness. Similarly, the more generally liberal upper classes showed more effect of liberalism on premarital sexual permissive levels, and they were a more sexually permissive group. In fact, all the liberal social classes were more permissive than the comparable conservative social classes (see Table 4.4). It has been generalized from this that a high degree of general liberalism (political, religious, and economic) not only creates an atmosphere where an individual will find sharp differences regarding sexual permissiveness among liberals and conservatives, but that it also creates a general receptivity to social attitudes and structures that maintain high levels of sexual permissiveness.

PROPOSITION THREE: TO THE EXTENT THAT INDIVIDUAL TIES TO THE MARITAL AND FAMILY INSTITUTIONS DIFFER, INDIVIDUALS WILL TEND TO DISPLAY A DIFFERENT TYPE OF SENSITIVITY OF PERMISSIVENESS TO SOCIAL FORCES   This propostion differs from Proposition One in that it refers to the ways that permissiveness relates to social forces but not to the strength of that relation. Basically, this proposition was supported by the checks noted in Chapter 5. These checks showed fundamental male-female differences in line with courtship-role differences. The relation of romantic love to permissiveness was significant mostly for females; the age of the individual at his first date was significant mostly for males; regular dating, steady dating, and falling in love were characteristics that were related differently with permissiveness for males and females.

PROPOSITION FOUR: THE HIGHER THE OVERALL LEVEL OF PERMISSIVENESS IN A GROUP, THE GREATER THE EXTENT OF EQUALITARIANISM WITHIN THE ABSTINENCE AND DOUBLE-STANDARD CLASSIFICATIONS   The data from Chapter 6 indicate that if a high church-attending group (low permissives) is compared with a low church-attending group (high permissives) on the basis of percent of those double-standard adherents who are orthodox, it is found that the high church-attenders have a higher percent who are orthodox double standard. Accordingly, if believers in abstinence in these two groups are compared, it is found that the high church-attenders have a higher percent who are nonequalitarian. These findings would make one believe that increases in permissiveness will promote equalitarianism. Male-female differences generally fit this proposition also, with females who are not abstinent being less equalitarian than are such males.

Perhaps the tendency reported in Chapter 2 for high-permissive groups to rank affectionless kissing and petting lower than low-permissive groups is relevant here. The emphasis on nonequalitarianism in the low-permissive groups may well promote a lower regard for the individual in kissing and petting (although perhaps not in coitus), and this may weaken opposition to affectionless kissing and petting.

PROPOSITION FIVE: DIFFERENCES IN THE POTENTIAL FOR PERMISSIVENESS IN ONE'S BASIC SET OF PARENTALLY DERIVED VALUES IS A KEY DETERMINANT OF THE NUMBER, RATE AND DIRECTION OF CHANGES IN ONE'S PREMARITAL SEXUAL STANDARDS AND BEHAVIOR   The distinguishing feature of low- and high-permissive individuals is not where they start sexually, for the findings indicated that for white college-educated females the starting point is almost always only the acceptance of kissing. Rather, the distinction is what the individual is willing to do behaviorally, for almost all sexual behavior is eventually repeated and comes to be accepted. It is assumed that an individual's basic values encourage or discourage participating in sexual behavior, and that differences in these basic values are the key distinctions between high and low permissives. The females who move upward in permissiveness most quickly are least likely to express guilt about kissing and petting behavior. The findings of Chapter 8 are relevant here, for the close similarity of perceived parental sex standards to the individual's own sex standards holds for both low- and high-permissive groups. This leads to the conclusion that high-permissive children are the offspring of high-permissive parents who instill, consciously or not, basic values conducive to high permissiveness.

Proposition Five is quite broad and subsumes part of the meaning of the first four propositions, but it differs in that it refers to parentally derived values that exist when dating begins, while the first four propositions refer to group, or contextual, characteristics and to changes that occur after dating starts. Also Proposition Five refers to a broader set of values than is covered in the first four propositions. When contextual pressures are the same (as expressed in Propositions One to Four), then the basic parentally derived values are the key determinant of sex behavior and standards. They set the initial amount of permissive "push" that can be altered by social forces.

PROPOSITION SIX: THERE IS A GENERAL TENDENCY FOR THE INDIVIDUAL TO PERCEIVE HIS PARENTS' PERMISSIVENESS AS A LOW POINT ON A PERMISSIVE CONTINUUM AND HIS PEERS' PERMISSIVENESS AS A HIGH POINT, AND TO PLACE HIMSELF CLOSER TO HIS PEERS, PARTICULARLY TO THOSE HE REGARDS AS HIS CLOSE FRIENDS   The data considered in Chapter 8 are relevant here. The findings indicated that those who perceive themselves as similar to their parents in their sexual standards are lower on permissiveness than those who do not. Those higher on permissiveness in a particular group report that they are different from their parents, thus indicating that generally parents are perceived of as being relatively low on permissiveness. On the other hand, those who perceive themselves as similar to peers or to close friends are *higher* on permissiveness than those who do not. This would indicate that peers and close friends are generally thought of as relatively high on permissiveness. The individual thus perceives himself as existing between a low-permissive parent and a high-permissive set of contemporaries. The additional finding that a higher percent of young people feel more similar to peers and to close friends than to parents supports the view that the tendency is toward the perceived viewpoint of one's contemporaries. Chapter 7 presented data showing that "parental guidance" was less likely to be the reason for older and/or more-permissive students accepting their current standards. This too is compatible with Proposition Six.

PROPOSITION SEVEN: THE GREATER THE RESPONSIBILITY FOR OTHER FAMILY MEMBERS AND/OR THE LESS THE COURTSHIP PARTICIPATION, THE GREATER THE LIKELIHOOD THAT THE INDIVIDUAL WILL BE LOW ON PERMISSIVENESS   The findings reported on in Chapters 7 and 9 are in part included here. It was found that older siblings are lower on permissiveness than younger siblings and that the only child is highest on permissiveness. Older siblings have the greatest responsibility for other siblings; the only child has no such responsibility. The findings also showed that as the number of children increase and their age increases, permissiveness of parents tends to decrease. Here again it might be said that as these events occur parental responsibility increases, and this drop in permissiveness is compatible with the proposition. In a related manner, as the individual is involved as a participant in the courtship process he is increasingly freed from parental domination; thus he has less responsibility for others and his permissiveness tends to increase.[2] The divorcée's reentry into courtship also is relevant here. Perhaps the greater sensitivity of the student sample to liberality, as reported in Chapter 4, is also due in part to the students' greater courtship involvement. Finally, it could be contended that male-female permissive differences,

[2] Perhaps the findings in Appendix D of the different ways that intensity works in the adult and student samples is related to the differential courtship participation of these two groups.

too, may in part result from the different responsibility the two sexes have in the family.[3] Proposition Three differs in that it speaks of how the different ties to the family create a different type of sensitivity to permissiveness. Proposition Seven speaks of how these ties create a lesser degree of permissiveness.

Certainly other propositions could possibly be added to or substituted for these seven. But these particular seven propositions were used because they offered the best explanation of more of the data in each of the substantive chapters than could any other proposition. Of course, they must be carefully checked out in future research. These seven propositions were not stated in formalized language, for this area is not sufficiently developed for that. It is hoped that they will be used as the base from which more formalized presentations will eventually emerge. Attempts are made throughout the book to show what each proposition implies on the group, family, and individual levels and thereby to give some dynamic processual quality to the propositions. The basic atempt at a sociocultural explanation underlies all the propositions.

A mere listing of hypothesized empirical relations and the test results is not enough.[4] If a science is to cumulate and grow there must be organized ways of unifying separate hypotheses.[5] Each proposition in this study unites a set of interrelated empirical findings. Hopefully they can be united into a theory, and it is this that will now be considered.

A Proposed Theory

At the most general level, a theory concerning sexual permissiveness would simply contend that sexual permissiveness is learned in a social setting in much the same formal and informal ways that other attitudes are learned. Accordingly, it would follow that just as religious, political, and

[3] It is believed that the connection of the female to offspring is one fundamental basis of the ancient double-standard. The responsibility for children makes it likely that society will limit the activities that are conceived as possibly interfering with such responsibility, and this often means sexual affairs after marriage or before marriage if they can lead to conception. It is true that modern contraception lessens the attachment of the female to reproduction, and the equalization of child-rearing roles may further help in this direction. But until males and females share this responsibility fully, it is doubtful whether societies will view the sexuality of the two in fully equalitarian ways. This view is elaborated later in this chapter.

[4] Short and Strodtbeck speak of "retroduction" as deliberate exposure to data to stimulate new perspectives and hypotheses. This approach is similar to that in this study in its stress on doing more than simply reporting test results. See James F. Short, Jr. and and Fred L. Strodtbeck, *Group Process and Gang Delinquency.* Chicago: University of Chicago Press, 1965, pp. 24–26.

[5] See Hans L. Zetterberg, *On Theory and Verification in Sociology.* New York: The Bedminister Press, 1965 (also see the 1954 and 1963 editions) for an excellent summary of the nature of social science theory and problems related to it.

economic attitudes vary by social groupings, so do sexual attitudes. Further, the extent to which the attitude was endorsed in a particular group would relate to other competing social and cultural factors. From a group-level perspective, shared attitudes may be referred to as group norms and sexual norms would be expected to be of the same general character as other substantive norms.

Within this broad sociological framework the seven propositions fit as specific statements concerning the nature of premarital sexual permissiveness as viewed from a sociological standpoint.

The meaning of these propositions may be elaborated as follows. The young person gains his basic set of values from his parents, his friends, and from the basic type of social groupings he is exposed to as he matures. As dating begins he comes increasingly under the influence of the more permissive peer values that dominate the courtship area. How quickly he responds to these permissive pressures depends on their strength as well as the type of basic values brought to the situation from his parental upbringing. These values in turn reflect his position in his own family, his race, sex, social class, city size, region, religious attitudes, level of general liberalism, and the traditional level of sexual permissiveness, among other factors. The biological sex drive acts to promote sexuality during this period. For the majority of individuals the courtship period witnesses an increase in permissiveness and equalitarianism, and a breakthrough of the adult-induced guilt feelings. Following marriage the individual comes more under the influence of the adult-run family institution and its relatively low premarital permissive values. Again, it would be predicted that most individuals would then change to a lower permissive level, and this too would be affected by such social factors as those just noted.

There are two basic institutions, then, that are of key importance for the development of premarital sexual attitudes and behavior—courtship and the family.[6] The fundamental orientation of the participant-run court-

---

[6] The term *institution* is used to mean an integrated set of customs that focus about one or more key functions (see Kingsley Davis, *Human Society*. New York: Crowell-Collier and Macmillan, 1950, p. 71). *Courtship customs* focus about the key function of mate selection. It is true that some of the more casual dating lacks this as an end in view, but it is functionally part of such a process, for such dating does seem to develop into more serious forms (see Ira L. Reiss, "Social Class and Campus Dating," *Social Problems*, 14 (Fall 1965), pp. 193–205). In a participant-run system, heterosexual interaction cumulates and culminates in mate selection, for marriage is the heart of courtship. The usual requirement is that those who mate be from different primary kinship groups. The *marital institution* involves the key function of legitimizing parenthood. This definition of marriage follows a long tradition from Malinowski to Davis and Gough. Finally, *family institution* is defined as a small kinship-structured group with the key function of the nurturant socialization of the newborn. *Kinship structure* refers to the special ties between individuals that imply real or fictive descent notions and that involves strong feelings of rights and duties toward each other. *Nurturant socialization* refers to the giving of emotional response and care to the newborn during the early part of his life. For a full discussion of these definitions see Ira L. Reiss, "The Universality of the Family: A Conceptual Analysis," *Journal of Marriage and the Family*, 26 (November 1965), pp. 443–453. Both the courtship

ship institution is one of relatively high premarital sexual permissiveness. In a related manner the orientation of the adult-run family institution is one of relatively low premarital sexual permissiveness. Other social institutions have their effects primarily through these two institutions. As the individual matures in American society the relative strength of influence of these two institutions varies in accord with his role positions, and his premarital sexual attitudes vary accordingly. The female appears to break away slower and in more gradual stages than the male.[7] The participation in the courtship institution leads to the breakthrough of the adult taboos on premarital sex. The later participation in the marital and family institution leads to at least a partial return to these adult taboos on premarital sexuality. The size of the "permissive gap" between the family and courtship institutions seems to be fairly similar for high- and low-permissive groups. Chapter 8 showed that there was no less of a perceived similarity to parents in high-permissive groups.

The basic theory may be stated somewhat more formally as follows: The courtship and family institutions are the two key, direct determinants of the norms regarding premarital sexual permissiveness. The sexual norms of the courtship institution will reflect the basic values of the family institution relevant to sexuality.[8] However, when participant-run, the courtship institution tends to normatively differentiate from the family institution and to react more to the permissive pressures of the courtship role and therefore to have relatively high permissive premarital norms. The biological sex drive pressures the individual toward more permissiveness when outside controls are weak. Due to the female's closer ties to the family institution, such differentiation tends to be different and less complete for her than for the male. The family institution, with its emphasis on the role of parental responsibility, tends to react less favorably to permissive courtship pressures, and thus the basic values inculcated by the family do help limit eventual permissiveness. Societal forces affect individual permissiveness in a group, both through pressures from other courtship and family groups with different permissive norms and through pressures of other institutions,

---

and marital institutions are "transitional institutions" in that they are transitions to the family institution. They are permanent on a societal basis but function on an individual basis as temporary steps to the family.

[7] The greater tendency for males to differentiate from the parental family was shown in Charles W. Hobart, "Emancipation from Parents and Courtship in Adolescents," *Pacific Sociological Review*, 1 (Spring 1958), pp. 25–29. A cross-cultural test of role differentiation of the sexes may be found in Herbert Barry *et al.*, "A Cross Cultural Survey of Some Sex Differences in Socialization," *Journal of Abnormal and Social Psychology*, 55 (April 1957), pp. 327–332. Barry reports that although sex-role differences are universal they vary with type of economy and family.

[8] George P. Murdock, *Social Structure*. New York: Crowell-Collier and Macmillan, 1949. Murdock developed the idea that by examining a family system one can predict the corresponding type of courtship system, since the two are functionally related. This notion is incorporated in the second sentence of the proposed theory. An illustration might be that from the stress on love in marriage and in the American family, the importance of love in courtship in America could be predicted.

tending to encourage or discourage the autonomy of the participant-run courtship system and the independence of thought of the young people themselves. In addition, the basic norms of these other institutions help define the range of acceptable sexuality and thereby help shape the ways in which sexual permissiveness will express itself when courtship autonomy is high. The basic tendency in a participant-run system is for the participant, due to his role position, to increase his permissiveness during courtship and to somewhat reverse his views after marriage and parenthood.

This theoretical conception can be briefly summarized, provided that the elaborate meanings of such a simplified statement be kept in mind: THE DEGREE OF ACCEPTABLE PREMARITAL SEXUAL PERMISSIVENESS IN A COURT-SHIP GROUP VARIES DIRECTLY WITH THE DEGREE OF AUTONOMY OF THE COURTSHIP GROUP AND WITH THE DEGREE OF ACCEPTABLE PREMARITAL SEXUAL PERMISSIVENESS IN THE SOCIAL AND CULTURAL SETTING OUTSIDE THE GROUP.

The question may be raised here as to why the courtship system should tend toward greater permissiveness than that permitted by adults in the family and in other institutions. Very simply put, the answer is that there is a biological sexual drive operating to promote sexual activity, and that within a given type of sociocultural setting the more autonomy the courtship system has the greater the likelihood that drive will gain expression. In addition, youth culture has other characteristics promoting permissiveness, such as adventurousness and general liberality. In American culture many values promote sexuality as well as inhibit it. The family institution is that part of the sociocultural system that most directly transmits the influence of that system to the young person. Even within the relatively autonomous American courtship system there are many limitations that young people themselves, particularly females, place upon their sexual behavior and attitudes. Thus, autonomy, while promoting permissiveness, need not promote promiscuity.

Of equal interest is the question of the adults' greater conservatism, and this can be simply answered as being due to the feeling of responsibility they have for the legitimacy of offspring born to their children. This is virtually a universal responsibility of adults. Furthermore, married adults are not exposed to the sexual constraints and temptations of the unmarried. Thus, when autonomous adolescent courtship is allowed in a society, it is to be expected that the adults will be relatively low on permissiveness and the youngsters, due to sexual interests, relatively high on permissiveness. This is precisely the case in America today. It may be concluded that to the extent that the courtship institution has high autonomy, the adult norms will not be so effective in controlling permissiveness.

Thus, it is not enough just to know the adult norms, one must also know the extent to which courtship autonomy promotes a liberal interpretation of these adult norms. Other peer groups also comprise the outside culture and can affect the permissive level of a particular group of individuals. Sex and race and other variables associated with sexual attitudes are thus fundamentally explainable in terms of the basic sociocultural setting and the degree of courtship autonomy. The seven propositions help spell out the workings of this theory. But very simply put, the theory states that where the sociocultural setting is the same, differences in courtship autonomy will lead to differences in courtship permissiveness. Also, where the courtship autonomy is the same, differences in the sociocultural setting will lead to differences in courtship permissiveness. This theory should apply to all cultures with adolescent courtship systems, and so the theory has cross-cultural relevance. For the full meaning of the theory one should not rely on the simplified statement but rather should check the more elaborate statements that precede it. In this way the theory will not be oversimplified.

Integration of Propositions and Theory ✓

There should be a logical connection between the propositions and the theory such that the propositions are deducible from the theory and/or that the theory should logically relate the propositions to one another. Moreover, the certainty of such relationships depends on the precision and completeness of the theory and on the degree to which the full implications of the theory and propositions have been worked out. Given the very early stages of research work in the sociology of premarital sexual permissiveness, it is too much to expect a fully developed theory with all levels of interrelation spelled out, but it is not too much to expect a reasonably clear theory that basically tends to show some logical connections with all seven of the propositions. This should afford a basic theory for future researchers to test. Some of the interrelations of each proposition with the theory will be dealt with briefly.

PROPOSITION ONE   The relation of Proposition One to the proposed theory is that it could be deduced that given a highly permissive courtship system, those who were traditionally low on permissiveness would be under the greatest pressures from the courtship system to change.[9] If each traditional level of permissiveness were isolated from all others, this might not be the case. But the interaction of different levels means the exposure to more permissive viewpoints.[10] Without certain structural constraints the permissive

---

[9] In reality, each courtship level is tied to a similar adult level, so that a low-permissive set of youngsters will have a low-permissive set of parents. However, the general courtship level would be above that of such a low-permissive group, whereas the general permissive level of the family would be much closer to such a low-permissive group. Also, it should be remembered that males are a high-permissive group *within every level.*

[10] Biological factors are, of course, also involved. They tend to strengthen the permissive pressures. However, the biology of an individual is heavily colored and

pressure will tend to prevail, for it is supported by the sexual and other interests of the young people.

PROPOSITION TWO   A generally liberal group, by the definitions used in Chapter 4, is one that stresses individual rights and autonomy and that underplays the importance of conformity and tradition. It would follow from the proposed theory that such an orientation would favor the autonomy of the courtship institution, and accordingly, in a generally liberal setting, a greater likelihood of maintaining high permissiveness due to the enhanced "pull" of this institution would be witnessed. This basically is the logical connection of Proposition Two to the proposed theory.[11]

PROPOSITION THREE   The fact that females are not as easily freed from family norms leads logically to this proposition.[12] The theory also states that the values of the family institution would affect courtship and thus it would be expected that the permissive pressures operate differently due to the different role the female performs in the family.

PROPOSITION FOUR   The proposed theory states that males customarily move away from restrictive norms more easily than females. Thus, it follows that female permissiveness must be increased if equalitarianism is to be achieved.[13] Such increased female permissiveness is most likely in a high-permissive group, and thus such a group should display more equalitarianism.

PROPOSITION FIVE   Given the basic theoretical position of the courtship-family competition, it would follow that the basic values of the family are the starting point of an individual's permissiveness as he enters the court-

---

shaped by his sociocultural environment in the area of sex, and thus pure biological factors do not help to explain why one subcultural group is much more permissive than another.

[11] It should be noted that the forces discussed in Proposition One and Two work in opposite directions. A low-permissive tradition *encourages* change and low general liberalism *discourages* change. Thus, a conservative group with a low-permissive tradition would have the conservatism working *against* change and the low-permissive tradition working *for* change. Exactly how to measure the strength of each force and predict which would prevail is an important and complicated area for research.

[12] For an interesting set of supporting data see Hobart, "Emancipation from Parents."

[13] The double standard is related in part to male power in a society and is a common compromise between the desire for legitimate offspring and for sexual pleasure. For some comments on the role of female power in sexuality see James Coleman, "Female Status and Premarital Sexual Codes," *American Journal of Sociology,* 72 (September 1966), p. 217, and Ira L. Reiss, "Some Comments on Premarital Sexual Permissiveness," *The American Journal of Sociology,* 72 (March 1967), pp. 558–559. For additional comments on the relation of equalitarianism to permissiveness see fn. 10 in Chapter 6.

ship institution. Further support comes from the premise that other institutions largely transmit their courtship values through the family system.

PROPOSITION SIX   This relates to a major part of the theory, in that it sets up the opposition of the family and courtship institution *as being perceived* and states the premarital tendency for the courtship institution to gain ground over the family institution. Given the theory, it would follow that the actors in a social system would see the system as such and would show the predicted tendencies.

PROPOSITION SEVEN   It follows from the theory that any role encouraging the inculcation of adult or parental type values would tend to encourage relatively low permissiveness. In effect, Proposition Seven states that this is so for roles in the family among siblings, parents, and children. Roles that tie one to the family would tend to reduce one's courtship autonomy and thereby also reduce one's permissiveness.

There is a general coherence and unity of these propositions with the proposed theory. However, the logical connections are surely not fully and perfectly worked out. It remains for other researchers to work out the interrelations, to deduce other propositions and to relate this theory to other theories at other levels.[14] Post-factum theorizing is essential to the growth of any science, but it is equally important that it be carefully tested and revised in light of future work and later theories. The key risk of such theorizing is of being unaware of the need for careful testing and revision to see if the plausible is also empirically supportable in other direct tests. The theory is developed for American society. It is an empirical question whether it applies to all courtship systems. Three major samples were used to develop the ideas, and not all propositions could be tested in all samples. So here too additional testing is surely called for.

There are causal implications in this set of propositions and in this theory. Two centuries ago David Hume made it clear that causality can be used only as a model for our thinking and not as something that can be fully established empirically. But to further the understanding of human society,[15] relationships must be examined and those that are "spurious" weeded out in order to find those that seem to be "causal" or "more important" or "more invariant."

The reader certainly is aware that the direction of causality is difficult to establish in a cross-sectional study such as this. Here too, certain directionality has been assumed that need not have been assumed. And surely

[14] Joseph Berger *et al.*, *Sociological Theories in Progress*. New York: Houghton Mifflin Co., 1966. This book contains some attempts to encourage axiomatic-type theories and the cumulative testing of such theories.

[15] For an elaboration of this view see Hubert M. Blalock, Jr., *Causal Inferences in Nonexperimental Research*. Chapel Hill: University of North Carolina Press, 1964.

there are feedback interactions between many of the variables, which would tend to make them operate as both cause and effect. As our knowledge becomes more precise, we can delve into these refinements more carefully. What seems to be the key "explanations" for the phenomena studied in the three basic samples of this study have been presented here. The evidence and reasons have also been presented. At the present theoretical stage of development it is important also to state the conditions under which a relationship holds. Future research will elaborate upon the explanation and, hopefully, will answer many of the important questions that cannot be finally dealt with at this point.[16] It is the search for such explanation that is at the heart of the search for theory.[17]

Some Implications of the Theory and Its Propositions

In a society where parents had fuller control over the courtship process of mate selection there would be less likelihood of divergence between the norms and behaviors sought by participants in these two institutions than there is in America. In such a case, if the parents were low on sexual permissiveness, they might chaperon the couples, encourage early marriage, segregate the sexes, or in other ways try to implement their low-permissive norms. If the parents were high on premarital sexual permissiveness, then more freedom generally would be given, except where it might lead to marriages that were undesired.[18] But in either case the parents' monopoly of power in these two institutions would likely lead to less change in the individual's attitudes about premarital sex after he had married and had children.

In a society such as America's the courtship and family institutions have differentiated, and the locus of power in the courtship system has shifted

[16] Michael Schofield, *The Sexual Behavior of Young People*. Boston: Little, Brown & Co., 1965. Schofield reports that the two key characteristics of his high-permissive group were high ethnocentrism and low restrictiveness. Basically these factors imply a high value on the peer group and a low value on parental or other restraints. Such findings are quite compatible with the theory just presented. F. Ivan Nye presents evidence on the relation of parental and other controls on delinquency in general. See his *Family Relationships and Delinquent Behavior*. New York: John Wiley & Sons, 1958.

[17] Cross-cultural and historical tests of this theory would indeed be valuable.

[18] William J. Goode, "The Theoretical Importance of Love," *American Sociological Review*, 24 (February 1959), pp. 38–47. Goode points out the ways in which love is controlled to maintain the existing status system. Goode does not deal with sex, but even though the societal fit of sex is different, it is often controlled the same way. When sex is allowed in double-standard fashion, it is deliberately aimed at achieving pleasure and avoiding permanent entanglements. Equalitarian sex is much more of a challenge to the status system, for it can lead to love more easily, and this can eventuate in marriage. Perhaps it is the fear of this that makes even permissive cultures, like Samoa, forbid premarital coitus to female royalty.

from the parents to the participants themselves. For this reason the American courtship institution has been referred to as a participant-run system, unlike the older parent-run systems that the European ancestors of Americans knew rather well. Of course, the fact that the parents *directly* interfere in mate-choices much less than they formerly did does not necessarily mean that they have also lost their *indirect* influence over this process. Studies of dating patterns clearly show that homogamy operates on sociocultural factors such as class, religion, education, and so on.[19] Thus, individuals often end up with marriages that are little different from what their parents would have arranged for them.

The area of sexual norms appears on the surface to be somewhat different, for here the "participants" have evolved a set of sexual codes that often clash with those their parents would have them accept. Witness the fact that in the adult sample the percentage who accepted abstinence as a premarital sexual standard was twice what it was for the student sample (see Chapter 2, Tables 2.5 and 2.7). The student group seems much more evenly divided among the four major premarital sexual standards than is the adult group. One reason for this clash on premarital sexual norms has been written into the theory of this study—namely, the role position of the participant encourages sexual freedom, whereas the role position of the adult parent does virtually the opposite. The premarital temptation level is present and high for the participant; it is nonexistent for the married parent. A second reason, also written into the theory may be worth noting—namely that the parents of today were the participants of yesterday. This means that it is likely that they were much more permissive during their own courtship period, and that in turn raises the possibility that their basic values are conducive to higher permissiveness than their parental-role position now specifies. Such a formerly permissive parent may well do a poor job of inculcating values that would promote low permissiveness. This may be one reason why the student sample felt close to their parents' standards even though the students were much more permissive. The courtship institution, though permanent on a societal basis, is *transitional* on an individual basis, and past membership in the courtship institution may limit the ability of the individual fundamentally to change his value position after entering the family institution. The actual basic values of the individual need not change greatly from courtship to marriage, but the role demands alter radically and highlight different aspects of his value system.

However, sight should not be lost of the strong relation of the family to premarital sex norms which can be seen in many different ways. The stress on love in the family is reflected in the type of premarital sex norms in American society, and thus the parents' indirect control is evident here also.[20] The type of sexuality most likely to lead to marriage—such as that involving engaged couples—is the type least socially condemned. The degree of male dominance in the family institution is reflected in the degree of his dominance in the dating system. Historically, as sexual satisfaction of the woman in marriage increased in importance so did the emphasis on sexual satisfaction in courtship. The increased marital-love orientation and interest of males is testified by the large reduction in age at the time of marriage and the large increase in the percent who marry. This also is reflected in the increased male premarital-love orientation. The role flexibility in marriage, wherein males will help out with housework and wives work outside the home, may also be reflected in the greater flexibility in courtship norms. An interesting problem, but one beyond the scope of this work, is to decide to what extent the changes in courtship helped produce the changes in the family institution and to what extent it was the other way around. Such changes as these, of course, also reflect the broader sociocultural context of both the family and courtship institutions.

The key societal function of marriage is to legitimize parenthood, not to legitimize sexuality. Sexual expression is common outside of marriage in the preliterate world.[21] However, because marriage legitimizes parenthood, premarital relations that eventuate in a conception without the probability of marriage are almost universally condemned. Thus, most societies are more tolerant of premarital intercourse between engaged couples, for they are likely to marry if pregnancy results. Also, prostitution gains some acceptance because it does not threaten to promote premarital pregnancy. Similarly, those careful couples who use contraceptives are less condemned than the careless ones.

Sexuality before marriage is not central to the key societal function of the marital institution (parenthood) if it is safely performed. Still, there is little reason to expect support for premarital sex from those interested in the marital institution, since it is not central to that institution except in its encouragement of courtship, which may eventuate in marriage. Premarital relations is in part a result of the American type of participant-run court-

---

[20] Murdock. See also the emphasis placed on the family as a means of understanding courtship norms by Kingsley Davis, "Sexual Behavior," *Contemporary Social Problems,* eds. Robert K. Merton and Robert A. Nisbet. New York: Harcourt, Brace & Co., 1966, pp. 322–372.

[21] R. A. LeVine has proposed that sexual changes are due to structural limits and inhibitions. Broadly conceived, this would be what is called the socioeconomic context and would be compatible with the theory presented here if the autonomy of the courtship system were signaled out more as an independent variable. He speaks of lack of structural barriers rather than of presence of courtship autonomy. See his "Gusii Sex Offenses: A Study in Social Control," *American Anthropologist,* 61 (December 1959), pp. 965–990. In a sense the "illegitimate opportunities" thesis of Richard A. Cloward and Lloyd E. Ohlin fits with the autonomy and permissiveness relation being proposed here. See *Delinquency and Opportunity.* New York: The Free Press, 1960.

ship system, and in other societies it also relates closely to the mate-finding function of the courtship institution. But since it has the potential of an unwanted pregnancy, it has the potential of upsetting those in the marital and family institutions who support the notions of legitimacy these institutions confer.[22] Thus, some conflict between the low permissiveness of married people and the high permissiveness of single people who are dating seems inevitable. The people in the courtship institution have less vested interest in societal maintenance. In addition, the courtship institution developed a high degree of functional autonomy.[23]

The high permissiveness of youngsters today is an unintended consequence of parental approval of the participant-run courtship system. Since parents still approve of this system there is little they can do about its permissive consequences. Of course, in actuality there is more than one courtship system and more than one peer group or youth culture. But with few exceptions the peer groups are more permissive than the parental groups (see tables in Chapter 2). The conflict between the family and the courtship systems illustrates the ways in which "deviant" sexual behavior (coital behavior) may be promoted by the very people who define it as deviant. Furthermore, it points up how an institution can promote such deviant behavior in an organized fashion among millions of young people. However, it has already been stressed that the sexual standards of the young are still highly integrated with the marital and family values of their parents. The most popular youth standards stress the connection of affection with sexuality. The deviancy of the young is thus one of degree, not of kind.[24]

The seven propositions of this study would lead to the belief that the traditionally low groups would be most sensitive to the permissive pressure resulting from the differentiation of the courtship institution from the family institution. To be more specific, white females, and particularly middle- and upper middle-class white females who come from the new middle-classes, have shown the greatest change in this century. The relation of the family to the stratification system is an important one that needs much

---

[22] It is interesting to note that as consequences like VD and pregnancy come under control parental worries often shift in the direction of possible psychological harm in sexual relations. It seems that parents responsible for sexually mature offspring are in an anxiety-promoting situation. Parental conservatism regarding sex may well be due to the lesser tensions parents feel if they believe their youngsters are not taking risks of any kind. An interesting analogy could be worked up with smoking and lung cancer. Even those parents who smoke probably prefer their offspring not to smoke.

[23] Alvin W. Gouldner, "Reciprocity and Autonomy in Functional Theory," *Symposium in Sociological Theory,* Llewellyn Gross, ed. New York: Harper & Row, Publishers, 1959, pp. 241–279. Gouldner utilizes the concept of functional autonomy to mean the degree to which a part can survive separation from the system.

[24] In line with this basic thesis Davis would argue that prostitution is condemned because such sex has little tie with the family except as a safety valve for unhappy husbands. The most highly valued sex ties most closely into the family, for example, sex among engaged couples. Davis overlooked the role of autonomy of courtship in his conception of sexuality, but he did stress, as is done here, the key role of the family and, by implication, of the entire sociocultural context.

further analysis. As the current courtship system emerged, the middle-class female group had to learn to cope with the demands of a participant-run courtship system more so than did the males. Males in the Western world had always been given greater freedom; their major change was an adjustment to the fact that the females they were drinking with at the bar and to whom they were offering a cigarette were not prostitutes or "easy" girls from the lower classes but rather girls from their own social level who might even be virgins. The female's change, then, was more radical, being an introduction to a free dating system, whereas the male's adjustment required recognition of a new type of dating partner—a dating partner with a much higher likelihood of ultimately being his mate.[25] However, the female still is more closely tied to the family normatively, and equality has been only partially achieved.

The "institutional gap" between the courtship and family institutions seems to have been at its height in the 1920s, for the participant-run system was then well on its way and yet the parental generation had been raised under a quite different system. The clash in more recent years should be considerably less, for there have been smaller changes, and the parents who were courting in the late 1940s were probably quite similar to their children courting in the late 1960s. The major studies show little evidence of behavior changes in coital rates, but they do show changes in petting rates. Basic changes in the last forty or fifty years have more likely been in the area of attitudes than in behavior.[26] Americans are more open in their discussion of sex, and permissiveness is more respectable today.[27]

It should be borne in mind here that recent historical studies indicate that the nineteenth-century courtship system was not as radically different from that of the twentieth century as one might think. Visitors to America in the nineteenth century were amazed at the degree of free mate choice, the high degree of equalitarianism, and the prevalence of the nuclear family.[28] The high rates of immigration, the frontier, and the large number of young immigrants all are factors here. Thus, change may have been more gradual than was thought.

[25] Despite the popular press, the research evidence indicates that males today are much "tamer" and more discriminate than their fathers or grandfathers. For example, Kinsey *et al.* report the incidence of intercourse with prostitutes was cut in half in his younger generation of males. See *Sexual Behavior in the Human Male*. Philadelphia: W. B. Saunders Co., 1948, pp. 410, 603.

[26] For a full summary and analysis of the evidence see Ira L. Reiss, "The Sexual Renaissance: A Summary and Analysis," *Journal of Social Issues*, 22 (April 1966), pp. 123–137. See also the other articles in this special issue of *Journal of Social Issues* entitled "The Sexual Renaissance in America." Also, Ira L. Reiss, *Premarital Sexual Standards in America*. New York: The Free Press, 1960, chap. 10.

[27] Jean Butman's study indicates that those nonvirgins who are least informed about contraception are most likely to become premaritally pregnant.

[28] Frank F. Furstenberg, Jr., "Industrialization and the American Family: A Look Backward," *American Sociological Review*, 31 (June 1966), pp. 326–337, and Daniel R. Miller and Guy E. Swanson, *The Changing American Parent*. New York: John Wiley & Sons, 1958, chap. 1.

Unless the family institution increases its permissiveness, the institutional gap may well widen soon, for there are signs of a likely increase in courtship permissiveness on the behavioral level and perhaps also on the attitudinal level.[29] Even under a stable set of sexual norms the courtship and family institutions would have disagreements in viewpoint due to their radically different role perspectives on the courtship process. The supervisor and the supervised probably never see eye to eye perfectly on such a personal issue.[30]

The newer sexual codes reflect the new courtship context. In place of the ancient double standard and abstinence classifications, the permissiveness-with-affection standard is increasingly found. Even within the double standard and abstinence classifications, the data show that the common thing is to choose the more permissive subtypes, which are petting with affection and the transitional double standard (see Tables 2.5, 2.6 and 2.7). Equalitarianism is more likely to be a factor today, together with much greater emphasis on affection, rather than the older male emphasis on pleasure. The student high permissives studied were most often permissiveness-with-affection adherents, secondarily transitional-double-standard adherents, and least often permissiveness-without-affection. It is well to keep in mind that from the point of view of "operational norms," the older society was double standard (orthodox) and only formally abstinent. The societal choice today is actually between that older system and a newer, more equalitarian, and more permissive system. An individual may choose abstinence as his standard, but he must recognize the fact that for two thousand years the Western world has failed to bring up the majority of even one generation of males in behavioral conformity to this code. In addition, it should be noted that the double standard is rooted in part in the role differentiation within the family. Unless the male-female roles in the family become identical it is likely that male and female sexuality will continue to differ. The realistic choice today is of the degree of equalitarianism the individual prefers rather than of full equalitarianism or of full double standard. The change in sexual standards during the last century has not been a sexual revolution, but rather, a gradual evolvement of a more equalitarian and more participant-run system, the basic parts of which were present a hundred years ago.

The new permissiveness in America is not a sign of increased anomie.[31]

---

[29] The sharpness of the parent-youth conflict has been questioned by several authors: David C. Epperson, "A Reassessment of Indices of Parental Influence in 'The Adolescent Society,' " *American Sociological Review,* 29 (February 1964), pp. 93–96; Frederick Elkin and William H. Westley, "The Myth of Adolescent Culture," *American Sociological Review,* 20 (December 1955), pp. 680–684. See also the author's "Sexual Codes in Teen-Age Culture," *The Annals,* 338 (November 1961), pp. 53–62.

[30] It is interesting to pursue this generalization and see how well it would apply to social classes, political groups, labor and management.

[31] Marshall B. Clinard, ed., *Anomie and Deviant Behavior.* New York: The Free Press, 1964. The classic essay by Merton and many other key ideas are examined in this book. Good references to other studies are given.

Merton's paradigm might possibly have been applicable in the 1920s, and the inability to obtain the cultural goals of "purity" and virginity at marriage by the existing means of the new courtship system may well have led to anomic reactions. The reactions included innovations such as "technical virginity," ritualism by those who became frigid spinsters, retreatism for those who withdrew, and rebellion for those who substituted new goals and means. The basic outcome was the eventual development of new subtypes and new sex codes, which by the 1960s have come to be accepted as a part of the courtship system by the participants even if not by all of their parents.

Surely there is today a type of high permissiveness founded on anomie, but there was little evidence of that in this study. What checks were done showed only a highly qualified general relation between personal happiness, family happiness, or social class and level of permissiveness.[32] The theory posited in this study leads to the conclusion that in a participant-run courtship system the high-permissive groups are those with social characteristics such as urbanism, low church-attendance, tradition of high sexual permissiveness and general liberality—all of which tend to strengthen the autonomy of the courtship institution and promote more-permissive adult values. Thus, a high-permissive level in a group is no more a sign of anomie than is a high percent of Democrats or Catholics. Those who argue that the high permissiveness of some lower-class groups results from the disorganized atmosphere of poverty must answer the question of why the same socioeconomic level often produces rigid conformists and low sexual permissives,[33] and why upper-class groups also may be highly permissive.

There is ample evidence that premarital permissiveness leads to consequences that are defined as social problems and to behavior that is defined as deviant. But that is different from saying it is produced by anomic conditions. Further, the nature of such consequences is often exaggerated, particularly when it refers to teen-age rates of venereal disease or to unwed motherhood.[34] Basically the high-permissive courtship groups lead to mar-

---

[32] In the student sample, some positive relation to family happiness was found by degree of permissiveness. Measures of personal satisfaction showed no strong relation. In the adult sample, for single white males and females there was some tendency for those who were personally unhappy to be high on permissiveness. This was only a small proportion of the total group of high permissives, however. These are all indirect measures, and their understanding will require further testing. What little research has been done on personality types gives slight support for a relation of personality integration and abstinence. See fn. 25 and 28, Chap. 9. The discussion in Chapter 9 on one-parent families and permissiveness may also be relevant here.

[33] Clinard, p. 55, raises this same question.

[34] The actual rate of syphilis has stayed about the same in the last ten years, but the proportion of this that involves infectious cases has risen considerably. Instead of reporting this fact, many simply report that infectious syphilis is rapidly increasing and see this as cause for alarm. It may well be that this sort of increase is a sign of better reporting of early cases and therefore not a cause for alarm but for celebration for those who oppose syphilis. The total syphilis rate was 60 per 100,000 in 1965 and was actually higher in 1955, when it was 76. However, the infectious rate was 12 in 1965 and only 4 in 1955. See Table 1, p. 20, in: American Social Health Associa-

riage just as do the low-permissive courtship groups; thus, though some may think of them as deviant, they are a functional part of the mate-selection process in a participant-run system. The clearest example of this is the fact that males are a high-permissive group compared to females, and yet they are not necessarily more anomic or deviant, and of course they marry just as often.

There is a type of more contraceptive-minded and affection-oriented permissiveness that has been developing among the new middle-classes, particularly within the professional occupational groups (see Chapter 4). Lenski gives some evidence of this new class system by noting the higher value placed on intellectual autonomy over obedience in the new upper middle class.[35] It is this more "respectable" permissiveness that is visible in many of the findings of this study. This is the type of permissiveness that is common today, and although it may well be viewed by parental groups as deviant behavior, it is not as often viewed as such by the youngsters themselves and is surely not an anomic reaction. Rather, as was previously stated, it may be contended that it is simply a result of the fact that currently in American society the courtship institution is highly autonomous, and as such the forces that promote permissiveness can have greater effects because the parental blockage is weak.

As has been previously noted, the family and its values have a profound influence on premarital sexual norms in all cultures. What of other social institutions and societal forces outside of the courtship and the family institutions? It should be clear from the findings and discussions in this study that these other institutions affect permissiveness directly and through the courtship and family institutions. Movies, books, and television have their impact by altering family or courtship customs, although it is known that they are mitigated by self-selection processes.[36] The political institution and the economic institution enter in with legislation that may declare birth control legal or that may promote contraceptive pills. But here too the

---

tion, *Today's VD Control Problem*. New York: February, 1966. Teen-age syphilis is stressed, but teen-agers account for only about 20 percent of the total syphilis reported. Teen-age unwed motherhood is also played up, but teen-agers make up only 40 percent of the unwed mothers while comprising 68 percent of all single females over fourteen years. See Clark Vincent, "Teen-age Unwed Mothers in American Society," *Journal of Social Issues*, 22 (April 1966), pp. 22–33. The illegitimacy rates for teen-age females have hardly shown any change from 1955 to 1965, whereas the rates for girls twenty-five and over have increased considerably. In 1964 the teen-age rate was 16.5 and the rate for twenty-five to twenty-nine years old was 50.1. See Department of Health, Education and Welfare, *Monthly Vital Statistics Reports Supplement*, 15, 3, June 14, 1966.

[35] Gerhard Lenski, *The Religious Factor*. New York: Doubleday & Co., 1961, p. 200. The emphasis on autonomy in the new middle class also may well promote courtship autonomy and thereby sexual permissiveness.

[36] Joseph Klapper, *The Effects of Mass Communication*. New York: The Free Press, 1960.

youngsters must be receptive and the self-selective factor is operative.[37] Religion was found in this study to be a key factor, although one wonders if it is religion per se or the conservative style of life the high church-attenders represent. In general these other forces affect permissive levels to the degree that they support the autonomous courtship system or put forth adult norms of permissiveness. This is best brought out in Proposition Two, which asserts that general liberalism regarding religion, politics, and economics promotes a high level of permissiveness.[38]

The entire social structure has its greatest impact on sexual norms in the sense that the basic values of an individual comes from the type of social system in which he grows up. Several of the propositions bear on this point. Values relating to freedom, pleasure, affection, autonomy, responsibility, and so forth are all relevant to the choice of a sexual code during the courtship period. The type of courtship system any one group has, and its basic values, generally reflect the overall social setting of that group.

Although the theory proposed in this study is addressed directly to premarital sexuality, it surely has relevance to marital, postmarital, and extramarital sexuality. Since the courtship, marital, and family institutions are functionally interdependent, what affects one should affect the other and should also reflect earlier feedback from the other institutions. For example, the importance of premarital affection is reflected in marital and family relations and in turn reinforces that importance. Equalitarianism within courtship both affects and reflects equalitarianism within marriage. Thus, the kind of social forces that affect premarital sexuality should have relevance for marital sexuality, and the propositions and the theory that explain the way such social forces operate should also be revelant. However, it will take considerable research to test empirically whether this plausible position is also a true position, and if so, to what extent.

In conclusion, it should be noted that the family, marital, and courtship institutions should *not* be treated as purely dependent variables of the social system. It has been clearly pointed out by many in recent years that the nuclear family, which fits so well with industrialism, may well have *preceded* industrialism in American rather than having been produced by industrialism.[39] Given the frontier and lack of traditions in America, the nuclear

[37] Ira L. Reiss, "Contraceptive Information and Sexual Morality," *Journal of Sex Research,* 2 (April 1966), pp. 51–57.

[38] A check of the "civil rights" questions used on the national sample (see Appendix C) showed that the relation between being high on civil rights and being high on sexual permissiveness, for whites was weak and not significant. The Negroes showed a much stronger and significant relation here. This was one of the few instances in which this occurred. The Negro relation was particularly strong for questions 10 and 13 in Appendix C. The way the respondent voted in the 1960 Kennedy-Nixon election was also checked and no significant relation to permissiveness was found for any race-sex grouping.

[39] For a recent article with good references see Frank F. Furstenberg, Jr. "Industrialization and the American Family."

family was a predictable phenomenon from the earliest settlements. Immigration waves were often composed of single individuals and young married couples rather than of three-generation families. Perhaps this historical setting led to the equalitarianism and autonomy of the nuclear family, and it in turn led to the industrialization and urbanization of America. In any case the evidence is sufficient to make any researcher approach the family, courtship, and marital institutions as both potential cause and effect in the social system in America.

Although premarital sexual permissiveness was treated in this study as the dependent variable, it should be remembered that it was so treated to simplify the research design; for premarital-sexual permissiveness also operates as a cause, as almost any important variable in a functionally integrated social system would. It is up to future researchers to spell out these interrelations more precisely.

Final Summary and Conclusions

At the beginning of this study the hesitancy of sociologists in the past to do legitimate research in the area of sex was commented upon. To many even today the question arises as to the value of this research area to sociology. The relevance of the study of premarital sexual permissiveness to institutional analysis, attitude formation, deviant behavior, primary group interaction, contextual effects, socialization, stratification, urbanization, cognative dissonance, reference-group behavior, social change, family-size theory, social control, and many other areas of sociological concern should by now be clear. The area of sexual permissiveness reflects in a very revealing way the nature of human society. It reveals man in a situation involving a culturally shaped biological drive that relates vitally to many of his human relationships. *In order to understand human sexual relationships we must understand in some sense how social order and human society itself is possible.* Indeed if the question of how society takes large groups of people who are relatively equal in their innate sexual drives and teaches them to be so different in their attitudes and behavior can be answered, then we will have come a long way toward understanding human society in general. This researcher will feel more than content, if he has demonstrated the strategic value of sex research sufficiently to encourage others to continue this search and to gather more complete data and formulate increasingly more precise propositions and theories concerning the nature of the human sexual relationship.

APPENDICES

APPENDIX A

Questionnaire Used
in Five-School Student Sample

General Introduction

You have been chosen at random to help make up the sample of this study. Your personal identity cannot be made known to anyone. Once your questionnaire has been returned to the research staff, there is no possible way in which any of the information involved can be traced to any individual subject. With this guarantee that your answers can be treated only as objects of data, we urge you to consider each of the questions carefully and with complete honesty. You can be of the greatest help in this project if you are as truthful as possible. Please do not exaggerate your answers. Take your time and answer all questions to the best of your knowledge. Thank you.

Part I   General Information

1. (a) Class in school (please check)
     (1) Freshman_____
     (2) Sophomore_____
     (3) Junior_____
     (4) Senior_____
   (b) Number of semesters in school including this one._____

2. Sex: male_____   female_____

3. Date of birth. _____
            (day)   (mo.)   (year)

4. (a) What do your parents consider to be their home state? Mother's home state _____   Father's home state _____
   (b) In what states did you spend the last fifteen years of your life and how long in each? _____

183

(c) Approximate size of city where you have spent most of your life

(1) Less than 1000 _____ (5) 50,000–100,000 _____
(2) 1000–10,000 _____ (6) 100,000–500,000 _____
(3) 10,000–25,000 _____ (7) 500,000–1,000,000 _____
(4) 25,000–50,000 _____ (8) Over 1,000,000 _____

(d) Would you consider most of your residence as urban _____ or rural _____?

5. (a) What is your religion? (please name specific denomination) _____

(b) How often do you attend church?

(1) More than once a week _____ (4) Once a month _____
(2) Once a week _____ (5) Seldom _____
(3) Once every two weeks _____ (6) Never _____

(c) Do you classify yourself as devout _____, moderately devout _____, or inactive _____?

(d) Is your parents' religion the same as yours? Yes_____ No_____

(e) Are both parents of the same _____ or different _____ religions? If different, what are they? _____

6. (a) Are your parents

(1) living together? _____ (3) divorced? _____
(2) separated? _____ (4) missing? _____

(b) Are you living with your parents? Yes_____ No_____
If you are living with your parents, do you live with them

(1) during the school year? _____
(2) during summer and vacations? _____
(3) all year? _____

(c) If you are not living with your parents, indicate with whom:

(1) Guardian _____
(2) Relative (please specify) _____
(3) Other (please specify) _____

7. (a) Father living? Yes_____ No_____

(b) Occupation of father or male guardian with whom you have lived the longest (be specific) _____

(c) Father or male guardian's education (be specific as to when he stopped his schooling; for example, 8th grade, 12th grade, 2d year in college, and so on) _____

8. (a) Mother living? Yes_____ No_____

(b) Occupation of mother or female guardian with whom you have lived the longest _____

(c) Mother or female guardian's education (be specific as to when she stopped her schooling; for example, 8th grade, 12th grade, 2d year in college, and so on) _____

9. What do you estimate your family income to be per year?

(1) Below $2000 _____ (5) $7500–$10,000 _____
(2) $2000–$3500 _____ (6) $10,000–$15,000 _____
(3) $3500–$5000 _____ (7) Over $15,000 _____
(4) $5000–$7500 _____

10. (a) Number of brothers _____ Their ages _____

(b) Number of sisters _____ Their ages _____

11. (For high-school students only)
    (a) Are you planning to go to college? Yes_____ No_____
    (b) If No, is it that you want to, but cannot. Explain any part of this answer which you feel it is necessary to explain. _____
12. (For college students only)
    When did you decide to go to college?
    (1) Before junior year in high school _____
    (2) Junior year in high school _____
    (3) Senior year in high school _____
    (4) After senior year in high school _____
13. (a) You are engaged to be married. How far do you believe it is proper to go sexually?
    (1) Kissing _____
    (2) Petting _____
    (3) Full sexual relations _____
    (b) How far do you believe it is proper for your partner to go?
    (1) Kissing _____
    (2) Petting _____
    (3) Full sexual relations _____

Part II

Instructions: Please keep in mind that we are not interested in your behavior or in your acceptance of other people's behavior, but in the values and standards which you personally hold.

After each question you will find six choices. First decide whether you agree or disagree with the view expressed. Then circle the degree of your agreement or disagreement with the views expressed in the situations described below. Do not feel that you have to check the same degree of agreement or disagreement for both parties involved in each situation, since it may happen that what you feel is acceptable for one person you may not feel is acceptable for the other in that situation. Thus, you may check them the same way or differently.

In order to be clear about the usage of certain terms we will define them as follows:

Petting: Sexually stimulating behavior more intimate than kissing and simple hugging but not including full sexual relations (*to be used this way throughout the questionnaire*).

Strong affection: Affection which is stronger than physical attraction or average fondness or "liking," but less strong than the emotional state which you would call love.

Love: The emotional state which is more intense than strong affection and which you would *define* as love.

WE REALIZE THAT MANY OF YOU ARE TOLERANT TOWARD WHAT OTHER PEOPLE DO OR BELIEVE. IN THIS SECTION, HOWEVER, WE ARE NOT INTERESTED IN WHETHER OR NOT YOU TOLERATE OTHER PEOPLES' ACTIONS AND BELIEFS. PLEASE ANSWER THESE QUESTIONS ON THE BASIS OF HOW YOU FEEL TOWARD THE VIEWS EXPRESSED.

1. John and Mary are engaged to be married. They kiss, since both feel that kissing is allowable when the couple is engaged.

(a) How do you feel about John's views in this situation?
Agree: (1) Strong, (2) Medium, (3) Slight
Disagree: (1) Strong, (2) Medium, (3) Slight

(b) How do you feel about Mary's views in this situation?
Agree: (1) Strong, (2) Medium, (3) Slight
Disagree: (1) Strong, (2) Medium, (3) Slight

2. John and Mary are in love. They kiss, since both feel that kissing is allowable when the couple is in love.

(a) How do you feel about John's views in this situation?
Agree: (1) Strong, (2) Medium, (3) Slight
Disagree: (1) Strong, (2) Medium, (3) Slight

(b) How do you feel about Mary's views in this situation?
Agree: (1) Strong, (2) Medium, (3) Slight
Disagree: (1) Strong, (2) Medium, (3) Slight

3. John and Mary have strong affection for each other. They kiss, since both feel that kissing is acceptable when the couple has strong affection.

(a) How do you feel about John's views in this situation?
Agree: (1) Strong, (2) Medium, (3) Slight
Disagree: (1) Strong, (2) Medium, (3) Slight

(b) How do you feel about Mary's views in this situation?
Agree: (1) Strong, (2) Medium, (3) Slight
Disagree: (1) Strong, (2) Medium, (3) Slight

4. John and Mary have no particular affection for each other. They kiss, since both believe that kissing does not necessitate any particular affection between the couple.

(a) How do you feel about John's views in this situation?
Agree: (1) Strong, (2) Medium, (3) Slight
Disagree: (1) Strong, (2) Medium, (3) Slight

(b) How do you feel about Mary's views in this situation?
Agree: (1) Strong, (2) Medium, (3) Slight
Disagree: (1) Strong, (2) Medium, (3) Slight

5. John and Mary are engaged to be married. They pet, since both believe that petting is acceptable when the couple is engaged to be married.

(a) How do you feel about John's views in this situation?
Agree: (1) Strong, (2) Medium, (3) Slight
Disagree: (1) Strong, (2) Medium, (3) Slight

(b) How do you feel about Mary's views in this situation?
Agree: (1) Strong, (2) Medium, (3) Slight
Disagree: (1) Strong, (2) Medium, (3) Slight

6. John and Mary are in love. They engage in petting, since both believe that petting is acceptable when the couple is in love.

(a) How do you feel about John's views in this situation?
Agree: (1) Strong, (2) Medium, (3) Slight
Disagree: (1) Strong, (2) Medium, (3) Slight

(b) How do you feel about Mary's views in this situation?
Agree: (1) Strong, (2) Medium, (3) Slight
Disagree: (1) Strong, (2) Medium, (3) Slight

7. John and Mary have strong affection for each other. They engage in pet-

ting, since both believe that petting is acceptable when the couple is strongly affectionate.

(a) How do you feel about John's views in this situation?
   Agree: (1) Strong, (2) Medium, (3) Slight
   Disagree: (1) Strong, (2) Medium, (3) Slight

(b) How do you feel about Mary's views in this situation?
   Agree: (1) Strong, (2) Medium, (3) Slight
   Disagree: (1) Strong, (2) Medium, (3) Slight

8. John and Mary have no particular affection for each other. They engage in petting, since both feel that petting does not require any particular affection between the couple.

(a) How do you feel about John's views in this situation?
   Agree: (1) Strong, (2) Medium, (3) Slight
   Disagree: (1) Strong, (2) Medium, (3) Slight

(b) How do you feel about Mary's views in this situation?
   Agree: (1) Strong, (2) Medium, (3) Slight
   Disagree: (1) Strong, (2) Medium, (3) Slight

9. John and Mary are engaged to be married. They have full sexual relations, since they both feel that full sexual relations is acceptable when the couple is engaged to be married.

(a) How do you feel about John's views in this situation?
   Agree: (1) Strong, (2) Medium, (3) Slight
   Disagree: (1) Strong, (2) Medium, (3) Slight

(b) How do you feel about Mary's views in this situation?
   Agree: (1) Strong, (2) Medium, (3) Slight
   Disagree: (1) Strong, (2) Medium, (3) Slight

10. John and Mary are in love. They engage in full sexual relations, since they both feel that full sexual relations is acceptable when the couple is in love.

(a) How do you feel about John's views in this situation?
   Agree: (1) Strong, (2) Medium, (3) Slight
   Disagree: (1) Strong, (2) Medium, (3) Slight

(b) How do you feel about Mary's views in this situation?
   Agree: (1) Strong, (2) Medium, (3) Slight
   Disagree: (1) Strong, (2) Medium, (3) Slight

11. John and Mary feel strong affection for each other. They engage in full sexual relations, since they both think that full sexual relations is acceptable when the couple is strongly affectionate.

(a) How do you feel about John's views in this situation?
   Agree: (1) Strong, (2) Medium, (3) Slight
   Disagree: (1) Strong, (2) Medium, (3) Slight

(b) How do you feel about Mary's views in this situation?
   Agree: (1) Strong, (2) Medium, (3) Slight
   Disagree: (1) Strong, (2) Medium, (3) Slight

12. John and Mary have no particular affection for each other. They engage in full sexual relations, since they both feel that having full sexual relations does not require any particular affection between the couple.

(a) How do you feel about John's views in this situation?
   Agree: (1) Strong, (2) Medium, (3) Slight
   Disagree: (1) Strong, (2) Medium, (3) Slight

    (b) How do you feel about Mary's views in this situation?
        Agree: (1) Strong, (2) Medium, (3) Slight
        Disagree: (1) Strong, (2) Medium, (3) Slight

13. John and Mary believe that full sexual relations done predominantly for sexual pleasure is just about as good as full sexual relations engaged in for the sake of love or similar emotional feelings.

    (a) How do you feel about John's views in this situation?
        Agree: (1) Strong, (2) Medium, (3) Slight
        Disagree: (1) Strong, (2) Medium, (3) Slight

    (b) How do you feel about Mary's views in this situation?
        Agree: (1) Strong, (2) Medium, (3) Slight
        Disagree: (1) Strong, (2) Medium, (3) Slight

14. I believe that there is something basically nasty and dirty about most sex before marriage.

    Agree: (1) Strong, (2) Medium, (3) Slight
    Disagree: (1) Strong, (2) Medium, (3) Slight

15. (a) Men should be allowed more freedom than women in sexual behavior before marriage. How do you feel about this attitude?
        Agree: (1) Strong, (2) Medium, (3) Slight
        Disagree: (1) Strong, (2) Medium, (3) Slight

    (b) If you agreed with the above statement, did you do so because you feel that it is morally right or because you feel that this is the way the world is and it's too difficult to change? _____

16. (a) Men and women should be allowed to participate equally in sex in accordance with the same standard. How do you feel about this attitude?
        Agree: (1) Strong, (2) Medium, (3) Slight
        Disagree: (1) Strong, (2) Medium, (3) Slight

    (b) If you disagreed with this statement, was it because you feel it is morally wrong or because you feel it is too difficult to change the way the world is? _____

Part III

Instructions: Please circle the degree of agreement or disagreement you have with the statements below. The first list contains statements concerning the male; the second contains statements concerning the female. Please read each one carefully and check your degree of agreement or disagreement with each statement in both lists. Remember, WE ARE NOT INTERESTED IN YOUR TOLERANCE OF OTHER PEOPLE'S BEHAVIOR OR BELIEFS. PLEASE ANSWER THESE QUESTIONS, AS BEFORE, ON THE BASIS OF HOW YOU FEEL TOWARD THE VIEWS EXPRESSED.

Male Standards (Both Men and Women Check This Section)

1. I believe that kissing is acceptable for the male before marriage if he is engaged to be married.
    Agree: (1) Strong, (2) Medium, (3) Slight
    Disagree: (1) Strong, (2) Medium, (3) Slight

2. I believe that kissing is acceptable for the male before marriage when he is in love.
    Agree: (1) Strong, (2) Medium, (3) Slight
    Disagree: (1) Strong, (2) Medium, (3) Slight

3. I believe that kissing is acceptable for the male before marriage when he feels strong affection for his partner.
Agree: (1) Strong, (2) Medium, (3) Slight
Disagree: (1) Strong, (2) Medium, (3) Slight

4. I believe that kissing is acceptable for the male before marriage when he is not particularly affectionate toward his partner.
Agree: (1) Strong, (2) Medium, (3) Slight
Disagree: (1) Strong, (2) Medium, (3) Slight

5. I believe that petting is acceptable for the male before marriage when he is engaged to be married.
Agree: (1) Strong, (2) Medium, (3) Slight
Disagree: (1) Strong, (2) Medium, (3) Slight

6. I believe that petting is acceptable for the male before marriage when he is in love.
Agree: (1) Strong, (2) Medium, (3) Slight
Disagree: (1) Strong, (2) Medium, (3) Slight

7. I believe that petting is acceptable for the male before marriage when he is strongly affectionate for his partner.
Agree: (1) Strong, (2) Medium, (3) Slight
Disagree: (1) Strong, (2) Medium, (3) Slight

8. I believe that petting is acceptable for the male before marriage when he is not particularly affectionate toward his partner.
Agree: (1) Strong, (2) Medium, (3) Slight
Disagree: (1) Strong, (2) Medium, (3) Slight

9. I believe that full sexual relations is acceptable for the male before marriage when he is engaged to be married.
Agree: (1) Strong, (2) Medium, (3) Slight
Disagree: (1) Strong, (2) Medium, (3) Slight

10. I believe that full sexual relations is acceptable for the male before marriage when he is in love.
Agree: (1) Strong, (2) Medium, (3) Slight
Disagree: (1) Strong, (2) Medium, (3) Slight

11. I believe that full sexual relations is acceptable for the male before marriage when he is strongly affectionate toward his partner.
Agree: (1) Strong, (2) Medium, (3) Slight
Disagree: (1) Strong, (2) Medium, (3) Slight

12. I believe that full sexual relations is acceptable for the male before marriage when he is not particularly affectionate for his partner.
Agree: (1) Strong, (2) Medium, (3) Slight
Disagree: (1) Strong, (2) Medium, (3) Slight

13. I believe that full sexual relations is acceptable for the male before marriage when there is no particular affection and that this type of relationship is just about as acceptable as full sexual relations which involve strong affection or love.
Agree: (1) Strong, (2) Medium, (3) Slight
Disagree: (1) Strong, (2) Medium, (3) Slight

Female Standards (*Both Men and Women Check This Section*)

1. I believe that kissing is acceptable for the female before marriage when she is engaged to be married.
Agree: (1) Strong, (2) Medium, (3) Slight
Disagree: (1) Strong, (2) Medium, (3) Slight

2. I believe that kissing is acceptable for the female before marriage when she is in love.
Agree: (1) Strong, (2) Medium, (3) Slight
Disagree: (1) Strong, (2) Medium, (3) Slight

3. I believe that kissing is acceptable for the female before marriage when she feels strong affection for her partner.
Agree: (1) Strong, (2) Medium, (3) Slight
Disagree: (1) Strong, (2) Medium, (3) Slight

4. I believe that kissing is acceptable for the female before marriage when she is not particularly affectionate toward her partner.
Agree: (1) Strong, (2) Medium, (3) Slight
Disagree: (1) Strong, (2) Medium, (3) Slight

5. I believe that petting is acceptable for the female before marriage when she is engaged to be married.
Agree: (1) Strong, (2) Medium, (3) Slight
Disagree: (1) Strong, (2) Medium, (3) Slight

6. I believe that petting is acceptable for the female before marriage when she is in love.
Agree: (1) Strong, (2) Medium, (3) Slight
Disagree: (1) Strong, (2) Medium, (3) Slight

7. I believe that petting is acceptable for the female before marriage when she is strongly affectionate for her partner.
Agree: (1) Strong, (2) Medium, (3) Slight
Disagree: (1) Strong, (2) Medium, (3) Slight

8. I believe that petting is acceptable for the female before marriage when she is not particularly affectionate toward her partner.
Agree: (1) Strong, (2) Medium, (3) Slight
Disagree: (1) Strong, (2) Medium, (3) Slight

9. I believe that full sexual relations is acceptable for the female before marriage when she is engaged to be married.
Agree: (1) Strong, (2) Medium, (3) Slight
Disagree: (1) Strong, (2) Medium, (3) Slight

10. I believe that full sexual relations is acceptable for the female before marriage when she is in love.
Agree: (1) Strong, (2) Medium, (3) Slight
Disagree: (1) Strong, (2) Medium, (3) Slight

11. I believe that full sexual relations is acceptable for the female before marriage when she is strongly affectionate for her partner.
Agree: (1) Strong, (2) Medium, (3) Slight
Disagree: (1) Strong, (2) Medium, (3) Slight

12. I believe that full sexual relations is acceptable for the female before marriage when she is not particularly affectionate for her partner.
Agree: (1) Strong, (2) Medium, (3) Slight
Disagree: (1) Strong, (2) Medium, (3) Slight

13. I believe that full sexual relations is acceptable for the female before marriage when there is no particular affection and that this type of relationship is just about as acceptable as full sexual relations which involve strong affection or love.
Agree: (1) Strong, (2) Medium, (3) Slight
Disagree: (1) Strong, (2) Medium, (3) Slight

After you have completed the questions above, place an X beside the one statement in the male list and the one statement in the female list which you feel most nearly expresses how far you feel the male should go and how far you feel the female should go.

Part IV

1. (a) Explain briefly in the space provided below your reasons for choosing the two statements beside which you placed an X above. Why do you think they were good?

   (b) Briefly state your reasons against those statements for both male and female which you rejected above. Why do you think they were not good?

2. (a) How do you feel your standards compare with those of your parents?

MOTHER	FATHER
(1) Very similar _____	(1) Very similar _____
(2) Similar _____	(2) Similar _____
(3) Somewhat similar _____	(3) Somewhat similar _____
(4) Somewhat dissimilar _____	(4) Somewhat dissimilar _____
(5) Dissimilar _____	(5) Dissimilar _____
(6) Very dissimilar _____	(6) Very dissimilar _____

   (b) If at all dissimilar, do you feel your standards are more _____ or less _____ strict than those of your parents?

3. (a) How do you feel your standards compare with those standards of others your own age?

(1) Very similar _____	(4) Somewhat dissimilar _____
(2) Similar _____	(5) Dissimilar _____
(3) Somewhat similar _____	(6) Very dissimilar _____

   (b) If at all dissimilar, are your standards more _____ or less _____ strict than those of others your own age?

4. (a) How do you feel your standards compare with those standards of your very close friends?

(1) Very similar _____	(4) Somewhat dissimilar _____
(2) Similar _____	(5) Dissimilar _____
(3) Somewhat similar _____	(6) Very dissimilar _____

   (b) If at all dissimilar, are your standards more _____ or less _____ strict than those of your very close friends?

Part V

1. Are you at present (1) unattached _____, (2) going fairly regularly with one person _____, (3) going steady _____, (4) in love _____, (5) pinned (for college students only) _____, (6) engaged _____, (7) other _____?

2. Counting the relationship (if any) marked above, have you gone fairly regularly with one person short of going steady ?_____

   (a) Number of times _____

    (b) Duration (in months) of each ⎯⎯⎯⎯⎯⎯⎯⎯⎯⎯⎯

    (c) Ages at occurrence ⎯⎯⎯⎯⎯⎯⎯⎯⎯⎯⎯⎯⎯⎯⎯

3. Counting the relationship marked above, have you gone steady? ⎯⎯⎯⎯⎯
    (a) Number of times ⎯⎯⎯⎯
    (b) Duration in months of each ⎯⎯⎯⎯⎯⎯⎯⎯⎯⎯⎯
    (c) Ages at occurrence ⎯⎯⎯⎯⎯⎯⎯⎯⎯⎯⎯⎯⎯

4. Counting the above-marked relationship, have you been pinned? ⎯⎯⎯⎯⎯
    (a) Number of times ⎯⎯⎯⎯
    (b) Duration in months of each ⎯⎯⎯⎯⎯⎯⎯⎯⎯⎯⎯
    (c) Ages at occurrence ⎯⎯⎯⎯⎯⎯⎯⎯⎯⎯⎯⎯⎯

5. Counting the above-marked relationship, have you been engaged? ⎯⎯⎯⎯⎯
    (a) Number of times ⎯⎯⎯⎯
    (b) Duration in months of each ⎯⎯⎯⎯⎯⎯⎯⎯⎯⎯⎯
    (c) Ages at occurrence ⎯⎯⎯⎯⎯⎯⎯⎯⎯⎯⎯⎯⎯

6. Have you been in love? ⎯⎯⎯⎯
    (a) Number of times ⎯⎯⎯⎯
    (b) Duration in months of each ⎯⎯⎯⎯⎯⎯⎯⎯⎯ — ⎯⎯⎯
    (c) Ages at occurrence ⎯⎯⎯⎯⎯⎯⎯⎯⎯⎯⎯⎯⎯

7. On the average, how many times per month do you date? ⎯⎯⎯⎯

8. At what age did you begin dating? ⎯⎯⎯⎯
    (b) At what age did you begin single dating? ⎯⎯⎯⎯
    (c) At what age did you begin dating regularly, short of going steady? ⎯⎯⎯
    (d) At what age did you begin dating in cars? ⎯⎯⎯⎯
    (e) Would you say that most of your dating activities were restricted to (1) "playing the field" ⎯⎯⎯⎯, (2) dating particular individuals fairly regularly ⎯⎯⎯⎯, or (3) about half and half ⎯⎯⎯⎯?

Part VI

Please circle the degree of agreement or disagreement you have with the following statements concerning love relationships between men and women.

1. True love leads to almost perfect happiness.
    Agree: (1) Strong, (2) Medium, (3) Slight
    Disagree: (1) Strong, (2) Medium, (3) Slight

2. There is only one real love for a person.
    Agree: (1) Strong, (2) Medium, (3) Slight
    Disagree: (1) Strong, (2) Medium, (3) Slight

3. True love is known at once by the people involved.
    Agree: (1) Strong, (2) Medium, (3) Slight
    Disagree: (1) Strong, (2) Medium, (3) Slight

4. Even though one's past love affair was not as strong as the present one, it may still have been a real love relationship.
    Agree: (1) Strong, (2) Medium, (3) Slight
    Disagree: (1) Strong, (2) Medium, (3) Slight

5. Doubt may enter into real love.
    Agree: (1) Strong, (2) Medium, (3) Slight
    Disagree: (1) Strong, (2) Medium, (3) Slight

6. True love is mysterious and cannot be understood by reason. It can only be felt, not explained.
   Agree: (1) Strong, (2) Medium, (3) Slight
   Disagree: (1) Strong, (2) Medium, (3) Slight

7. True love will last forever.
   Agree: (1) Strong, (2) Medium, (3) Slight
   Disagree: (1) Strong, (2) Medium, (3) Slight

8. Conflict can be a part of real love.
   Agree: (1) Strong, (2) Medium, (3) Slight
   Disagree: (1) Strong, (2) Medium, (3) Slight

9. It is possible to love two people at the same time.
   Agree: (1) Strong, (2) Medium, (3) Slight
   Disagree: (1) Strong, (2) Medium, (3) Slight

10. When one is in love, the person whom he loves becomes the only goal in his life. One lives almost solely for the other.
    Agree: (1) Strong, (2) Medium, (3) Slight
    Disagree: (1) Strong, (2) Medium, (3) Slight

Part VII

1. Which phrase below best characterizes most of your relations with your family?
   (1) Very happy ——————— (4) Somewhat dissatisfactory ——
   (2) Happy ——————— (5) Unhappy ———————
   (3) Somewhat satisfactory —— (6) Very unhappy ———————

2. Would you say that most of the time you are closer to your mother ——— or your father ———?

3. Do you feel for the most part that your life goals are being achieved ——— or not being achieved ———?

4. Do you find that there are sufficient pastimes and types of entertainment for your use ——— or that it is difficult to find things to do ———?

5. Do you think that your standards regarding sex before marriage
   (1) are very likely to change in the future? ———
   (2) are somewhat likely to change in the future? ———
   (3) are slightly likely to change in the future? ———
   (4) are slightly unlikely to change in the future? ———
   (5) are somewhat unlikely to change in the future? ———
   (6) are very unlikely to change in the future? ———

6. (a) Have your attitudes toward sexual behavior changed since you have begun dating? Yes——— No———
   (b) If yes, have they become more strict ——— or less strict———?
   (c) Please explain how many times they have changed and at what ages.
   ———

7. (a) I believe that my sexual *behavior* and the sexual *standards* in which I believe are
   in agreement with each other: (1) Strong, (2) Medium, (3) Slight
   in disagreement with each other: (1) Strong, (2) Medium, (3) Slight
   (b) Please explain your answer if your sexual behavior differs from your sexual standards.

8. (a) For an engaged woman it is proper to allow
   (1) Kissing _____
   (2) Petting _____
   (3) Full sexual relations _____
   (b) For an engaged man it is proper to allow
   (1) Kissing _____
   (2) Petting _____
   (3) Full sexual relations _____

9. Summarize your feelings toward your past serious relationships as a whole. Do you feel that they have been helpful or harmful in the formation of your present attitudes?

10. Do you think your standards should apply to others? Yes_____ No_____
    Explain _____

11. Would you define petting to include only certain types of sexual behavior and not others? Yes_____ No_____ If Yes, explain. _____

12. Any additional comments you have which might further explain your attitudes may be listed below.

(*For the New York college the following questions were added*)

13. How many semesters have you been at this school? _____

14. (a) Have your sexual *standards* changed since you came here? _____ If Yes, are they more or less strict now? _____
    (b) Has your sexual *behavior* changed since you have been here? _____ If Yes, is it more or less strict now? _____

APPENDIX B

Questionnaire Used
in Iowa College Student Sample

This questionnaire is fully anonymous. You will *not* put your name on it. We are interested in overall patterns and not in any particular individual. There is no way to identify you with your answers. Please be as truthful as you can, for it is important that we have a valid test of this questionnaire. You can be of great help to us if you will be kind enough to fill out this questionnaire and do so in full honesty. Feel free to write in any qualifications of your answers you deem relevant. Thank you for your cooperation.

Part I

1. Class in school: _____ Freshman
   _____ Sophomore
   _____ Junior
   _____ Senior

2. Sex: _____ Male
   _____ Female

3. Circle the number corresponding to your age to your *nearest* birthday:
   _____, 18, 19, 20, 21, 22, 23, 24, 25, _____

4. Marital status: _____ Married
   _____ Single
   _____ Divorced
   Other: _____

5. (a) What state does your *mother* consider to be her home state? _____ Iowa
   Other: _____
   (b) What state does your *father* consider to be his home state? _____ Iowa
   Other: _____

6. What state have you lived in the longest? _____ Iowa
   Other: _____

7. What is the approximate size of the place you have lived in the most?
   _____ 0–999
   _____ 1000–2499
   _____ 2500–9999
   _____ 10,000–24,999
   _____ 25,000–49,999
   _____ 50,000–99,999
   _____ 100,000–249,999
   _____ 250,000 up
   _____ Rural farm, ranch, and so on

8. What is your major?
   _____ Sociology
   _____ Nursing
   _____ Psychology
   _____ Education
   Other: _____

9. What is your religion (please name specific denomination)?
   _____ None
   _____ Catholic
   _____ Methodist
   _____ Lutheran
   _____ Presbyterian
   Other denomination: _____

10. In an *average month,* how many times do you attend church?
    _____ Never
    _____ Once a month
    _____ Twice
    _____ Three times
    _____ Four times
    _____ Five or more times a month

11. Do you classify yourself as:
    _____ Devout?
    _____ Moderately devout?
    _____ Inactive?

12. Are both of your parents living?
    _____ Yes
    _____ Father living
    _____ Mother living

13. If Yes to question 12, are they living together?
    _____ Yes
    _____ No   (please explain): _____

14. Do you live with one or both of your parents when you are not in school?
    _____ Yes
    _____ No

15. (a) What is (or was) the title of your father's main occupation (be specific)? _____
    (b) What kind of work does this involve? _____

16. How many other jobs does he currently have for which he is paid? _____

17. What is your mother's occupation (be specific)?

_____ Housewife only

Other: _____

18. Father's education.

_____ None

_____ Some elementary school (1–7 years)

_____ Completed elementary school (8 years)

_____ Some high school (1–3 years)

_____ Graduated from high school (4 years)

_____ Some college (1–3 years)

_____ Graduated from college (4 plus years)

_____ Has at least some postgraduate college credits

Other (please explain): _____

19. Mother's education.

_____ None

_____ Some elementary school (1–7 years)

_____ Completed elementary school (8 years)

_____ Some high school (1–3 years)

_____ Graduated from high school (4 years)

_____ Some college (1–3 years)

_____ Graduated from college (4 plus years)

_____ Has at least some postgraduate college credits

Other (please explain): _____

20. What would you estimate your yearly family income to be?

_____ Under $2000

_____ $2000–$2999

_____ $3000–$3999

_____ $4000–$4999

_____ $5000–$5999

_____ $6000–$6999

_____ $7000–$7999

_____ $8000–$9999

_____ $10,000 and over

21. (a) Please circle the number of brothers you have. None, 1, 2, 3, 4, 5, ____

(b) How many are older than you? _____

22. (a) Please circle the number of sisters you have: None, 1, 2, 3, 4, 5, ____

(b) How many are older than you? _____

23. For how many years before you entered college were you sure you would go to college?

_____ Always

_____ One year

_____ Two years

_____ Three years

Other (please specify): _____

24. Are you a member of a social sorority or fraternity?   _____ Yes

_____ No

Part II[1]

Male Sexual Standards (Everyone Should Answer This Section Regardless of Their Sex)

Instructions: In this section we are interested in obtaining your personal beliefs. After each question decide first whether you agree or disagree; then circle the degree of your agreement or disagreement (strong, medium, slight).

Definitions: In order to be sure we are defining terms the same way, we will define *petting:* sexually stimulating behavior more intimate than kissing and simple hugging but not including full sexual relations. *Strong affection:* affection which is stronger than physical attraction or average fondness or "liking," but less strong than the emotional state which you would call love. *Love:* the emotional state which is more intense than strong affection and which you would define as love.

Remember, we are not interested in what you tolerate in others, we are interested in your personal beliefs. Please answer that way. Please also keep in mind the above definitions.

Please check how strongly you feel about each of the following statements:

1. I believe that petting is acceptable for the male before marriage when he is in love.
   Agree: (1) Strong, (2) Medium, (3) Slight
   Disagree: (1) Strong, (2) Medium, (3) Slight

2. I believe that full sexual relations is acceptable for the male before marriage when he is not particularly affectionate for his partner.
   Agree: (1) Strong, (2) Medium, (3) Slight
   Disagree: (1) Strong, (2) Medium, (3) Slight

3. I believe that kissing is acceptable for the male before marriage when he is engaged to be married.
   Agree: (1) Strong, (2) Medium, (3) Slight
   Disagree: (1) Strong, (2) Medium, (3) Slight

4. I believe that petting is acceptable for the male before marriage when he is strongly affectionate for his partner.
   Agree: (1) Strong, (2) Medium, (3) Slight
   Disagree: (1) Strong, (2) Medium, (3) Slight

5. I believe that full sexual relations is acceptable for the male before marriage when he is engaged to be married.
   Agree: (1) Strong, (2) Medium, (3) Slight
   Disagree: (1) Strong, (2) Medium, (3) Slight

6. I believe that kissing is acceptable for the male before marriage when he is in love.
   Agree: (1) Strong, (2) Medium, (3) Slight
   Disagree: (1) Strong, (2) Medium, (3) Slight

7. I believe that petting is acceptable for the male before marriage when he is not particularly affectionate toward his partner.
   Agree: (1) Strong, (2) Medium, (3) Slight
   Disagree: (1) Strong, (2) Medium, (3) Slight

[1] Only some of these questionnaires had the male and female scale items in Part II in the order given to the five schools. This was done in order to compare differences due to item order.

8. I believe that full sexual relations is acceptable for the male before marriage when he is in love.
   Agree: (1) Strong, (2) Medium, (3) Slight
   Disagree: (1) Strong, (2) Medium, (3) Slight

9. I believe that kissing is acceptable for the male before marriage when he is not particularly affectionate toward his partner.
   Agree: (1) Strong, (2) Medium, (3) Slight
   Disagree: (1) Strong, (2) Medium, (3) Slight

10. I believe that petting is acceptable for the male before marriage when he is engaged to be married.
    Agree: (1) Strong, (2) Medium, (3) Slight
    Disagree: (1) Strong, (2) Medium, (3) Slight

11. I believe that kissing is acceptable for the male before marriage when he feels strong affection for his partner.
    Agree: (1) Strong, (2) Medium, (3) Slight
    Disagree: (1) Strong, (2) Medium, (3) Slight

12. I believe that full sexual relations is acceptable for the male before marriage when he is strongly affectionate toward his partner.
    Agree: (1) Strong, (2) Medium, (3) Slight
    Disagree: (1) Strong, (2) Medium, (3) Slight

Female Sexual Standards (*Everyone Should Answer This Section Regardless of Their Sex. Remember the Definitions Given at the Beginning of Part Two.*) Please check how strongly you feel about each of the following statements.

1. I believe that petting is acceptable for the female before marriage when she is in love.
   Agree: (1) Strong, (2) Medium, (3) Slight
   Disagree: (1) Strong, (2) Medium, (3) Slight

2. I believe that full sexual relations is acceptable for the female before marriage when she is not particularly affectionate for her partner.
   Agree: (1) Strong, (2) Medium, (3) Slight
   Disagree: (1) Strong, (2) Medium, (3) Slight

3. I believe that kissing is acceptable for the female before marriage when she is engaged to be married.
   Agree: (1) Strong, (2) Medium, (3) Slight
   Disagree: (1) Strong, (2) Medium, (3) Slight

4. I believe that petting is acceptable for the female before marriage when she is strongly affectionate for her partner.
   Agree: (1) Strong, (2) Medium, (3) Slight
   Disagree: (1) Strong, (2) Medium, (3) Slight

5. I believe that full sexual relations is acceptable for the female before marriage when she is engaged to be married.
   Agree: (1) Strong, (2) Medium, (3) Slight
   Disagree: (1) Strong, (2) Medium, (3) Slight

6. I believe that kissing is acceptable for the female before marriage when she is in love.
   Agree: (1) Strong, (2) Medium, (3) Slight
   Disagree: (1) Strong, (2) Medium, (3) Slight

7. I believe that petting is acceptable for the female before marriage when she is not particularly affectionate toward her partner.

Agree: (1) Strong, (2) Medium, (3) Slight
Disagree: (1) Strong, (2) Medium, (3) Slight

8. I believe that full sexual relations is acceptable for the female before marriage when she is in love.
Agree: (1) Strong, (2) Medium, (3) Slight
Disagree: (1) Strong, (2) Medium, (3) Slight

9. I believe that kissing is acceptable for the female before marriage when she is not particularly affectionate toward her partner.
Agree: (1) Strong, (2) Medium, (3) Slight
Disagree: (1) Strong, (2) Medium, (3) Slight

10. I believe that petting is acceptable for the female before marriage when she is engaged to be married.
Agree: (1) Strong, (2) Medium, (3) Slight
Disagree: (1) Strong, (2) Medium, (3) Slight

11. I believe that kissing is acceptable for the female before marriage when she feels strong affection for her partner.
Agree: (1) Strong, (2) Medium, (3) Slight
Disagree: (1) Strong, (2) Medium, (3) Slight

12. I believe that full sexual relations is acceptable for the female before marriage when she is strongly affectionate toward her partner.
Agree: (1) Strong, (2) Medium, (3) Slight
Disagree: (1) Strong, (2) Medium, (3) Slight

Part III

A. Do you personally feel that men and women should be allowed the same amount of sexual freedom?

_____ No, men more freedom
_____ No, women more freedom
_____ Yes, I feel strongly they should have the same amount of freedom
_____ Yes, I feel moderately strongly that men and women should be allowed the same amount of sexual freedom
_____ Yes, I feel slightly that men and women should be allowed the same amount of sexual freedom

B. Below are defined several premarital sexual standards. Please circle the name of the one which you find most acceptable.

(1) ABSTINENCE—KISSING WITH AFFECTION: The furthest males or females are allowed to go is to kiss someone they feel strong affection for.

(2) ABSTINENCE—KISSING WITHOUT AFFECTION: The furthest males or females are allowed to go is to kiss, but this can be done with anyone regardless of affection.

(3) ABSTINENCE—PETTING WITH AFFECTION: The furthest males or females are allowed to go is petting, and this can be done only when there is strong affection present.

(4) ABSTINENCE—PETTING WITHOUT AFFECTION: The furthest males or females are allowed to go is petting, and this can be done with anyone regardless of affection.

(5) ABSTINENCE—UNEQUAL SUBTYPES:
    (a) Check here if you will give males more freedom in regard to kissing and petting but would restrict females somewhat.
    (b) Check here if you will give females more freedom in regard to kissing and petting, but would restrict males somewhat.

(6) TRANSITIONAL DOUBLE STANDARD: Males are allowed full sexual relations even if not in love or engaged; females, only if in love and/or engaged.

(7) ORTHODOX DOUBLE STANDARD: Males are allowed full sexual relations; females are not.

(8) PERMISSIVENESS WITH AFFECTION—LOVE OR ENGAGED: Both males and females may have full sexual relations when love is present or when engaged.

(9) PERMISSIVENESS WITH AFFECTION—STRONG AFFECTION: Both males and females may have full sexual relations when strong affection is involved.

(10) PERMISSIVENESS WITHOUT AFFECTION—TYPE ONE: Both males and females are allowed full sexual relations regardless of the amount of affection, and this type of relationship can occur quite frequently.

(11) PERMISSIVENESS WITHOUT AFFECTION—TYPE TWO: Both males and females can have full sexual relations regardless of the amount of affection present, but this should occur rarely.

(12) REVERSE DOUBLE STANDARD—TRANSITIONAL: Females allowed full sexual relations even if not in love or engaged; males, only if in love and/or engaged.

(13) REVERSE DOUBLE STANDARD—ORTHODOX: Females are allowed full sexual relations; males are not.

(14) OTHER: Write in and explain your standard, if your standard does not clearly fit the categories.

C. List the name and number of the standard you circled in part three:

Part IV

All of your questions in the following section refer to the time you have accepted your present standard (that is, the one you circled in Part III).

1. During the time that you have accepted your present standard, have you engaged in *kissing*?
    _____ Yes
    _____ No

2. In relation to kissing behavior, would you say you have done
    _____ less than your standard would allow you to do?
    _____ as much as your standard would allow you to do?
    _____ or would you say your kissing behavior has exceeded your standard?

3. If your kissing behavior differs from your standard, does it do so
    _____ rarely?
    _____ sometimes?
    _____ frequently?
    _____ It does not differ

4. If there is a difference between your kissing behavior and your standard, please briefly explain the nature of the difference and why you feel this has occurred. _____

If you have engaged in kissing (that is, answered Yes to question 1), answer questions 5 and 6. If not, go to question 7.

5. Have you felt guilty about the above described behavior?
   _____ No
   _____ Some
   _____ Moderately
   _____ A lot

6. Do you feel that your partner(s) should be more condemned for this behavior than you?
   _____ Yes, mostly
   _____ Yes, a little
   _____ No

7. During the time you have accepted your present standard, have you engaged in *petting?*
   _____ Yes
   _____ No

8. In relation to petting behavior, would you say you have done
   _____ less than your standard would allow you to do?
   _____ as much as your standard would allow you to do?
   _____ or would you say your petting behavior has exceeded your standard?

9. If your petting behavior differs from your standard, does it do so
   _____ rarely?
   _____ sometimes?
   _____ frequently?
   _____ It does not differ

10. If there is a difference between your petting behavior and your standard, please explain briefly the nature of the difference and why you feel this has occurred.

If you have engaged in petting (that is, answered Yes to question 7 above), answer questions 11 and 12. If not, go to question 13.

11. Have you felt guilty about your petting behavior?
    _____ No
    _____ Some
    _____ Moderately
    _____ A lot

12. Do you feel that your partner(s) should be more condemned for this behavior than you?
    _____ Yes, mostly
    _____ Yes, a little
    _____ No

13. Comparing kissing and petting, which of these two types of behavior, would you say, in your entire dating history was most likely to exceed your standard?
    _____ Kissing
    _____ Petting
    Other (explain): _____

14. Which of these two types of behavior was most likely *not to* occur as much as your standard would allow?

        _____ Kissing
        _____ Petting
        Other (explain): _____

15. Would you clarify your answers by some comments here:

16. During the time that you have accepted your present standard, have you engaged in *full sexual relations?*

        _____ Yes
        _____ No

17. In regard to full sexual relations, would you say you have done

        _____ less than your standard would allow you to do?
        _____ as much as your standard would allow you to do?
        _____ or would you say your behavior with regard to full sexual relations has exceeded your standard?

18. If your behavior with regard to full sexual relations differs from your standard, does it do so

        _____ rarely?
        _____ sometimes?
        _____ frequently?
        _____ It does not differ

19. If there is a difference between your behavior with regard to full sexual relations and your standard, please explain briefly the nature of the difference and why you feel this has occurred.

    If you have engaged in full sexual relations (that is, answered Yes to question 16, above), please answer questions 20 and 21. If not, go to question 22.

20. Have you felt guilty about the above described behavior?

        _____ No
        _____ Some
        _____ Moderately
        _____ A lot

21. Do you feel that your partner(s) should be more condemned for this behavior than you?

        _____ Yes, mostly
        _____ Yes, a little
        _____ No

22. Comparing kissing, petting and full sexual relations—which of these three types of behavior, would you say, in your entire dating history was most likely to exceed your standard?

        _____ Kissing
        _____ Petting
        _____ Full sexual relations
        Other (explain): _____

23. Which of these three types of behavior was most likely *not* to occur as much as your standard would allow?

        _____ Kissing
        _____ Petting
        _____ Full sexual relations
        Other (explain): _____

24. Would you clarify your answers by some comments here: _____

25. How likely to change are your present standards?
  _____ Very likely to change
  _____ Moderately likely to change
  _____ Slightly likely to change
  _____ They will probably not change

26. How frequently is it permissible for males to have intercourse without affection?
  _____ Never
  _____ Rarely
  _____ Frequently

27. How frequently is it permissible for females to have intercourse without affection?
  _____ Never
  _____ Rarely
  _____ Frequently

28. How romantic do you think your love beliefs are?
  _____ Very romantic
  _____ Moderately romantic
  _____ Slightly romantic
  _____ Not at all romantic

29. For precisely what length of time have you accepted your present standard?
  _____ years

30. About how old were you during this time?   _____ years

31. During the time you accepted your present standard were you ever (check as many as appropriate)
  _____ engaged?
  _____ in love?
  _____ very fond of someone?
  Other (explain)?   _____

Part V

1. Are your present sexual standards the ones you have always held?
  _____ Yes
  _____ No

2. Please fill in the numbers of the standards (from Part III) above the ages at which you held these standards. For example, if you held standard 3 from ages 12 to 17 and changed to standard 5 and hold that today, you might fill in the question as in the example below.

Standards   None__←(3)_____→ ←__(5)____

Ages   10 11 12 13 14 15 16 17 18 19 20 21 22 23 24 25
   If you feel that you held no standard at some age, state *none*; and and if you gradually changed, write that in also. Now, fill this information in on the chart.

Standards

Ages   10 11 12 13 14 15 16 17 18 19 20 21 22 23 24 25

Part VI

This section is only for those who have earlier in their life held a different standard than their present one. If you have never changed your standard, proceed to Part VII.

1. For the standard you accepted just before the one you now hold, please explain how you came to accept it.

2. Please state why you changed to your current standard?
   (a) What is the standard you held previous to your present one? (Refer to your answer to question 2 in Part V, on the chart just completed.)

   _____   _____
   Number   Full descriptive title from Part III
   (b) How long a time did you accept this standard?   _____ years

3. How old were you during this time? _____

4. During the time you accepted this standard were you
   _____ engaged?
   _____ in love?
   _____ very fond of someone?
   other (explain)?   _____

5. During the time that you accepted this standard did you engage in *kissing*?
   _____ Yes
   _____ No

6. In regard to kissing behavior, would you say you did
   _____ less than your standard would allow you to do?
   _____ as much as your standard would allow you to do?
   _____ or would you say your kissing behavior during that time exceeded your standard?

7. If your kissing behavior differed at that time from your standard, did it do so
   _____ rarely?
   _____ sometimes?
   _____ frequently?
   _____ It did not differ

8. If there was a difference between your kissing behavior and your standard, please explain briefly the nature of the difference and why you feel this occurred.

   If you engaged in kissing (i.e., answered Yes to question 5), answer questions 9 and 10. If not, go to question 11.

9. Did you feel guilty about your kissing behavior at that time?
   _____ No
   _____ Some
   _____ Moderately
   _____ A lot

10. Did you feel at that time that your partner(s) should be more condemned for this behavior than you?
    _____ Yes, mostly
    _____ Yes, a little
    _____ No

11. During the time you accepted this standard (the one you held just before the one you now hold), did you engage in *petting*?

    _____ Yes

    _____ No

12. In regard to petting behavior, would you say you did

    _____ less than your standard would allow you to do?

    _____ as much as your standard would allow you to do?

    _____ or would you say your petting behavior during that time exceeded your standard?

13. If your petting behavior at that time differed from your standard, did it do so

    _____ rarely?

    _____ sometimes?

    _____ frequently?

    _____ It did not differ

14. If there was a difference between your petting behavior and your standard, please explain briefly the nature of the difference and why you feel this occurred.

If you engaged in petting (that is, answered Yes to question 11 above), answer Questions 15 and 16. If not, go to question 17.

15. Did you feel guilty at that time about your petting behavior?

    _____ No

    _____ Some

    _____ Moderately

    _____ A lot

16. Did you feel that your partner(s) should be more condemned for this behavior than you?

    _____ Yes, mostly

    _____ Yes, a little

    _____ No

17. During the time you held this standard (the standard just before your current one), did you engage in *full sexual relations*?

    _____ Yes

    _____ No

18. In regard to full sexual relations, would you say you did

    _____ less than your standard would allow you to do?

    _____ as much as your standard would allow you to do?

    _____ or would you say your behavior in regard to full sexual relations during that time exceeded your standard?

19. If your behavior in regard to full sexual relations differed from your standard during that time, did it do so

    _____ rarely?

    _____ sometimes?

    _____ frequently?

    _____ It did not differ

20. If there was a difference between your behavior regarding full sexual relations and your standard, please briefly explain the nature of the difference and why you feel this occurred.

If you engaged in full sexual relations (that is, answered Yes to question 17 above), then answer questions 21 and 22. If not, go to Part VII.

21. Did you feel guilty at that time about your behavior regarding full sexual relations?

      _____ No
      _____ Some
      _____ Moderately
      _____ A lot

22. Did you feel that your partner(s) should be more condemned for this behavior than you?

      _____ Yes, mostly
      _____ Yes, a litlte
      _____ No

Part VII[2]

1. Which of those sexual acts that once made you feel guilty have you come to accept? _____

2. Which of those sexual acts that once made you feel guilty have you stopped performing? _____

3. How well do you think you live up to your *present* standard?

      _____ Very closely
      _____ Closely
      _____ Not so well
      _____ Pretty badly

4. If you had a different standard before your present one, how well do you think you lived up to that one?

      _____ Very closely
      _____ Closely
      _____ Not so well
      _____ Pretty badly
      _____ No different previous standard

5. Are you content today with the level of agreement between your behavior and your standard?

      _____ Almost fully so
      _____ Mostly
      _____ Somewhat
      _____ Not content

6. I believe that petting is acceptable for the male before marriage even if he is not particularly affectionate toward his partner.
Agree: (1) Strong, (2) Medium, (3) Slight
Disagree: (1) Strong, (2) Medium, (3) Slight

7. I believe that full sexual relations is acceptable for the male before marriage even if he is not particularly affectionate for his partner.
Agree: (1) Strong, (2) Medium, (3) Slight
Disagree: (1) Strong, (2) Medium, (3) Slight

[2] Questions 6 to 11 of Part VII of this questionnaire slightly altered the wording of three of the male and female scale questions in order to see if responses would differ as compared with the usual wording contained in Part II of this questionnaire. No difference was noted. The new wording, though only a very slight change, seemed clearer and was partly used in the questionnaire for the adult sample (Appendix C).

8 I believe that kissing is acceptable for the male before marriage even if he is not particularly affectionate toward his partner.
Agree: (1) Strong, (2) Medium, (3) Slight
Disagree: (1) Strong, (2) Medium, (3) Slight

9. I believe that petting is acceptable for the female before marriage even if she is not particularly affectionate for her partner.
Agree: (1) Strong, (2) Medium, (3) Slight
Disagree: (1) Strong, (2) Medium, (3) Slight

10. I believe that full sexual relations is acceptable for the female before marriage even if she is not particularly affectionate for her partner.
Agree: (1) Strong, (2) Medium, (3) Slight
Disagree: (1) Strong, (2) Medium, (3) Slight

11. I believe that kissing is acceptable for the female before marriage even if she is not particularly affectionate toward her partner.
Agree: (1) Strong, (2) Medium, (3) Slight
Disagree: (1) Strong, (2) Medium, (3) Slight

12. With how many different people of the opposite sex have you had very regular or exclusive dating relationships?

13. Please describe what you feel the most important factors were in the development of your present sexual standard.

14. Do you feel that this questionnaire has gotten at the essence of your beliefs in this area?
_____ Yes
_____ No (if not, please explain your own standard in your own words)

15. Do you feel that a serious investigator could rely on the truthfulness of answers that members of this class are giving to this questionnaire?
_____ Yes
_____ No (if not, why not? Do you have any suggestions?)

THANK YOU FOR YOUR COOPERATION

APPENDIX C

Questionnaire Used
in National Adult Sample[1]

SURVEY RESEARCH SERVICE

National Opinion Research Center

University of Chicago

SRS-160

1. Taken all together, how would you say things are these days—would you say that you are *very happy, pretty happy,* or *not too happy?*___
     Very happy _____
     Pretty happy _____
     Not too happy _____

2. When you think of the things you want from life, would you say that you're *doing pretty well* or you're *not doing too well* now in getting the things you want?
     Doing pretty well now _____
     Not doing too well now _____

(ASK QUESTIONS 3–8 IF RESPONDENT IS WHITE. SKIP TO QUESTION 8 IF RESPONDENT IS NEGRO.)

The next few questions deal with some topics of current interest.

3. Do you think white students and Negro students should go to the same schools or to separate schools?
     Same schools _____
     Different schools _____
     Don't know _____

4. Generally speaking, do you think there should be separate sections for Negroes in street cars and buses?
     Yes _____
     No _____

5. If a Negro with the same income and education as you moved into your block, would it make any difference to you?

[1] The questionnaire in its present form contains only part of the questions asked by NORC interviewers. Some of the questions asked for other researchers have been omitted. These other questions were on the following topics: attitude and behavior toward alcohol, attitudes toward some problem areas in the public schools, magazine reading habits, and a few other miscellaneous questions. Of the questions used, the following were made available by courtesy of other researchers participating in this study: questions 1 and 2, by Norman Bradburn; questions 3 to 8, by Herbert Hyman and Paul B. Sheatsley; questions 9 to 14, by Norman Miller.

Yes (unfavorable or no comment volunteered) _____
No (favorable comment volunteered) _____
No, no difference _____
Don't know _____

6. In general, would you say you have become *more favorable* toward racial integration in recent years, or are you *less favorable* to integration?
    More favorable _____
    Less favorable _____
    About the same _____

IF MORE OR LESS FAVORABLE:

(a) why is that? (what are some of the things that have led you to become more or less favorable to integration now?)

7. In general, do you think Negroes are as intelligent as white people; that is, can they learn things just as well if they are given the same education and training?
    Yes _____
    No _____
    Don't know _____

8. (a) (ASK EVERYONE.) Do you think the day will ever come in the South when whites and Negroes will be going to the same schools, eating in the same restaurants, and generally sharing the same public accommodations?
    Yes _____ (ASK "b")
    No _____
    Don't know _____

IF YES:

(b) How many years do you think it will take before this comes about?

SKIP TO QUESTION 14 IF RESPONDENT IS WHITE. ASK QUESTIONS 9–13 ONLY IF RESPONDENT IS NEGRO.

The next few questions deal with some topics of current interest.

9. (a) I'm going to read some names of people and organizations. Please tell me whether you've ever heard of them. There may be some here you're not familiar with. First, the NAACP? Have you ever heard of them? (ASK ABOUT EACH NAME, AND CODE "YES" OR "NO" FOR EACH IN TABLE BELOW. ASK QUESTION 9b ABOUT EACH NAME CODED "YES" BELOW.)

(b) Now, please tell me whether your general opinion of the people or groups you know about is *favorable* or *unfavorable*. First, how about _____ (ASK FIRST ONE CODED "YES")? Is your opinion favorable or unfavorable?

	Ever heard of:		General Opinion of:		
	YES	NO	FAVORABLE	NEUTRAL	UNFAVORABLE
(a) The NAACP?					
(b) The Black Muslims?					
(c) SNCC? (Student Nonviolent Coordinating Committee)					
(d) Rev. Martin Luther King?					
(e) Malcolm X or Jeremiah X?					
(f) Southern Christian Leadership Conference?					
(g) Rev. Paul Davis?					
(h) CORE?					

10. Some people feel that in working for equal rights for Negroes, Rev. King is moving too fast; others think he is not working fast enough. What do you think?

He is moving too fast _____

He is moving at the right speed. _____

He isn't moving fast enough _____

11. I'm going to read four different ways that might be used to get equal rights for Negroes. Which one do you think is best? (READ CODES.)

(1) Marches, picketing, or sit-ins in which Negroes would be *ready to use* violence if necessary _____

(2) Marches, picketing, or sit-ins in which *no violence* would be used under *any* circumstances _____

(3) Use of the courts and the laws _____

(4) Rely on white people to gradually change their ideas _____

12. Here is a list of the things that Negro groups working for equal rights frequently want. (HAND RESPONDENT CARD C.) Which do you think is the most important to work for now? (RECORD ANSWER.) And which do you think is least important to work for now?

	MOST IMPORTANT	LEAST IMPORTANT
(a) Equal job opportunities		
(b) No discrimination in housing		
(c) Desegregation of public schools		
(d) Desegregation of public places, like restaurants, stores, and parks		
(e) Voting rights		
(f) Other (Specify)		
(g) Cannot choose one as the most or least important		

13. If there were to be a peaceful parade, a march, or picketing here in this town or area in favor of equal rights for Negroes, would you take part?

Yes _____ (ASK "a" and "b.")

No _____

IF YES:

(a) Would you take part even if you knew it might land you in jail?

Yes _____

No _____

(b) Would you take part even if you knew there might be violence?

Yes _____

No _____

(ASK EVERYONE REMAINING QUESTIONS.)

14. In general, are you satisfied or dissatisfied with the way the Kennedy administration is handling the problem of civil rights for Negroes?

Satisfied _____

Dissatisfied _____ (ASK "a.")

IF DISSATISFIED:

(a) Why?

15. The following questions concern some attitudes of yours regarding courtship behavior. We realize that you may be tolerant of what others do and think, but we are not interested now in that. We are interested in your own personal views about the questions we will ask. These questions do *not* concern what you do—they all concern what you believe about courtship. (HAND RESPONDENT BLUE SHEET, SIDE "A.") On this sheet we'd like you to circle the degree of agreement or disagreement you have with each state-

ment. For example, if you agree slightly with a statement, you would circle "3." If you disagree strongly, you would circle "6."[2] (THE FOLLOWING IN-STRUCTIONS ARE ON THE BLUE SHEET. YOU NEED NOT READ THEM ALOUD EXCEPT IF RESPONDENT HAS DIFFICULTY READING.) Just answer these statements on the basis of how you feel toward the views expressed. Your name will never be connected with these answers, so please be as honest as you can. We use the words to mean just what they do to most people, but some may need definition:

Love means the emotional state which is more intense than strong affection and which you would define as love.

Strong affection means affection which is stronger than physical attraction, average fondness, or "liking," but less strong than love.

Petting means sexually stimulating behavior more intimate than kissing and simple hugging, but not including full sexual relations.

(WHEN RESPONDENT FINISHES SIDE "A," BE SURE HE TURNS THE SHEET OVER AND COMPLETES SIDE "B." WHEN RESPONDENT FINISHES SIDE "B," TAKE BACK BLUE SHEET AND GO TO NEXT QUESTION. Questions *a* to *x* comprise the "blue sheet.")

(a) I believe that kissing is acceptable for the male before marriage when he is engaged to be married.
Agree: (1) Strong, (2) Medium, (3) Slight
Disagree: (1) Strong, (2) Medium, (3) Slight

(b) I believe that kissing is acceptable for the male before marriage when he is in love.
Agree: (1) Strong, (2) Medium, (3) Slight
Disagree: (1) Strong, (2) Medium, (3) Slight

(c) I believe that kissing is acceptable for the male before marriage when he feels strong affection for his partner.
Agree: (1) Strong, (2) Medium, (3) Slight
Disagree: (1) Strong, (2) Medium, (3) Slight

(d) I believe that kissing is acceptable for the male before marriage even if he does not feel particularly affectionate toward his partner.
Agree: (1) Strong, (2) Medium, (3) Slight
Disagree: (1) Strong, (2) Medium, (3) Slight

(e) I believe that petting is acceptable for the male before marriage when he is engaged to be married.
Agree: (1) Strong, (2) Medium, (3) Slight
Disagree: (1) Strong, (2) Medium, (3) Slight

(f) I believe that petting is acceptable for the male before marriage when he is in love.
Agree: (1) Strong, (2) Medium, (3) Slight
Disagree: (1) Strong, (2) Medium, (3) Slight

(g) I believe that petting is acceptable for the male before marriage when he feels strong affection for his partner.
Agree: (1) Strong, (2) Medium, (3) Slight
Disagree: (1) Strong, (2) Medium, (3) Slight

(h) I believe that petting is acceptable for the male before marriage even if he does not feel particularly affectionate toward his partner.
Agree: (1) Strong, (2) Medium, (3) Slight
Disagree: (1) Strong, (2) Medium, (3) Slight

[2] In the questionnaire the "disagree" subcategories were numbered 4, 5, and 6.

(i) I believe that full sexual relations are acceptable for the male before marriage when he is engaged to be married.
Agree: (1) Strong, (2) Medium, (3) Slight
Disagree: (1) Strong, (2) Medium, (3) Slight

(j) I believe that full sexual relations are acceptable for the male before marriage when he is in love.
Agree: (1) Strong, (2) Medium, (3) Slight
Disagree: (1) Strong, (2) Medium, (3) Slight

(k) I believe that full sexual relations are acceptable for the male before marriage when he feels strong affection for his partner.
Agree: (1) Strong, (2) Medium, (3) Slight
Disagree: (1) Strong, (2) Medium, (3) Slight

(l) I believe that full sexual relations are acceptable for the male before marriage even if he does not feel particularly affectionate toward his partner.
Agree: (1) Strong, (2) Medium, (3) Slight
Disagree: (1) Strong, (2) Medium, (3) Slight

(m) I believe that kissing is acceptable for the female before marriage when she is engaged to be married.
Agree: (1) Strong, (2) Medium, (3) Slight
Disagree: (1) Strong, (2) Medium, (3) Slight

(n) I believe that kissing is acceptable for the female before marriage when she is in love.
Agree: (1) Strong, (2) Medium, (3) Slight
Disagree: (1) Strong, (2) Medium, (3) Slight

(o) I believe that kissing is acceptable for the female before marriage when she feels strong affection for her partner.
Agree: (1) Strong, (2) Medium, (3) Slight
Disagree: (1) Strong, (2) Medium, (3) Slight

(p) I believe that kissing is acceptable for the female before marriage even if she does not feel particularly affectionate toward her partner.
Agree: (1) Strong, (2) Medium, (3) Slight
Disagree: (1) Strong, (2) Medium, (3) Slight

(q) I believe that petting is acceptable for the female before marriage when she is engaged to be married.
Agree: (1) Strong, (2) Medium, (3) Slight
Disagree: (1) Strong, (2) Medium, (3) Slight

(r) I believe that petting is acceptable for the female before marriage when she is in love.
Agree: (1) Strong, (2) Medium, (3) Slight
Disagree: (1) Strong, (2) Medium, (3) Slight

(s) I believe that petting is acceptable for the female before marriage when she feels strong affection for her partner.
Agree: (1) Strong, (2) Medium, (3) Slight
Disagree: (1) Strong, (2) Medium, (3) Slight

(t) I believe that petting is acceptable for the female before marriage even if she does not feel particularly affectionate toward her partner.
Agree: (1) Strong, (2) Medium, (3) Slight
Disagree: (1) Strong, (2) Medium, (3) Slight

(u) I believe that full sexual relations are acceptable for the female before marriage when she is engaged to be married.
Agree: (1) Strong, (2) Medium, (3) Slight
Disagree: (1) Strong, (2) Medium, (3) Slight

(v) I believe that full sexual relations are acceptable for the female before marriage when she is in love.
Agree: (1) Strong, (2) Medium, (3) Slight
Disagree: (1) Strong, (2) Medium, (3) Slight

(w) I believe that full sexual relations are acceptable for the female before marriage when she feels strong affection for her partner.
Agree: (1) Strong, (2) Medium, (3) Slight
Disagree: (1) Strong, (2) Medium, (3) Slight

(x) I believe that full sexual relations are acceptable for the female before marriage even if she does not feel particularly affectionate toward her partner.
Agree: (1) Strong, (2) Medium, (3) Slight
Disagree: (1) Strong, (2) Medium, (3) Slight

16. Finally, we have a few background questions.
What do you usually do—work full-time, work part-time, keep house, or something else?

Work full-time _____
Work part-time _____
Unemployed _____
Laid off, or on strike _____
Retired _____
Housewife (SKIP TO QUESTION 18)
Student (SKIP TO QUESTION 18)
Other (specify) _____

17. What kind of work (do you) (did you normally) do?
Occupation: _____.
(PROBE, IF VAGUE) What do you actually do on that job?
Industry: _____.

18. What is the last grade you completed in school?
0–7 years _____
8 years (completed grade school) _____
9–11 years _____
12 years (completed high school) _____
13–15 years (some college) _____
16 years (completed college) _____
More than 16 years _____

19. What is your marital status?

MALE RESPONDENT	FEMALE RESPONDENT
Single, never married— (SKIP TO QUESTION 23)	Single, never married— (SKIP TO QUESTION 23)
Currently married— (SKIP TO QUESTION 22)	Currently married— (SKIP TO QUESTION 20)
Separated, divorced— (SKIP TO QUESTION 22)	Separated, divorced— (SKIP TO QUESTION 21)
Widowed—(SKIP TO QUESTION 22)	Widowed—(SKIP TO QUESTION 21)

20. FOR CURRENTLY MARRIED WOMEN: What does your husband do—work full-time, is he laid off, or something else?

Works full-time _____
Works part-time _____
Unemployed _____
Laid off, or on strike _____
Retired _____
Student _____
Other (specify _____

21. What kind of work (does your husband) (did your husband normally) do?
Occupation: _____ .
Industry: _____ .

22. We'd like a little information about each of your children. This would include any that you might have had by a previous marriage.
(a) First, what are the age and sex of each of your children? Let's start
with the oldest and go to the youngest. (RECORD AGE AND SEX UNDER
"A" BELOW.)
(b) For each one, I'd like the following information:
(1) What grade of school is he/she in?
(ASK ABOUT EACH CHILD 18 OR YOUNGER:)
(2) Is that a public or parochial school?
(ASK ABOUT EACH CHILD 14 OR OLDER:)
(3) Has he/she ever been married?

A	B(1)	B(2)		B(3)	
Age Sex	*Grade of School*	*Type of School*		*Ever Married?*	
M F		PUBLIC	PAROCHIAL	YES	NO
(1)					
(2)					
(3)					
(4)					
(5)					
(6)					
(7)					
(8)					

23. What is your religious preference?
Protestant _____ (ASK "a.")
Catholic _____
Jewish _____
Other (specify) _____
IF PROTESTANT
(a) What denomination is that?

24. What is your age?

25. What is your main nationality background?
(a) First, how about your father's side? _____
(b) What is your main nationality background on your mother's side?
_____

26. Is there anyone in your immediate family who is blind?
Yes _____ (ASK "a" and "b.")
No _____
IF YES:

   (a) How is that person related to you?

        Parent _____

        Sibling _____

        Spouse _____

        Child _____

   (b) Could we have his name and address? (We may be planning a study of the blind sometime in the future, and it would be helpful to have his/her name and address.)

        Name _____

        Address _____

              (city)   (state)

27. Have you, yourself, ever lived in or outside the South?

    FOR NORTHERNERS OR WESTERNERS:

        Yes, have lived in South _____ (ASK "a")

        No, haven't lived in South _____

    FOR SOUTHERNERS:

        Yes, have lived in South _____ (ASK "A")

        No, haven't lived outside South _____

    IF YES:

   (a) Where was that? _____ _____

              (city or town)   (state)

28. (HAND RESPONDENT CARD "D.") Adding up the income from all sources, which category on this card comes closest to your total family income before taxes in 1962?

        Under $3000 _____

        $3000 to $3999 _____

        $4000 to $4999 _____

        $5000 to $5999 _____

        $6000 to $6999 _____

        $7000 to $7999 _____

        $8000 to $9999 _____

        $10,000 to $14,999 _____

        $15,000 or over _____

29. In the 1960 election, did you prefer Nixon or Kennedy for president?

        Nixon _____

        Kennedy _____

        Other (specify) _____

        Don't know _____

30. Did you happen to vote in that election or were you unable to for some reason?

        Did vote _____

        Did not vote _____

        Not eligible _____

Interviewer Remarks

1. Sex of respondent.

        Male _____

        Female _____

2. Race of respondent.
    White _____
    Negro _____

3. CODE THE MOST APPROPRIATE STATEMENT BELOW.
    (a) No Negro children attend school with whites in the public schools where respondent resides.
    (b) A few Negro children attend school with whites in the public schools where respondent resides.
    (c) A considerable number of Negro children attend school with whites in the public schools where respondent resides.

APPENDIX D

Reliability and Validity

General Reliability and Validity

To the extent that there is agreement that the dependent variable is adequately measured by the Guttman scales used in this study, there is support for the validity of this study. (See second part of this appendix for a full discussion of the validity of the scales.) The use of five schools in the student sample, of one school in the Iowa sample, and of a national sample means that there are really seven separately gathered samples on which to test many of the results. All relationships tested in the student sample were checked for each of the five schools in this sample. This too should promote confidence in the results of the study. The fact that the scales worked in all samples and that many similar relations were found is of importance in judging reliability. But the ultimate question of the honesty of the respondent remains. The aim was to get at informal, operational norms rather than merely at formal norms. Was this achieved? To reiterate what was said in Chapter 1, many married women in population surveys seem more willing to talk about their premarital and marital sex life than about their husband's income. In the past twenty years the general public has gained a vast amount of experience with survey researchers. Sex in particular has become a topic of public conversation on the college campuses, at PTA meetings, in ladies' magazines, and even in the church discussion groups. Thus, it would seem that there is a much greater willingness today to talk about sex and to talk about it candidly.[1]

The student sample probably has more validity in most people's judgment, because students are rather well known to be frank and outspoken concerning their attitudes. Further, it should be borne in mind that it was primarily attitudes that were being asked about and behavior was only secondary (except in the Iowa sample—see Appendix B). This too should promote confidence in the results of the study, for one would expect less hesitancy to reveal the truth on attitudinal questions than on behavioral questions. The adult sample was asked only attitudinal questions.

The student samples were given anonymous questionnaires by student assistants either in their rooms (the two Virginia colleges and the New York college) or in a group with ample space between seats and with teacher supervision (the

[1] For a coverage of recent developments in depth see Ira L. Reiss, ed., "The Sexual Renaissance in America," *Journal of Social Issues,* 22 (April 1966), pp. 1–140.

two high schools and the Iowa college). When the questionnaire was given out in private rooms the interviewer left the questionnaire and came back several hours later to pick up the completed form. The sex and race of interviewer and respondent were the same in these cases. In the adult sample the questions on sexual permissiveness were given to the respondent to fill out on a separate sheet. The interviewer did not see or record the answers but merely took back the sheet. The other questions were asked orally. The adult interviewers were almost all highly trained female interviewers employed by the National Opinion Research Center, and in most all cases they matched their respondents in race.[2] The questions were pretested in both the adult and student samples.

It may be argued that even trained female interviewers such as those used in the National Adult Sample could not help but inhibit the respondent, even if they just handed the respondent a sheet with items to check on sexual permissiveness (see Appendix C). However, the interviewers were specifically instructed to be careful not to give any impression of judging the respondent and to stress anonymity and the importance of the answers to social science research. There are certain advantages to the depth interview approach used by Kinsey and others, but the anonymous questionnaire also has unique advantages of its own. Ultimately, no matter what approach is used, there still is doubt about the honesty of the responses.

Some other checks on validity were done. There were two ways of measuring permissiveness in the student sample that involved a total of forty-eight questions (see Appendix A, Parts II and III). Both ways yielded very similar results. It would take some effort for the respondent to fabricate in a similar way on forty-eight questions—however, it is possible that some respondents did just that. Similar questions were asked in somewhat different ways at the beginning and at the end of the questionnaire, and this too yielded comparable responses (Appendix A, Part I, question 12, and Part VII, question 8). In the Iowa sample the respondents were asked to rate the truthfulness of their fellow students and to judge if the questionnaire had gotten at the essence of their own beliefs. About eighty percent said the questionnaire got at their beliefs and was answered truthfully by others. Many of these respondents admitted having guilt feelings, which also created confidence in their honesty.

Other validity checks involved examining previously established relationships. Granted that there are not many of these, the scale responses showed males more permissive than females, Negroes more permissive than whites, and students more permissive than adults. All of this tends to strengthen faith in the trustworthiness of the data.

If all the respondents had lied equally, it would, of course, have made no difference for purposes of comparing the high- and low-permissive individuals. The real danger is that some segments of the sample will lie more than other segments.[3] But if, for example, the high-permissive females had answered in a low-permissive fashion, then the range of response would have been narrow, and

---

[2] Nine of the 171 interviewers were males. Their results were not significantly different.

[3] Clark, John P. and Larry L. Tifft, "Polygraph and Interview Validation of Self Reported Deviant Behavior," *American Sociological Review,* 31 (August 1966), pp. 516–523, report that "there is no relationship between questionnaire validity (accuracy) and extent of involvement in deviant behavior" (p. 522). They found that people do cover up on things they actually did but do not accept, but that people differ on what is acceptable so that all types of people are involved in this sort of cover-up. This finding qualifies Allen L. Edwards' warnings in *Social Desirability Variable in Personality Assessment and Research.* New York: Holt, Rinehart and Winston, 1957.

this was not the case. Also, the differences between high- and low-permissive individuals would have been blurred, and it was found to be very sharp in many instances.

Less formal support for the validity of the findings comes from this researcher's having lived in the area of the five schools in the student sample for several years and having judged the responses to be in accord with his impressions of these students. Based on all the above evidence and recognizing the possibilities for error that remain, this researcher thinks he obtained basically truthful responses from the vast majority of respondents.[4]

Reliability and Validity of the Scales

The original twelve questions selected for the male and female scales formed a Guttman scale without any combination or dropping of questions.[5] This result lends support to the subjective choice of items in the scale and the reasoning supporting that choice. If it had been necessary to drop about half the items from the original questions, then the accuracy of the original conceptions would have been questionable. The questions were treated as dichotomous. Like any other scaling technique, the Guttman approach can be abused. If the researcher starts with a large group of items and then drops and combines them many times, the likelihood of finding a scale is quite high. However, such a scale would not be a meaningful one, for Guttman scaling requires that the researcher have a conception of the underlying dimension in mind, and if he must drop any items he ought to explain why he had to do so and alter the original conception accordingly.[6] Thus, it is worth noting that the original twelve-item male and female scales fit the Guttman-scale model.

The reliance on the researcher's conception of the dimension being measured is one insurance against pseudo Guttman scales. Other precautions involve the use of additional measures besides the coefficient of reproducibility. An item-by-item analysis was performed on the twelve items in each of the two scales. Each item was run in its dichotomized form against every other item in its scale.[7]

---

[4] All computations were checked several times. No major changes are necessary in any previously published reports on this study, but in a few tables some cases had to be reclassified.

[5] Other questions were experimented with but none were an essential part of the scales. For example see Appendix A, Part III question 13, which was added to check some specific ideas but is clearly not part of the scale.

[6] H. Christensen and G. Carpenter, "Value Behavior Discrepancies Regarding Premarital Coitus," *American Sociological Review,* 27 (February 1962), pp. 66–74. These authors started with twenty-one items and threw away eleven of them in order to get a .90 coefficient of reproducibility from the remaining ten items. It is clear from a perusal of these ten items that they are not unidimensional either. They involve questions of attitudes toward obscenity, toward the permissiveness of one's daughter, toward one's own permissiveness, toward marrying a virgin, and toward premarital pregnancy. It seems apparent that although these dimensions may be related (and that is why there is the appearance of a Guttman scale) they are not all tapping a single attitudinal dimension. To use such items and state what they are is permissible, but it seems misleading to call them a Guttman scale simply because after extensive manipulation they fit one criterion (the coefficient of reproducibility) of such a scale.

[7] It was possible to trichotomize several of the twelve items in the scale and still meet all the Guttman requirements. However, for the sake of simplicity all questions were dichotomized into *agree* or *disagree* regardless of the intensity of such feeling.

The two criteria suggested by Toby and Toby were utilized: (1) the zero cell should be no more than 10 percent of the total number of cases and (2) it should be no more than half of the + + or − − cells adjoining it.[8] This method checks for the cumulative quality that should be found in a set of intercorrelated items comprising a Guttman scale. The "zero" cell is the cell containing those responses that show agreement with a "higher" question and disagreement with a "lower" question. On a perfect Guttman scale, everyone who agrees with a question that indicates a higher position on the dimension must accept all questions that indicate a lower position on that dimension.

The item that showed up poorest in this test was item 4 (kissing without affection). This was expected since this item had the least stability in the various samples—moving from rank 5 to rank 10. There seemed to be a great deal of diversity regarding the relative permissiveness involved in this item. Question 4 produced the highest percent error in both the male and female scales in each sample, which further shows that even within one sample there was not a clear conception as to the rank in which this question belonged. There were similar difficulties with item 8, but to a smaller extent.

As a further check the coefficient of reproducibility (CR) was estimated using only those questions that did not have marginals as extreme as 80 or 20 percent. In all these checks, and in those using all twelve items, the coefficient of reproducibility was about .95, which is relatively high, and quite a bit higher than the coefficient of reproducibility of scales devised by Guttman during World War II.[9] The National Adult Sample had coefficients of reproducibility that were a few percentage points higher than the student sample on both male and female scales.

The coefficient of scalability (CS) was designed by Herbert Menzel (while he was working on his Ph.D.) to indicate the proportion of the total possible improvement that a particular Guttman scale affords over what could be predicted by knowing only the extremeness of individual responses and the extremeness of the marginals to each question.[10] In short, the coefficient of scalability informs the researcher as to what proportion of the remaining indeterminateness is removed by the scale in use. Menzel suggests that the coefficient of scalability should be about .60 to .65, which was the average coefficient of scalability that he estimated Guttman achieved from his World War II scales. Both the male and female scales in the student and the adult samples had coefficients of scalability that were between .80 and .90, indicating that more than eighty percent of the indeterminateness had been removed by the use of the Guttman-scale model.

Similar to the coefficient of scalability is the minimal marginal reproducibility

---

In research it is still advisable to use the six-way choice after each question, for without such an elaborate choice some respondents feel that they are not able to elaborate fully their beliefs in this area. Such a concession to respondent satisfaction is a small price to pay for cooperation.

[8] Jackson Toby and Marcia L. Toby, "A Method of Selecting Dichotomous Items by Cross Tabulation," *Sociological Studies in Scale Analysis,* John Riley *et al.,* ed. New Brunswick, New Jersey: Rutgers University Press, 1954, pp. 339–355.

[9] Samuel A. Stouffer, Louis Guttman, Edward A. Suchman, Paul F. Lazarsfeld, Shirley A. Star, and John A. Clausen, *Studies in Social Psychology in World War II,* Vol. 4. Princeton, N. J.: Princeton University Press, 1950. Carlfred Broderick of The Pennsylvania State University, devised the computor program for Guttman-scaling that was used in the present study.

[10] Herbert Menzel, "A New Coefficient for Scalagram Analyses," *Public Opinion Quarterly* (Summer 1953), pp. 268–280.

(MMR) devised by Edwards.[11] This measure simply takes the modal response for each scale item and divides it by the number of items, to obtain a reproducibility level that could be operated on just with knowledge of the extremeness of the item modes. A comparison of the minimal marginal reproducibility with the coefficient of reproducibility of the scale yields a measure of the improvement afforded by fitting the items to the Guttman-scale model. The minimal marginal reproducibility differed from the coefficient of reproducibility in the twelve-item male and female scales by about twenty percentage points. Minimal marginal reproducibility differs from a coefficient of scalability by not including any measure of the extremeness of individual responses, but it involves a similar type of logic.

In arranging scale responses into a Guttman-scale cumulative pattern, a considerable amount of juggling often occurs. It is well to have some measure of this because the less of it, the more the researcher can feel that the results were not artificially produced by simply an elaborate rearrangement of the responses. One way to measure this is to see what percentage of the respondents give pure scale-type responses, that is, give responses that fit perfectly one of the scale types in the particular scale. The percentage of respondents with pure scale responses to the twelve-item male and female scales was slightly over fifty percent in the student sample and almost sixty percent in the adult sample.[12] Relative to other scales, this is a good level of pure scale response. Many of the other respondents had only one error in their response patterns, and this also reduces the amount of "juggling" involved. As noted above, the two items with the greatest error were items 4 and 8, with item 4 being the largest producer of error. In both samples, item 4 averaged about fifteen to twenty percent error, while item 8 averaged about half of this amount or less, and all other items averaged very low in errors.

In sum, then, all the samples, both student and adult, showed a coefficient of reproducibility of about .95, a coefficient of scalability of about .85, a minimal marginal reproducibility of about .75 and a percent pure scale type of about .55. Compared to other scales used by Guttman and others, these results are very much on the high side. Taken together with the fact that no question had to be dropped, it lends strong support to the validity of the twelve-item male and female scales.

The explanation for the errors in items 4 and 8 that seems most persuasive is that there simply is a lack of clarity in American cultural values regarding the relation of these questions to some of the other scale questions. For example, there is *no* lack of clarity regarding the place of item 4 when it is compared only to the other kissing questions, and there is no lack of clarity concerning the rank of item 8 when it is compared to the other petting questions. The lack of ranking consensus occurs when item 4 is compared with items on petting or coitus and when item 8 is compared with items on coitus. Thus, it is in the interrelation of the three physical areas of kissing, petting, and coitus that the errors occur. Whether affectionless kissing is more permissive than affectionate petting or affectionate coitus is the sort of question that does not seem to be clearly answered by the American value system.

American values clearly define the subdimensions involved in the four kissing

[11] Allen L. Edwards, *Techniques of Attitude Scale Construction*. New York: Appleton-Century-Crofts, 1957, pp. 191–193.

[12] Since the Iowa College Sample was small and not a probability sample, it is not mentioned here. However, results in this sample were comparable to those in the other samples.

items, the four petting items, and the four coital items. However, when these three subdimensions are joined, the boundary areas are not so clear, and the extreme kissing and the extreme petting ranks create some error. This is not to say that the twelve-item scale is not measuring a single dimension. Rather, it is to recognize that there may well be variation within one basic dimension in terms of the clarity with which the ranks are conceived of by the respondents. Overall, there is one rank order that will scale all respondents quite well on the male and on the female scales. However, there is lesser universality regarding the ranking of items 4 and 8.

There are a few things the researcher can do to accommodate to the finding that items 4 and 8 are less anchored than the other items. First, he may use three separate permissiveness scales: one each for kissing, petting, and coitus. This is useful for some research problems, but generally it involves three times as many tables. Another choice is to disregard the movement of these items, since it does not fundamentally alter the scales' usefulness, and still to use all twelve questions. Further, he can use items 4, 8, and 12 as a nonaffection scale and use the other nine questions as an affection scale. Finally, he can select from the twelve items only those items that scale in exactly the same rank order in all samples and thereby discard such items as 4 and 8. This latter choice was the one taken in this study, and so a "contrived" *five-item scale* was developed.

The first three kissing items obtain well over 90 percent support, and thus are not needed in any subscale. Items 5 and 6 are so close that they can be combined and treated as one question, and all who agree to either one or both may be counted as agreeing to this contrived item. The same thing can be done to items 9 and 10. This leaves five basic items that scale identically in all samples: (5, 6), 7, (9, 10), 11, 12. Scale-type zero would reject all of these questions and would in almost all cases be composed of those who agreed only with kissing (items 1, 2, and 3). Scale-type one would accept (5, 6), and scale-type two would also accept (7), and so forth up to scale-type five, which would agree with all these items. This is the basic subscale that is used throughout the analysis in this study. It is universal in that every sample scales in the exact same way on this scale. Appendix E elaborates a simple method of scoring answers in accord with this scale. Although samples differ in their level of permissiveness, the rank order of the questions in this subscale are always the same. Thus, it has a universal quality that makes it particularly useful in comparing diverse groups, and it is recommended for future researchers. However, it should be added that the full twelve-question version of the scale is still valuable and should be used in research questionnaires for several reasons. First, it is important to check the various statistical measures of Guttman scales on the full twelve-item scale. Secondly, it is informative to note the rank of items 4 and 8, for they tell the level of group permissiveness in a way that is comparable with other samples and less direct than simply looking at the coital support in a group. It is well to use all twelve so that no differences in finding can be attributed to the contextual effect of using fewer questions. Finally, the researcher may want to use other subscales, such as the three kissing, petting, and coital subscales discussed previously, and they cannot be used unless all question responses are available. Some other subscales have also been used and will be referred to later.

In estimating an individual's permissiveness, the researcher must use the responses to the scale of the same sex as the person (male scale for men, female scale for women). To do otherwise is to contaminate potentially the individual's permissiveness with his equalitarianism. For example, a double-standard male may come out very low on permissiveness if his responses to the female scale are looked at, and a double-standard female may come out high on permissiveness if her responses to the male scale are looked at. The "same-sex scale" must be used to obtain a person's permissiveness level for himself, and that is what was used throughout the study.

All the scale statistics used on the twelve-item scales were computed on all the various subscales discussed above.[13] Every one of the subscales came out even "higher" on these statistics than did the twelve-item scale. This would be expected, since the fewer the number of items, the easier it is for chance to produce favorable results; for example, there are only thirty-two possible combinations of five dichotomous items, whereas there are 4096 possible combinations of twelve dichotomous items.[14]

Further checks on the scales were made by seeing if they would show what previous research had shown: that males and Negroes are respectively more permissive than females and whites. The scales did show this quite clearly, as the tables in Chapter 2 indicate. The Negro-white differences are clearly seen in the school comparisons, although it is also noticeable that one white school (the New York college) was equal to the Negro level of permissiveness. In point of fact the New York college was chosen, in part, as a validity test, since it was felt on other grounds that it was a highly permissive school, and thus it could be seen whether or not the scales would show this high level of permissiveness.

Male-female differences show up in comparison of rankings. Just as the more-permissive groups rank item 4 lower than the less-permissive groups; so males rank this item lower (less relative support) than do females.[15] Women respond on the male scale in ways indicating they give men more permissiveness than they do themselves; whereas men respond to the female scale in ways that indicate that they give women less permissiveness than they do themselves.[16] This basic set of male-female differences is just what one would predict on the basis

---

[13]The reader may be interested in using the twelve-item scales to arrive at premarital sexual standards. See fn. 13 in Chapter 2 for instructions.

[14] On the five-item universal scale discussed above, CR = .97, CS = .89, MMR = .70, and the percent pure scale type = .87 in the student sample. In the adult sample CR = .99, CS = .95, MMR = .72 and percent pure scale type = .96. These figures are averages for the male and female scales. Only slight differences appear between these two scales. The figures are *not* same-sex figures but rather total response to each scale. However, same-sex statistics are very similar. A chi-square test of the probability of the results was also performed and found to support the scales in every case. This check was suggested in Leon Festinger, "The Treatment of Quantitive Data by Scale Analysis," *Psychological Bulletin,* 44 (March 1947), pp. 149–161.

[15] However, item 8 does not show the same "mobility" as it did between Negro and white groups.

[16] The ways respondents of both sexes, when taken together, respond to the male scale and the female scale is taken as indicative of the general cultural view of this area. The way each sex responds separately may, of course, be taken as that particular sex's way of conceiving male or female sexual values. The way an individual responds to questions regarding his own sex is taken to be a measure of his own personal permissiveness. Thus, cultural values, in the area of sex particularly, must be specified as to who holds the values and toward what groups. Such specification is necessary in order to add meaning to any assertions that are made. In dealing with any value area wherein certain groups differ sharply, this same requirement would hold, despite the fact that it is often overlooked in the sociological literature.

Table D.1
PERCENTAGE AGREEING TO QUESTIONS IN THE MALE AND FEMALE FIVE-ITEM SCALES BY MEN AND WOMEN

Questions	Student Sample				Adult Sample			
	MEN		WOMEN		MEN		WOMEN	
	Male Scale	*Female Scale*	*Male Scale*	*Female Scale*	*Male Scale*	*Female Scale*	*Male Scale*	*Female Scale*
5 and/or 6	92.3	91.9	82.9	76.8	76.6	71.0	53.1	47.9
7	79.3	70.1	55.8	45.5	68.2	60.0	41.8	32.7
9 and/or 10	68.9	63.8	42.4	32.3	31.4	25.5	11.3	8.7
11	50.4	42.3	24.9	14.1	25.0	19.1	8.0	6.7
12	30.9	19.2	12.7	4.1	18.1	11.0	5.3	3.9
N	(405)	(395)	(434)	(440)	(691)	(697)	(751)	(749)

of other knowledge of the American double-standard heritage.[17] (See Table D.1.)

Given the low level of knowledge about the area of sexual permissiveness, there is not much more that could be done to check the validity of these scales. Reliability is not an issue in Guttman scales, since the finding of a cumulative scale pattern means that the items have a singular meaning to the respondents and would evoke the same response whenever given. Unidimensionality with high reproducibility means that little error in measurement is possible.[18]

Some writers, such as Donald Hayes,[19] have suggested that the response of individuals is sensitive to the contextual factor of the order in which the items are asked. Although it is doubtful as to whether this effect has been fully demonstrated, it is worth noting.[20] In order to check on this possibility an experiment was made with the Iowa College Sample to see what effect a change of item order would have on matched groups of students. The group taking the items in the order given in Exhibit 2.2 did come out somewhat more permissive than those taking the items in a random order. However, the individual rank order was not affected except in a very small number of cases; that is, the relative position of individuals remained the same, and thus the ordinal qualities of the Guttman scale were not affected.[21] Nevertheless, it is probably a good idea, especially for comparing groups, that each group be given the scale items in the same order so as to control for any possible contextual effects that may contaminate the researcher's analysis.

[17] Ira L. Reiss, *Premarital Sexual Standards in America*. New York: The Free Press, 1960. Chap. 4 is a detailed discussion of the double-standard.

[18] Louis Guttman, "Problems of Reliability," *Studies in Social Psychology in World War II*, Vol. 4, Stouffer *et al.*, eds., pp. 277–312.

[19] Donald P. Hayes, "Item Order and Guttman Scales," *American Journal of Sociology*, 70 (July 1964), pp. 51–58.

[20] Ira L. Reiss, "Hayes' Item Order and Guttman Scales," *American Journal of Sociology*, 70 (March 1965), p. 629.

[21] Others have found similar results showing that although scale scores may change, individual rankings remain more constant. See John P. Clark and Larry L. Tifft, "Polygraph and Interview Validation of Self Reported Deviant Behavior," *American Sociological Review*, 31 (August 1966), p. 521.

One way that Guttman has suggested for handling the issue of the effect of question order, question wording, and such is to use "intensity analysis" to establish an invariant zero point in the scale, which will separate those favorable to the attitude being measured from those unfavorable on the attitude and at exactly the same point regardless of questionnaire item order.[22] In effect, the researcher cross-classifies each respondent by scale type on the content dimension and by intensity of his response, indicated by whether he said his feelings were strong (two points), medium (one point) or slight (zero points) on each question. Thus a search is made for a patterned way that scale type relates to intensity. Guttman states that the resultant curve will usually be U- or J-shaped,

Table D.2
FEMALE SCALE INTENSITY SCORES IN STUDENT SAMPLE

Intensity Level	Low						Scale Type						High		
	0	1	2	3	4	5	6	7	8	9	10	11	12	Total N
24 (high)			22	1	5	3	5	1	2	6	2	2	12	61
23			14		6	2	6		2	2	1	1	3	37
22		_3_	26	6	6	2	3		5	8	4	5	(3)	71
21		1	(14)	3	10	2	12		1	10	2		4	59
20		1	8	8	15	2	9	1	5	6	3	3	1	62
19			14	7	12	12	11	4	7	14	3	(2)	3	89
18	(1)	1	8	(7)	(19)	7	(14)	5	6	(11)	(5)	6	2	92
17			4	7	17	(9)	5		_6_	13	2	1	2	66
16			8	5	8	7	4	1	13	12	3			61
15			3	2	10	5	9	(4)	6	4	2	2	1	48
14				4	9	4	6	5	5	11	1			45
13			1	3	6	2	5	3	1	3	2		1	27
12			1		4	1	2	2	1	3	1		1	16
11			1	2	1	1	2	3	3	1	1			15
10				2	2	3	1	1	3			1	1	14
9				2	1	1	3		1	2	1			11
8			1	1		1	1					1		5
7						2	1							3
6			1		1									2
5					1		2							3
4										1				1
3							1							1
2						1								1
1														0
0 (low)														0
Total N	1	6	126	60	133	67	102	30	68	106	33	24	34	790

[a] Median intensity is circled within each scale type. Underlines represent median intensities that fall between two intensity levels. The numbers in the table represent the number of respondents. This applies to Tables D.3, D.4, and D.5 also.

[22] Louis Guttman, "The Intensity Component in Attitude and Opinion Research," *Studies in Social Psychology in World War II*, Vol. 4, Stouffer *et al.*, eds., pp. 213–277.

showing high intensity at both the low and high scale types typically. The zero point is taken to be the low point of the curve, the bottom of the U or J. The following four graphs show the intensity-content curves formed by the student and adult samples on both the male and female scales.[23] One interesting difference is that the student sample is generally more intense at all levels than the adult sample.[24] In addition, the student sample shows more of a U-shaped curve, with both low *and* high permissives being intense. However, in the adult sample only those who were low on permissiveness were likely to be intense

Table D.3
MALE SCALE INTENSITY SCORES IN STUDENT SAMPLE

Intensity	Low					Scale Type						High			Total N
	0	1	2	3	4	5	6	7	8	9	10	11	12	
24 (high)			21	1	4	3	2		2	7	2	4	23	69
23			6	1	4	2	5		1	4	2	3	9	37
22		1	11	5	8	4	7	1	3	5	7	4	3	59
21		1	7	7	7	3	11	1	4	3	3	5	(9)	61
20		(3)	6	4	16	4	15		6	7	4	6	11	82
19			13	5	12	4	11	2	7	12	6	4	7	83
18			10	(9)	7	5	(18)	4	5	(10)	6	7	4	85
17		1	5	3	12	5	5	2	3	8	7	4	4	59
16	(1)		3	3	12	8	8	3	(15)	7	4	3	5	72
15			1	1	6	5	4	4	5	4	4	4	2	40
14			2	2	4	2	7	4	5	6	6	2	1	41
13				1	5	7	3		4	4	3		2	29
12			2	3	1	1	4	1	5	2	2	3		24
11			1	2	1	3	2	2	1	3	3	1		19
10			1		1	2	2	1	2	3				12
9				1							1			2
8					1	2	1		1	1		2		8
7													1	1
6							1		1				1	3
5					1					1				2
4		1							1					2
3								1		1				2
2														0
1														0
0 (low)														0
Total N	1	7	89	48	102	60	106	26	71	88	60	52	82	792

[23] It is interesting to note that item 4 in both scales, in both samples, has the lowest intensity of any question. This is congruent with its high degree of error, for it shows possible respondent uncertainty.

[24] Using same-sex intensity scores did not radically alter the results, since it seems that the key difference here is between students and adults and not between sexes.

Table D.4
FEMALE SCALE INTENSITY SCORES IN ADULT SAMPLE

Intensity	Low						Scale Type					High		
	0	1	2	3	4	5	6	7	8	9	10	11	12	Total N
24 (high)	(29)	2	4	40	2		7	14			6		15	119
23		3	3	39	1	2	3					3	2	56
22			(2)	11	47	3	3	10	8	1		2	2	89
21	2	2	6	60		1	12	10					3	96
20	1	1	(6)	(72)	2	7	5	22	3	2		3	4	128
19	1		7	40	8	7	15	19		1		1	5	103
18	1		3	34	3	7	21	19	1	2	3	2	4	100
17	1	1	1	24	8	(8)	18	16	(2)	1		3	1	84
16	4	1	1	43	(5)	5	(14)	(41)	1	4	4	6	3	132
15		1		8	6	8	12	28		6	4	5	4	82
14		1	2	6	4	3	15	26		(3)	1	2	1	64
13		1	1	5	2	3	7	15		2	2	6	3	47
12	2		2	14	6	2	17	17		3	4	3	(12)	82
11			1	8		2	7	14		2	1	7	3	45
10	2		2	3	1	3	5	13	1	1	4	3	7	45
9				3		1	5	7		2	1	1	3	23
8	2			6	2		2	12	1	3	1		6	35
7				3	1		1	1		1	1	1	5	14
6	1			5		1	1	4		1	1	2	2	18
5	1			3			1	2			1			8
4	1			3		1		1			1		1	8
3			1		1		2						1	5
2			2	2									1	5
1		1											1	2
0 (low)	4			3	3			2	1	1		1		6	21
Total N	52	16	56	471	55	64	181	290	10	35	36	50	95	1411

about their beliefs. The female scale in the adult sample seems to have three separate levels of intensity: the highest for those who are in the kissing types, medium for those in the petting scale types, and lowest for those in the coital scale types. This forms a rather unusual intensity curve, for it is not fully U- or J-shaped, but divides intensity along content lines of kissing, petting, and coitus, which makes sense in American society. Finally, it is noticeable from these graphs that the zero point seems generally to come between scale types 7 and 9, or at the point where the acceptance of coitus occurs. This cutting point is also, on other grounds, a good place to divide the high- and low-permissiveness respondents and is the general cutting point most in use throughout this study.

It is interesting to speculate on the meaning of these intensity differences between the adult and student samples. *It is possible that intensity is highest when the individual conceives of his or her position as being socially threatened in some way.* Adults are highest on intensity when low on permissiveness because they fear that their youngsters are prone to violate the adult conservative standards. Students are high on intensity when low on permissiveness for similar reasons to those of the adults, and the students are intense when high on per-

Table D.5
MALE SCALE INTENSITY SCORES IN THE ADULT SAMPLE

Intensity	Low 0	1	2	3	4	5	Scale Type 6	7	8	9	10	High 11	12	Total N
24 (high)	16	3	4	27	1	2	4	13	1			4	27	102
23			3	29		1	6	3	1	1			8	52
22		5	7	37	3		2	10		1		3	3	71
21	3		8	38		6	8	9				2	2	76
20	2	2	4	37	1	5	11	36	1	3	2	2	9	115
19	1	1	4	59		6	11	24	1	2	3	1	7	120
18	1	1	4	48	2	9	10	27		2	4	2	5	115
17	4	1	1	25	3	7	18	31	2	1	1	7	7	108
16	3	2	3	21	1	5	7	45		2		3	7	99
15	2		1	18	3	5	13	29	1	2	2	5	8	89
14	2		1	10	1	7	6	28	1	1	1	8	6	72
13		1	1	10	1	3	5	23	1	2	2	6	3	58
12	2		1	12	2	4	17	26	1	6		2	18	91
11	1		1	4			8	15	1	1	1	2	5	39
10	1					1	3	9	1	1		3	3	33
9			2			1	2	12	2	1	1	4	2	27
8	2	1	3	4	1		5	12			3	1	4	36
7	2			4		2		5	2	1		1	4	21
6	1		1	5		1	2	2				2	4	18
5								2				2	2	6
4				4			3	3					1	11
3		1		3	1		1				1			7
2			1	1			1		2			1	3	9
1							1						2	3
0 (low)	4		2	1	1								3	11
Total N	47	18	50	410	21	65	144	364	18	27	21	61	143	1389

missiveness because they perceive the adult challenge to their high level of permissiveness. Chapters 7, 8 and 9 present some suggestive evidence showing adult-student attitudinal differences in this area.

One final check on the conceptualization of the premarital sexual permissiveness dimension was made by asking the same substantive questions using different wording. For example, the respondent was asked not about himself but about his response to the attitude of a hypothetical couple (John and Mary) toward kissing, petting, and coitus under various states of affection. (See Appendix A, Part II, for the full set of questions). The different wording did not significantly change the results. These "John and Mary" scales came out very close in all measures applied. However, they were slightly lower in the coefficient of reproducibility, coefficient of scalability, and percentage of pure scale types. In addition, the male and female scales contained somewhat larger proportions of high-permissiveness individuals and more double-standard responses. This difference was taken as an index of the greater validity of the male and female scales, because it was felt that respondent deception would tend to be in the direction of reducing reported permissiveness and nonequalitarianism.

Ultimately, after all the checks are made, the validity of the scales depends on the subjective judgment of the individual who made up the scales. This is true of all scales. In this regard all this researcher can say is that he reviewed all the key research in this area in his 1960 book, has carefully studied the conceptualization of permissiveness, and believes this to be a valid scale.

APPENDIX E

Simple Instructions for Use of Reiss Premarital Sexual Permissiveness Scales

These instructions are not intended to replace or substitute for the full Guttman-scaling procedures that can be used with these scales. Rather, they are intended as a guide for those who want an efficient way of handling the scales that does not involve much technical background or reading.

First, always use all twelve items in each of the two scales (male scale and female scale) when administering them to respondents. The reasons for this are many. With all twelve items available, the researcher can select the four dealing with petting and use them alone for a petting scale. He can do the same with the four items concerning coitus or kissing. Also, he can select the three items dealing with situations where affection is not present (4, 8 and 12) and use them as a nonaffection scale.

Secondly, also use the six-way choice after each item, for that makes the respondent feel he can present his feelings more accurately, and you may at some future time want to use this full information. Most respondents can make this six-way choice for all twelve questions in a scale in a matter of a few minutes, so not much time is taken up by asking for a full answer to each of the twelve items.

After administering both the male and female scales in full form, the researcher may assume that he has a Guttman scale, since these scales have been tested on thousands of individuals in various groupings and always have worked properly. However, as noted previously, ideally the researcher should test for a Guttman scale using one of the Guttman-scaling procedures available on computers (there is one at the University of Iowa Computer Center that you may write for) or using a hand method such as that described by Louis Guttman in "The Cornell Technique for Scale and Intensity Analysis," *Educational and Psychological Measurement*, 7 (Summer 1947), pp. 247–280. Treat all responses as dichotomies so that any degree of agreement is counted as *agree* and any degree of disagreement is counted as *disagree*. This greatly simplifies the procedures involved. For other purposes, such as intensity analysis, use the open responses; but for simply testing for a Guttman scale, use the dichotomous form.

These instructions have been prepared under the assumption that the researcher will sometime make the above official Guttman-scale check, but that he wants a quick method for the moment. A scale that uses items 5, 6, 7, 9, 10, 11, and 12—seven of the twelve items—is recommended. Scores would be assigned to individual respondents on the basis of the following diagram.

	SCALE TYPE[a]					
ITEM NUMBER	0	1	2	3	4	5
5 or 6 or both	—	+	+	+	+	+
7	.—	—	+	+	+	+
9 or 10 or both	—	—	—	+	+	+
11	—	—	—	—	+	+
12	—	—	—	—	—	+

[a] A plus sign indicates agreement with the item.

The diagram indicates that respondents would be assigned to one of the six scale types on the basis of how he or she answered the seven items. For example, a person would be given a scale type of zero if he disagreed with all items. He would get a scale type of five if he agreed with all items. The other scale types fall in-between these two extremes. Items 5 and 6 have been combined, so that if a person answered Yes to one or both of these, he would be counted as agreeing; in short, only those who answered No to both of these would be counted as disagreeing. Items 9 and 10 have also been combined into one item in exactly the same way. This was done because the responses to these four items were so close that it was not important to separate them from each other.

You can simply look at how each respondent answered these questions and place him in one scale type or another accordingly. There are a few minor problems that may arise. First, the researcher should drop all respondents who have not answered all twelve questions; even though he uses only seven of them here, it is best not to include those who have not fully replied, for he cannot be sure he possesses their complete attitude. Second,—and this is more complicated —is the question of what to do with those respondents who are not "pure" scale types, that is, who do not fit perfectly into any of these scale types. In reality the researcher should not have to handle many error types, for more than ninety percent should be pure scale types. But when error types do appear, he should try to place the person in the scale type closest to his response, and in so doing try to place him nearer the center of the scale than toward either extreme (scale-types zero or five). For example, if a person agreed with items 5 and 6, disagreed with item 7 and agreed with item 9, he would have a scale-type three response with one error (item 7), and he could simply be called a scale-type three, which is the middle of the scale. However, if in addition to the above response the person had disagreed with item 11 and agreed with item 12, he would not be called scale-type five, for that is an extreme type, and it is best not to put people there unless they clearly fit. Instead he would be called scale-type three and placed in the middle of the scale. One other example: if a person responds Yes to items 5 and 6 and also agrees with items 7 and 12, he would be called scale-type two, which would keep him near the middle of the scale and would also produce only one "error" in his pattern. (The error would be his agreeing to item 12.) If he were called scale-type five, he would have two errors, for he would be missing on agreement to item 11 and to the combined item (9, 10). Thus, he fits better (has less error) in scale-type two. Making better fits and keeping toward the center of the scale are the two guides to use in assigning cases that are not pure scale types. A little practice and it should be quite easy. This sort of thing is required in the "Cornell" method of Guttman-scaling described in the article by Guttman noted above. Thus, this practice is useful for learning Guttman-scaling techniques.

There is another very important point. When the researcher obtains answers for both the male scale and the female scale for each respondent, he should first give scale types for each respondent on the scale that is the same sex as the respondent (women on the female scale and men on the male scale) and call this their same-sex permissiveness scale type. Then he should scale the respondent on the scale type of the sex opposite to himself and call this the opposite-sex permissiveness scale type. To do this most easily, it would be best to group separately all questionnaires answered by men and all answered by women respondents. If the researcher wants to measure the permissiveness of his respondents, he should use the same-sex scale types. If he wants to measure equalitarianism, he should compare the same-sex scale types with the opposite-sex scale types and classify the people who differ as nonequalitarian. He could distinguish the nonequalitarians by direction and by how many scale types they differed on the two scales. If he wants to measure the permissiveness allowed the opposite sex, he would use the opposite-sex scale types.

For the researcher's own purposes, he may want to reduce the six scale types to two or three groups of scale types. He should then combine all those who are scale-types zero, one, and two and call them low permissives and all those who are scale types three, four, and five and call them high permissives. That would afford a dichotomy of the scale. For a trichotomy, call scale-type zero low, scale-types one and two medium, and scale-types three, four, and five high. This is useful for dealing with a sexually conservative group. With a high-permissive group, trichotomize by combining scale-types zero, one, and two as low, three and four as medium, and five as high. Note that scale-type zero will be mostly those who only accept kissing; scale-types one and two also accept petting, and scale types three, four, and five also accept coitus.

By following these instructions the researcher should be able to handle responses to both the male scale and the female scale quite easily and to assign each respondent a scale type for each of these two scales.[1]

---

[1] If one is interested in using sexual standards, see fn. 13 in Chapter 2 for instructions.

Bibliography

American Social Health Association. *Today's VD Control Problem*. New York: February, 1966.

Aries, Philip. *Centuries of Childhood*. New York: Alfred A. Knopf, 1962.

Ashmore, Harry S. *The Negro and the Schools*. Chapel Hill: University of North Carolina Press, 1954.

————. *An Epitaph for Dixie*. New York: W. W. Norton & Co., 1957.

Ball, John C. and Nell Logan. "Early Sexual Behavior of Lower-Class Delinquent Girls," *Journal of Criminal Law, Criminology, and Police Science,* 51 (July–August 1960), pp. 209–214.

Barry, Herbert, Margaret K. Bacon, and Irvin L. Child. "A Cross-cultural Survey of Some Sex Differences in Socialization," *Journal of Abnormal and Social Psychology,* 55 (April 1957), pp. 327–332.

Beigel, Hugo, ed. *Advances in Sex Research*. New York: Harper & Row, Publishers, 1963.

Bell, Robert R. and Leonard Blumberg, "Courtship Stages and Intimacy Attitudes," *Family Life Coordinator,* 8 (March 1960), pp. 61–63.

———— and Jack V. Buerkle. "Mother and Daughter Attitudes to Premarital Sexual Behavior," *Marriage and Family Living,* 23 (November 1961), pp. 309–392.

———— and Jack V. Buerkle, "The Daughter's Role during the 'Launching State,' " *Marriage and Family Living,* 24 (November 1962), pp. 384–388.

————. "Parent-Child Conflict in Sexual Values," *Journal of Social Issues,* 22 (April 1966), pp. 34–44.

Bendix, Reinhard and Seymour M. Lipset, eds. *Class, Status, and Power*. New York: The Free Press, 1953.

Berger, Joseph, Morris Zelditch, Jr., and Bo Anderson. *Sociological Theories in Progress*. New York: Houghton Mifflin Co., 1966.

Bernard, Jessie, ed. "Teen-Age Culture," *Annals of the American Academy of Political and Social Science*, 338 (November 1961).

————. *Marriage and Family Among Negroes*. Englewood Cliffs, N.J.: Prentice-Hall, 1966.

————. "Marital Stability and Patterns of Status Variables," *Journal of Marriage and the Family*, 28 (November 1966), pp. 421–439.

Berry, Brewton. *Race and Ethnic Relations*. Boston: Houghton Mifflin Co., 1958.

Blalock, Jr., Hubert M. *Causal Inferences in Nonexperimental Research*. Chapel Hill: University of North Carolina Press, 1964.

Bossard, James H. S. *Parent and Child*. Philadelphia: University of Pennsylvania Press, 1953.

———— and Eleanor Stoker Boll. *The Large Family System*. Philadelphia: University of Pennsylvania Press, 1956.

Bradburn, Norman M. and David Caplovitz. *Reports on Happiness*. Chicago: Aldine Publishing Co., 1965.

Breed, Warren. "Sex, Class, and Socialization in Dating," *Marriage and Family Living*, 18 (May 1956), pp. 137–144.

Brim, Jr., Orville G. "Family Structure and Sex-Role Learning by Children: A Further Analysis of Helen Koch's Data," *Sociometry*, 21 (March 1958), pp. 1–16.

Brink, William and Louis Harris. *The Negro Revolution in America*. New York: Simon and Schuster, 1964.

Broderick, Carlfred. "Sexual Behavior Among Pre-Adolescents," *Journal of Social Issues*, 22 (April 1966), pp. 6–21.

————. "Socio-Sexual Development in a Suburban Community," *Journal of Sex Research*, 2 (April 1966), pp. 1–24.

Bromley, Dorothy and Florence Britten. *Youth and Sex*. New York: Harper & Row, Publishers, 1938.

Bronfenbrenner, Urie. "Socialization and Social Class Through Time and Space," *Readings in Social Psychology*, Eleanor E. Maccoby, Theodore W. Newcomb, and Eugene L. Hartley, eds. New York: Holt, Rinehart and Winston, 1958, pp. 400–425.

Brown, Julia S. "A Comparative Study of Deviation from Sexual Mores," *American Sociological Review*, 17 (April 1952), pp. 135–146.

Burchinal, Lee G. "The Premarital Dyad and Love Involvement," *Handbook of Marriage and the Family*, Harold T. Christensen, ed. Chicago: Rand McNally & Co., 1964, pp. 623–674.

Burgess, Ernest W. and Paul Wallin. *Engagement and Marriage*. New York: J. B. Lippincott Co., 1953.

Butman, Jean W. and Jane A. Kamm. "The Social Psychological and Behavioral World of the Teen Age Girl," University of Michigan, Institute for Social Research, June, 1965, unpublished.

Christensen, Harold T. and George R. Carpenter. "Value-Behavior Discrepancies Regarding Premarital Coitus," *American Sociological Review*, 27 (February 1962), pp. 66–74.

————, ed. *Handbook of Marriage and the Family.* Chicago: Rand McNally & Co., 1964.

————. "Scandinavian and American Sex Norms: Some Comparisons with Sociological Implications," *Journal of Social Issues,* 22 (April 1966), pp. 60–75.

Clark, John P. and Larry L. Tifft. "Polygraph and Interview Validation of Self Reported Deviant Behavior," *American Sociological Review,* 31 (August 1966), pp. 516–523.

Clinard, Marshall B., ed. *Anomie and Deviant Behavior.* New York: The Free Press, 1964.

Cloward, Richard A. and Lloyd E. Ohlin. *Delinquency and Opportunity.* New York: The Free Press, 1960.

Cochran, William G., Frederick Mostellar, and John W. Tukey. *Statistical Problems of the Kinsey Report on Sexual Behavior in the Human Male.* Washington, D.C.: The American Statistical Association, 1954.

Coleman, James. "Female Status and Premarital Sexual Codes," *American Journal of Sociology,* 72 (September 1966), p. 217.

————. *The Adolescent Society.* New York: The Free Press, 1960.

Davenport, Beverly Scott. "Premarital Sexual Permissiveness and Dating Behavior," Unpublished M. A. thesis, University of Iowa, 1966.

Davis, Allison, Burleigh B. Gardner and Mary R. Gardner. *Deep South.* Chicago: University of Chicago Press, 1941.

———— and John Dollard. *Children of Bondage.* New York: Harper Torchbooks, 1964.

Davis, Kingsley. *Human Society.* New York: Crowell-Collier and Macmillan, 1950.

————. "Sexual Behavior," *Contemporary Social Problems,* 2d ed., Robert K. Merton and Robert A. Nesbit, eds. New York: Harcourt, Brace & World, 1966, pp. 322–372.

Dedman, Jean. "The Relationship Between Religious Attitude and Attitude toward Premarital Sex Relations," *Marriage and Family Living,* 21 (May 1959), pp. 171–176.

DeMartino, M. F., ed. *Sexual Behavior and Personality Characteristics.* New York: The Citadel Press, 1963.

Dentler, Robert A. and Lawrence J. Monroe. "The Family and Early Adolescent Conformity and Deviance," *Marriage and Family Living,* 23 (August 1961), pp. 241–247.

Deutscher, Irwin. "Words and Deeds: Social Science and Social Policy," *Social Problems,* 13 (Winter 1966), pp. 235–254.

Dollard, John. *Caste and Class in a Southern Town.* New York: Doubleday & Co., Anchor Books, 1957.

Drake, St. Clair and Horace R. Cayton. *Black Metropolis.* New York: Harper Torchbooks, 1962.

Drucker, Peter F. "The New Majority," *Reading in Sociology,* 2d ed., Edgar A. Schuler, Thomas F. Hoult, Duane L. Gibson, Maude L. Fiero, and Wilbur B. Brookover, eds. New York: Thomas Y. Crowell Co., 1960, pp. 309–317.

Duncan, Otis Dudley. "A Socioeconomic Index for all Occupations" and "Properties and Characteristics of the Socioeconomic Index," *Occupations and Social Status,* Albert J. Reiss, Jr., ed. New York: The Free Press, 1963, chap. 6 and 7.

Durkheim, Emile. *The Rules of Sociological Method*. New York: The Free Press, 1938.

Edwards, Allen L. *Techniques of Attitude Scale Construction*. New York: Appleton-Century-Crofts, 1957.

————. *The Social Desirability Variable in Personality Assessment Research*. New York: Holt, Rinehart and Winston, 1957.

Ehrmann, Winston H. *Premarital Dating Behavior*. New York: Holt, Rinehart and Winston, 1959.

Elder, Jr., Glen H., and Charles E. Bowerman. "Family Structure and Child Rearing Patterns: The Effect of Family Size and Sex Composition," *American Sociological Review*, 28 (December 1963), pp. 891–905.

Elfin, Mel, ed. "Morals on the Campus," *Newsweek*, (April 6, 1964), pp. 52–59.

Elkin, Frederick and William H. Westley. "The Myth of Adolescent Culture," *American Sociological Review*, 20 (December 1955), pp. 680–684.

————. *The Child and Society: The Process of Socialization*. New York: Random House, 1960.

Ellis, Havelock. *Studies in the Psychology of Sex*. New York: New American Library, A Mentor Book, 1938.

Epperson, David C. "A Reassessment of Indices of Parental Influence in 'The Adolescent Society,'" *American Sociological Review*, 29 (February 1964), pp. 93–96.

Erikson, Erik H. *Childhood and Society*. New York: W. W. Norton & Co., 1963.

————, ed. *The Challenge of Youth*. Garden City, N. Y.: Doubleday & Co., 1965.

Festinger, Leon. "The Treatment of Quantitative Data by Scale Analysis," *Psychological Bulletin*, 44 (March 1947), pp. 149–161.

————. *A Theory of Cognitive Dissonance*. New York: Harper & Row, Publishers, 1957.

Feuer, Lewis S. *The Scientific Intellectual*. New York: Basic Books, 1963.

Frazier, E. Franklin. *The Negro Family in the United States*. New York: Holt, Rinehart and Winston, 1951.

————. *The Negro in the United States*. New York: Crowell-Collier and Macmillan, 1957.

Freedman, Mervin B. "The Sexual Behavior of American College Women: An Empirical Study and an Historical Survey," *Merrill-Palmer Quarterly of Behavior and Development*, 11 (January 1965), pp. 33–39.

Freedman, Ronald, Pascal K. Whelpton, and Arthur A. Campbell. *Family Planning, Sterility and Population Growth*. New York: McGraw-Hill, 1959.

Freud, Sigmund. *Three Contributions to the Theory of Sex*. New York: E. P. Dutton & Co., 1962.

Fuchs, Lawrence H. *The Political Behavior of American Jews*. New York: The Free Press, 1956.

Furstenberg, Frank F., Jr. "Industrialization and the American Family: A Look Backward," *American Sociological Review*, 31 (June 1966), pp. 326–337.

Gagnon, John H. "Sexuality and Sexual Learning in the Child," *Psychiatry*, 28 (August 1965), pp. 212–228.

Gebhard, Paul H., Wardell B. Pomeroy, Clyde E. Martin, and Cornelia V.

Christenson. *Pregnancy, Birth, and Abortion.* New York: Harper & Row, Publishers, and Paul B. Hoeber, Medical Books, 1958.

————, John H. Gagnon, Wardell B. Pomeroy, and Cornelia V. Christenson. *Sex Offenders.* New York: Harper & Row, Publishers, and Paul B. Hoeber, Medical Books, 1965.

Gilmartin, Brian G. "Relationship of Traits Measured by the California Psychological Inventory to Premarital Sexual Standards and Behaviors," Unpublished M.S. thesis, University of Utah, 1964.

Glick, Paul C. *American Families.* New York: John Wiley & Sons, 1957.

Glidewell, John C., ed. *Parental Attitudes and Child Behavior.* Springfield, Ill.: Charles C. Thomas, Publisher, 1961.

Glock, Charles Y. and Rodney Stark. *Religion and Society in Tension.* Chicago: Rand McNally & Co., 1965.

Goldsen, Rose K., Morris Rosenberg, Robin M. Williams, Jr., and Edward A. Suchman. *What College Students Think.* New York: D. Van Nostrand Co., 1960.

Goode, Erich. "Social Class and Church Participation." *American Journal of Sociology,* 72 (July 1966), pp. 102–111.

Goode, William J. *After Divorce.* New York: The Free Press, 1956.

————. "The Sociology of the Family," *Sociology Today,* Robert K. Merton, Leonard Broom, and Leonard S. Cottrell, eds. New York: Basic Books, 1959, pp. 178–191.

————. "The Theoretical Importance of Love," *American Sociological Review,* 24 (February 1959), pp. 38–47.

Goodman, Leo A. "Simple Methods for Analyzing Three-Factor Interaction in Contingency Tables," *Journal of the American Statistical Association,* 59 (June 1964), pp. 319–352.

———— and William H. Kruskal. "Measures of Association for Cross Classification," *Journal of the American Statistical Association,* 49 (December 1954), pp. 732–764.

————. "Measures of Association for Cross Classifications II: Further Discussion and Reference," *Journal of the American Statistical Association,* 54 (March 1959), pp. 123–163.

————. "Measures of Association for Cross Classification III: Approximate Sampling Theory," *Journal of the American Statistical Association,* 58 (June 1963), pp. 310–364.

Gordon, Robert A., James F. Short, Jr., Desmond S. Cartwright, and Fred L. Strodtbeck. "Values and Gang Delinquency: A Study of Street-Corner Groups," *American Journal of Sociology,* 69 (September 1963), pp. 109–128.

Gottlieb, David and Charles Ramsey. *The American Adolescent.* Homewood, Ill.: Dorsey Press, 1964.

————, Jon Reeves, and Warren D. Ten Houten, *The Emergence of Youth Societies: A Cross-Cultural Approach.* New York: The Free Press, 1966.

Gouldner, Alvin W. "Reciprocity and Autonomy in Functional Theory," *Symposium in Sociological Theory,* Llewellyn Gross, ed. New York: Harper & Row, Publishers, 1959.

Gross, Llewellyn. "A Belief Pattern Scale for Measuring Attitudes Toward Romanticism," *American Sociological Review,* 9 (December 1944), pp. 463–472.

Group for the Advancement of Psychiatry. *Sex and the College Student.* New York: Atheneum Publishers, 1966.

Guttman, Louis. "The Cornell Technique for Scale and Intensity Analysis," *Educational and Psychological Measurement,* (Summer 1947), pp. 247–280.

————. "The Intensity Component in Attitude and Opinion Research," *Studies in Social Psychology in World War II,* Vol. 4. Samuel A. Stouffer, Louis Guttman, Edward A. Suchman, Paul F. Lazarsfeld, Shirley A. Star, and John A. Clausen. Princeton, N. J.: Princeton University Press, 1950, pp. 213–277.

Hampe, Gary D. "Mixed Faith Dating," Unpublished M.A. thesis, University of Iowa, 1967.

Hayes, Donald P. "Item Order and Guttman Scales," *American Journal of Sociology,* 70 (July 1964), pp. 51–58.

Hernton, Calvin C. *Sex and Racism in America.* New York: Doubleday & Co., 1965.

Himelhoch, Jerome and Sylvia Fava, eds. *Sexual Behavior in American Society.* New York: W. W. Norton & Co., 1955.

Hobbs, Jr., Daniel F. and Marvin B. Sussman. "Impediments to Family Research: A Symposium," *Journal of Marriage and The Family,* 27 (August 1965), pp. 410–416.

Hobart, Charles W. "The Incidence of Romanticism During Courtship," *Social Forces,* 36 (May 1958), pp. 362–367.

————. "Emancipation from Parents and Courtship in Adolescents," *Pacific Sociological Review,* 1 (Spring 1958), pp. 25–29.

Hodge, Robert W., Paul M. Siegel, and Peter H. Rossi. "Occupational Prestige in the United States, 1925–1963," *American Journal of Sociology,* 70 (November 1964), pp. 286–302.

Hoffman, Martin L., and Lois W. Hoffman, eds. *Review of Child Development Research.* New York: Russell Sage Foundation, 1964.

Hollingshead, August B. *Elmtown's Youth.* New York: John Wiley & Sons, 1949.

Hunt, Morton M. *The World of the Formerly Married.* New York: McGraw-Hill, 1966.

Hyman, Herbert. *Survey Design and Analysis.* New York: The Free Press, 1955.

Irish, Donald P. "Sibling Interaction: A Neglected Aspect in Family Life Research," *Social Forces,* 42 (March 1964), pp. 279–288.

Jacobson, Paul H. *American Marriage and Divorce.* New York: Holt, Rinehart and Winston, 1959.

Johnson, Miriam M. "Sex Role Learning in the Nuclear Family," *Child Development,* 34 (June 1963), pp. 319–333.

Kagan, Jerome. "Acquisition and Significance of Sex Typing and Sex Role Identity," *Review of Child Development Research,* Martin L. Hoffman and Lois W. Hoffman, eds. New York: Russell Sage Foundation 1964, pp. 137–168.

Kammeyer, Kenneth. "Birth Order and the Feminine Sex Role among College Women," *American Sociological Review,* 31 (August 1966), pp. 508–515.

Kanin, Eugene A. and David H. Howard. "Postmarital Consequences of Premarital Sex Adjustments," *American Sociological Review,* 23 (October 1958), pp. 556–562.

Kardiner, Abram and Lionel Ovesey. *The Mark of Oppression.* New York: Meridian Books, 1962.

Kendall, Patricia and Paul F. Lazarsfeld. "Problems of Survey Analysis," *Continuities in Social Research,* Robert K. Merton and Paul F. Lazarsfeld, eds. New York: The Free Press, 1950, pp. 133–196.

Kinsey, Alfred C., Wardell B. Pomeroy, and Clyde E. Martin. *Sexual Behavior in the Human Male.* Philadelphia: W. B. Saunders Co., 1948.

————, and Paul H. Gebhard. *Sexual Behavior in the Human Female.* Philadelphia: W. B. Saunders Co., 1953.

Kirkendall, Lester A. *Premarital Intercourse and Interpersonal Relationships.* New York: The Julian Press, 1961.

Kirkpatrick, Clifford, Sheldon Stryker, and Philip Buell. "An Experimental Study of Attitudes Toward Male Sex Behavior with Reference to Kinsey Findings," *American Sociological Review,* 17 (October 1952), pp. 580–587.

Kish, Leslie. "Some Statistical Problems in Research Design," *American Sociological Review,* 24 (June 1959), pp. 328–338.

Klapper, Joseph. *The Effects of Mass Communication.* New York: The Free Press, 1960.

Kluckhohn, Clyde. "Values and Value Orientations in the Theory of Action," *Toward a General Theory of Action,* Talcott Parsons and Edward Shils, eds. Cambridge, Mass.: Harvard University Press, 1954, pp. 388–433.

Kohn, Melvin. "Social Class and Parental Values," *American Journal of Sociology,* 64 (January 1959), pp. 337–351.

Komarovsky, Mirra. "Functional Analysis of Sex Roles," *American Sociological Review,* 15 (August 1950), pp. 508–516.

Krich, Aron, ed. *Pioneer Writings on Sex (The Sexual Revolution, Vol. I).* New York: A Delta Book, 1964.

Kuhn, Manford A. "Kinsey's View of Human Behavior," *Sexual Behavior in American Society,* Jerome Himelhoch and Sylvia Fava, eds. New York: W. W. Norton & Co., 1955, pp. 29–38.

Landis, Judson T. and Mary G. Landis. *Building a Successful Marriage.* 3d ed. Englewood Cliffs, N. J.: Prentice-Hall, 1958.

Lansing, John B. and Leslie Kish. "Family Life Cycle as an Independent Variable," *American Sociological Review,* 22 (October 1957), pp. 512–519.

Lazarsfeld, Paul F., Bernard Berelson, and Hazel Gaudet. *People's Choice: How the Voter Makes up His Mind in a Presidential Campaign.* New York: Columbia University Press, 1948.

————. "Interpretation of Statistical Relations as a Research Operation," *The Language of Social Research,* Paul F. Lazarsfeld and Morris Rosenberg, eds. New York: The Free Press, 1955, pp. 115–125.

———— and Morris Rosenberg, eds. *The Language of Social Research.* New York: The Free Press, 1955.

Lenski, Gerhard. *The Religious Factor.* New York: Doubleday & Co., 1961.

Leslie, Gerald R. and Kathryn P. Johnsen. "Changed Perceptions of the Maternal Role," *American Sociological Review,* 28 (December 1963), pp. 919–928.

LeVine, Robert A. "Gusii Sex Offenses: A Study in Social Control," *American Anthropologist,* 61 (December 1959), pp. 965–990.

Lindenfeld, Frank. "A Note on Social Mobility, Religiosity and Student's Attitudes towards Premarital Sexual Relations," *American Sociological Review,* 25 (February 1960), pp. 81–84.

Lipset, Seymour M. *Political Man.* New York: Doubleday & Co., 1960.

Lott, Albert J., and Bernice E. Lott. *Negro and White Youth.* New York: Holt, Rinehart and Winston, 1963.

Lowrie, Samuel H. "Early and Late Dating: Some Conditions Associated with Them," *Marriage and Family Living,* 23 (August 1961), pp. 284–291.

Maccoby, Eleanor E., Theodore M. Newcomb, and Eugene L. Hartley, eds. *Readings in Social Psychology.* New York: Holt, Rinehart and Winston, 1958.

Malinowski, Bronislaw. *The Sexual Life of Savages in North-Western Melanesia.* New York: Eugenica Publishing Co., 1929.

Maslow, Abraham A. "Self Esteem (Dominance-Feeling) and Sexuality in Women," *Journal of Social Psychology,* 16 (November 1942), pp. 259–294.

Masters, William and Virginia Johnson. *Human Sexual Response.* Boston: Little, Brown & Co., 1966.

McKinley, Donald G. *Social Class and Family Life.* New York: The Free Press, 1964.

McTavish, Donald G. "A Method for More Reliably Coding Detailed Occupations into Duncan's Socioeconomic Categories," *American Sociological Review,* 29 (June 1964), pp. 402–406.

Mead, George Herbert. *Mind, Self, and Society.* Chicago: University of Chicago Press, 1934.

Menzel, Herbert. "A New Coefficient for Scalagram Analyses," *Public Opinion Quarterly,* (Summer 1953), pp. 268–280.

Merton, Robert K. and Paul F. Lazarsfeld, eds. *Continuities in Social Research.* New York: The Free Press, 1950.

————, Leonard Broom, and Leonard S. Cottrell, eds. *Sociology Today.* New York: Basic Books, 1959.

———— and Robert A. Nesbit, eds. *Contemporary Social Problems* 2d ed. New York: Harcourt, Brace & World, 1966.

Milbrath, L. W. "Latent Origins of Liberalism-Conservatism and Party Identification," *Journal of Politics,* 24 (November 1962), pp. 679–688.

Miller, Daniel R. and Guy E. Swanson. *The Changing American Parent.* New York: John Wiley & Sons, 1958.

Moore, Bernice M. and Wayne H. Holtzman. *Tomorrow's Parents.* Austin, Texas: University of Texas Press, 1965.

Morgan, Lewis H. *Ancient Society.* Chicago: Charles H. Kerr and Co., 1877.

Moynihan, Daniel Patrick. *The Case for National Action: The Negro Family.* Washington, D.C.: Office of Policy Planning and Research, U.S. Department of Labor, March, 1965.

Murdock, George P. *Social Structure.* New York: Crowell-Collier and Macmillan, 1949.

Myrdal, Gunner. *An American Dilemma.* New York: Harper & Row, Publishers, 1944.

Newcomb, Theodore M. and Everett K. Wilson, eds. *College Peer Groups.* Chicago: Aldine Publishing Co., 1966.

Nye, F. Ivan. *Family Relationships and Delinquent Behavior.* New York: John Wiley & Son, 1958.

Parsons, Talcott and Robert Bales. *Family, Socialization, and Interaction Process*. New York: The Free Press, 1955.

Podell, Lawrence and John C. Perkins. "A Guttman Scale for Sexual Experience—A Methodological Note," *Journal of Abnormal and Social Psychology,* 54 (May 1957), pp. 420–422.

Rainwater, Lee and William Yancy. "Black Families and the White House," *Transaction,* (July-August 1966), pp. 6–11 and 48–53.

Reisman, David. *The Lonely Crowd.* New York: Doubleday & Co., 1953.

Reiss, Albert, Jr. *Occupations and Social Status.* New York: The Free Press, 1963.

Reiss, Ira L. "The Double Standard in Premarital Sexual Intercourse: A Neglected Concept," *Social Forces,* 34 (March 1956), pp. 224–230.

————. "The Treatment of Premarital Coitus in Marriage and Family Texts," *Social Problems,* 4 (April 1957), pp. 334–338.

————. *Premarital Sexual Standards in America.* New York: The Free Press, 1960.

————. "Toward A Sociology of the Heterosexual Love Relationship," *Marriage and Family Living,* 22 (May 1960), pp. 139–145.

————. "Standards of Sexual Behavior," *Encyclopedia of Sexual Behavior,* A. Ellis and A. Abarbanel, eds. New York: Hawthorne, 1961, pp. 996–1004.

————. "Sexual Codes in Teen-Age Culture," *The Annals of the American Academy of Political and Social Science,* 338 (November 1961), pp. 53–62.

————. "Consistency and Sexual Ethics," *Marriage and Family Living,* 24 (August 1962), pp. 264–269.

————. "Personal Values and the Scientific Study of Sex," *Advances in Sex Research,* Hugo Beigel, ed. New York: Harper & Row, Publishers, 1963, chap. One.

————. "Sociological Studies of Sexual Standards," *Determinants of Human Sexual Behavior.* George Winokur, ed. Springfield, Ill.: C. C. Thomas, 1963, Chap. 6.

————. "The Scaling of Premarital Sexual Permissiveness," *Journal of Marriage and the Family,* 26 (May 1964), pp. 188–198.

————. "Premarital Sexual Permissiveness Among Negroes and Whites," *American Sociological Review,* 29 (October 1964), pp. 688–698.

————. "Hayes' Item Order and Guttman Scales," *American Journal of Sociology,* 70 (March 1965), p. 629).

————. "Social Class and Campus Dating," *Social Problems,* 13 (Fall 1965), pp. 193–205.

————. "Social Class and Premarital Sexual Permissiveness: A Re-Examination," *American Sociological Review,* 30 (October 1965), pp. 747–756.

————. "The Universality of the Family: A Conceptual Analysis," *Journal of Marriage and The Family,* 26 (November 1965), pp. 443–453.

————. "Contraceptive Information and Sexual Morality," *Journal of Sex Research,* 2 (April 1966), pp. 51–57.

————, ed. "The Sexual Renaissance in America," *Journal of Social Issues,* 22 (April 1966).

————. "The Sexual Renaissance: A Summary and Analysis," *Journal of Social Issues,* 22 (April 1966), pp. 123–137.

————. "Some Comments on Premarital Sexual Permissiveness," *American Journal of Sociology,* 72 (March 1967), pp. 558–559.

Remmers, H. H. "Early Socialization of Attitudes," *American Voting Behavior,* Eugene Burdick and Arthur J. Brodbeck, eds. New York: The Free Press, 1959, pp. 55–67.

———— and D. H. Radler. *The American Teenager.* New York: The Bobbs-Merrill Co., 1957.

Riley, John and Mathilda Riley. *Sociological Studies in Scale Analysis.* New Brunswick, N. J.: Rutgers University Press, 1954.

Rockwood, Lemo D. and Mary E. Ford. *Youth, Marriage, and Parenthood.* New York: John Wiley & Sons, 1945.

Rodman, Hyman. "The Lower Class Value Stretch," *Social Forces,* 42 (December 1963), pp. 205–215.

Roher, John H. and Munro S. Edmonson, eds. *The Eighth Generation Grows Up.* New York: Harper Torchbooks, 1960.

Rokeach, Milton. "Attitude Change and Behavior Change," *Public Opinion Quarterly,* 30 (Winter 1966–67), pp. 529–550.

Rosenberg, Morris. "Test Factor Standardization as a Method of Interpretation," *Social Forces,* 41 (October 1962), pp. 53–61.

————. *Society and the Adolescent Self-Image.* Princeton, N. J.: Princeton University Press, 1965.

Rossi, Alice S. "Naming Children in Middle-Class Families," *American Sociological Review,* 30 (August 1965), pp. 499–513.

Schmuck, Richard. "Sex of Siblings, Birth Order Position, Female Disposition to Conform in Two-Child Families," *Child Development,* 34 (December 1963), pp. 913–918.

Schofield, Michael. *The Sexual Behavior of Young People.* Boston: Little, Brown & Co., 1965.

Schuler, Edgar A., Thomas F. Hoult, Duane L. Gibson, Maude L. Fiero, and Wilbur B. Brookover, eds. *Readings in Sociology.* 2d ed. New York: Thomas Y. Crowell Co., 1960.

Sears, Robert F., Eleanor E. Maccoby, and Harry Levin. *Patterns of Child Rearing.* New York: Harper & Row, Publishers, 1957.

"Second Sexual Revolution," *Time,* 83 (January 24, 1964), pp. 54–60.

Seidman, Jerome M., ed. *The Adolescent.* New York: Holt, Rinehart and Winston, 1960.

Selvin, Hanan C. "A Critique of Tests of Significance in Survey Research," *American Sociological Review,* 22 (October 1957), pp. 519–527.

Shanas, Ethel and Gordon F. Streib, eds. *Social Structure and the Family: Generational Relations.* Englewood Cliffs, N. J.: Prentice-Hall, 1965.

Sherif, Muzafer and Carolyn W. Sherif, eds. *Problems of Youth: Transition to Adulthood in a Changing World.* Chicago: Aldine Publishing Co., 1965.

Short, James F., Jr. and Fred L. Strodtbeck. *Group Process and Gang Delinquency.* Chicago: The University of Chicago Press, 1965.

Simpson, George E. and J. Milton Yinger. *Racial and Cultural Minorities.* New York: Harper & Row, Publishers, 1953.

Somers, Robert H. "A New Asymmetric Measure of Association for Ordinal Variables," *American Sociological Review,* 27 (December 1962), pp. 799–811.

Spiro, Melford. *Kibbutz: Venture in Utopia*. Cambridge, Mass.: Harvard University Press, 1956.

———. *Children of the Kibbutz*. Cambridge, Mass.: Harvard University Press, 1958.

Stouffer, Samuel A., Louis Guttman, Edward A. Suchman, Paul F. Lazarsfeld, Shirley A. Star, and John A. Clausen. *Studies in Social Psychology in World War II*, Vol. 4. Princeton, N. J.: Princeton University Press, 1950.

Suchman, Edward A. "The Logic of Scale Construction," *Educational and Psychological Measurement,* (Spring 1950), pp. 79–93.

Terman, Lewis M. *Psychological Factors in Marital Happiness*. New York: McGraw-Hill, 1938.

Toby, Jackson and Marcia L. Toby. "A Method of Selecting Dichotomous Items by Cross Tabulation," *Sociological Studies in Scale Analysis,* John Riley and Mathilda Riley, eds. New Brunswick, N. J.: Rutgers University Press, 1954, pp. 339–355.

U.S. Bureau of the Census. *Trends in the Income of Families and Persons in the United States: 1947–1960*. Technical Paper 8, Washington, D.C.: U.S. Government Printing Office, 1963.

U.S. Department of Agriculture. *Characteristics of School Dropouts and High School Graduates: Farm and Non Farm 1960*. Report 65, Washington, D.C.: December, 1965.

U.S. Department of Health, Education, and Welfare. *Retention and Withdrawal of College Students*. Washington, D.C.: 1957.

U.S. Department of Health, Education, and Welfare. *Monthly Vital Statistics Report. Advance Report Final Marriage Statistics, 1963*. Vol. 15, suppl. 3, Washington, D.C.: May 31, 1966.

U.S. Department of Health, Education and Welfare. *Monthly Vital Statistics Reports Supplement,* Vol. 15, #3, Washington, D.C.: June 14, 1966.

Vincent, Clark E. "Teen-Age Unwed Mothers in American Society," *Journal of Social Issues*, 22 (April 1966), pp. 22–33.

———. *Unmarried Mothers*. New York: The Free Press, 1961.

———. "Socialization Data in Research on Young Marrieds," *Acta Sociologica,* 8 (No. 1–2, 1964), pp. 118–127.

Von Krafft-Ebing, Richard. *Psychopathia Sexualis*. New York: G. P. Putnam's Sons, 1965.

Ward, David A. and Gene G. Kasselbaum. *Women's Prison*. Chicago: Aldine Publishing Co., 1965.

Webb, Eugene J., Donald T. Campbell, Richard D. Schwartz, and Lee Sechrest. *Unobtrusive Measures*. Chicago: Rand McNally & Co., 1966.

Westermarck, Edward. *The History of Human Marriage*. 3 vols. New York: Allerton Book Co., 1922.

Whyte, William Foote. "A Slum Sex Code," *Class, Status, and Power,* Reinhard Bendix and Seymour M. Lipset, eds. New York: The Free Press, 1953, pp. 308–315.

Whyte, Jr., William H. *The Organization Man*. New York: Doubleday & Co., 1956.

Williams, Jr., Robin M. *American Society*. New York: Alfred A. Knopf, 1951.

Winch, Robert F. "Courtship in College Women," *American Journal of Sociology*, 55 (November 1949), pp. 269–278.

Wolff, Kurt H., ed. *The Sociology of Georg Simmel*. New York: The Free Press, 1950.

Wright, Charles R. and Herbert H. Hyman. "Voluntary Association Memberships of American Adults: Evidence from National Sample Surveys," *American Sociological Review*, 23 (June 1958), pp. 284–294.

Zeisel, Hans. *Say It With Figures*. New York: Harper & Row, Publishers, 1957.

Zetterberg, Hans L. *On Theory and Verification in Sociology*. 3d ed. New York: The Bedminster Press, 1965.

INDICES

Author Index

Subject Index